Tera-Tom on Teradata SQL for V2R6

Understanding is the key!

Published by

Coffing Publishing

Third Edition August, 2006

Written by W. Coffing
Web Page: www.CoffingDW.com
E-Mail address:
Tom.Coffing@CoffingDW.Com

International Standard Book Number ISBN 0-9768302-1-3

Printed in the United States of America

About our CEO Tom Coffing and Coffing Data Warehousing

Tom is President, CEO, and Founder of Coffing Data Warehousing. He is an internationally known consultant, facilitator, speaker, trainer, and executive coach with an extensive background in data warehousing. Tom has helped implement data warehousing in over 40 major data warehouse accounts, spoken in over 20 countries, and has provided consulting and Teradata training to over 8,000 individuals involved in data warehousing globally.

Tom has co-authored the following eight books on Data Warehousing:

- *Secrets of the Best Data Warehouses in the World*
- *Teradata SQL - Unleash the Power*
- *Tera-Tom on Teradata Basics*
- *Tera-Tom on Teradata E-business*
- *Teradata SQL Quick Reference Guide - Simplicity by Design*
- *Teradata Database Design - Giving Detailed Data Flight*
- *Teradata Users Guide -The Ultimate Companion*
- *Teradata Utilities - Breaking the Barriers*

Mr. Coffing has also published over 20 data warehousing articles and has been a contributing columnist to DM Review on the subject of data warehousing. He wrote a monthly column for DM Review entitled, "Teradata Territory". He is a nationally known speaker and gives frequent seminars on Data Warehousing. He is also known as "The Speech Doctor" because of his presentation skills and sales seminars.

Tom Coffing has taken his expert speaking and data warehouse knowledge and revolutionized the way technical training and consultant services are delivered. He founded CoffingDW with the same philosophy more than a decade ago. Centered around 10 Teradata Certified Masters, this dynamic and growing company teaches every Teradata class, provides world class Teradata consultants, offers a suite of software products to enhance Teradata data warehouses, and has eight books published on Teradata.

Tom has a bachelor's degree in Speech Communications and over 25 years of business and technical computer experience. Tom is considered by many to be the best technical and business speaker in the United States. He has trained and consulted at so many Teradata sites that students affectionately call him Tera-Tom.

Teradata Certified Master

- Teradata Certified Professional
- Teradata Certified Administrator
- Teradata Certified Developer
- Teradata Certified Designer
- Teradata Certified SQL Specialist
- Teradata Certified Implementation Specialist

Table of Contents

Table of Contents

Table of Contents

Table of Contents

Table of Contents

Table of Contents

Chapter 1 — The Rules of Data Warehousing

"Let me once again explain the rules. Teradata rules!"

Tera-Tom Coffing

The Teradata RDBMS was designed to eliminate the technical pitfalls of data warehousing and it is parallel processing that allows Teradata to rule this industry. The problem with Data Warehousing is that it is so big and so complicated that there literally are no rules. Anything goes! Data Warehousing is not for the weak or faint of heart because the terrain can be difficult and that is why 75% of all data warehouses fail. Teradata provides the users the ability to build a data warehouse for the business without having to compromise because the database is unable to meet the challenges and requirements of constant change. That is why 90% of all Teradata data warehouses succeed.

Teradata allows businesses to quickly respond to **changing conditions**. **Relational databases** are more **flexible** than other database types and flexibility is Teradata's middle name. Here is how Teradata Rules:

- 8 of the Top 13 Global Airlines use Teradata

- 10 of the Top 13 Global Communications Companies use Teradata

- 9 of the Top 16 Global Retailers use Teradata

- 8 of the Top 20 Global Banks use Teradata

- 40% of Fortune's "US Most Admired" companies use Teradata

- Teradata customers account for more than 70% of the revenue generated by the top 20 global telecommunication companies

- Teradata customers account for more than 55% of the revenue generated by the top 30 Global retailers

- Teradata customers account for more than 55% of the revenue generated by the top 20 global airlines

- More than 25% of the top 15 global insurance carriers use Teradata

Teradata Certification

"If you want to have the potential to be rich then get a medical degree, a law degree or pass the six Teradata Certification Tests!"

– Tera-Tom Coffing

There are six Teradata Certification tests and they are listed below. **Pass all six tests makes you a Teradata Certified Master.** You will be on a Teradata Master Email list where you can post or answer questions from every Teradata Certified Master around the globe. To take a Teradata test you sign up online at **Prometric.com**. Once at the website Prometric.com then select the hyperlink **"Schedule a Test"**. You will be taken to a 3-step menu. Select **Information Technology** as your **AREA of STUDY**. Select **NCR Teradata** as the **TESTING PROGRAM**. Fill in your location of **STATE** and **COUNTRY** and then select NCR Teradata again and pick the test you want to take. You will be given **TEST SITE** locations to choose from and make an appointment to take your examination.

Teradata Certification Tests

1 – Teradata Basics
2 – Teradata Physical Implementation
3 – Teradata SQL
4 – Teradata Database Administration (DBA)
5 – Teradata Designer
6 – Teradata Application Development

Pass all six tests and you are a Teradata Certified Master for life!

Pass the Teradata Basics and you are a Teradata Certified Professional
Pass Tests 1 and 2 and you are a Teradata Certified Implementation Specialist
Pass Tests 1 and 3 and you are a Teradata Certified SQL Specialist
Pass Tests 1, 2, and 4 and you are a Teradata Certified Administrator
Pass Tests 1, 2, and 5 and you are a Teradata Certified Designer
Pass Tests 1, 3, and 6 and you are a Teradata Certified Application Developer

---

A Logical View of the Teradata Architecture

"Kites rise highest against the wind – not with it."

– Sir Winston Churchill

Many of the largest data warehouses in the world are on Teradata. Teradata provides customers a centrally located architecture. This provides a single version of the truth and it minimizes synchronization. Having Teradata on your side is a sure win-ston. If Churchill had been a data warehouse expert, he would agree that most data warehouses eventually receive the blitz and stop working while Teradata has the strength from parallel processing to "never give up".

Many data warehouse environments have an architecture that is not designed for decision support, yet companies often wonder why their data warehouse failed. The winds of business change can be difficult and starting with Teradata is the biggest key to rising higher.

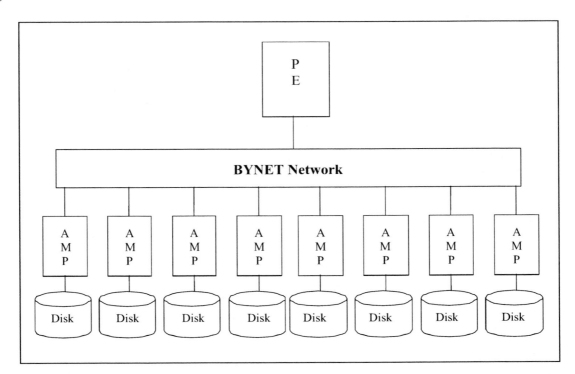

The Parsing Engine (PE)

"The greatest weakness of most humans is their hesitancy to tell others how much they love them while they're alive."

– O.A. Battista

If you haven't told someone lately how much you love them you need to find a way. Leadership through love is your greatest gift. Teradata has someone who greets you with love with every logon. That person is the Parsing Engine (PE), which is often referred to as the optimizer. When you logon to Teradata the Parsing Engine is waiting with tears in its eyes and love in its heart ready to make sure your session is taken care of completely.

The Parsing Engine does three things every time you run an SQL statement.
- Checks the syntax of your SQL
- Checks the security to make sure you have access to the table
- Comes up with a plan for the AMPs to follow

The PE creates a PLAN that tells the AMPs exactly what to do in order to get the data. The PE knows how many AMPs are in the system, how many rows are in the table, and the best way to get to the data. The Parsing Engine is the best optimizer in the data warehouse world because it has been continually improved for over 25 years at the top data warehouse sites in the world.

The **Parsing Engine** verifies SQL requests for **proper syntax**, checks security, maintains up to **120 individual user sessions**, and breaks down the **SQL requests into steps.**

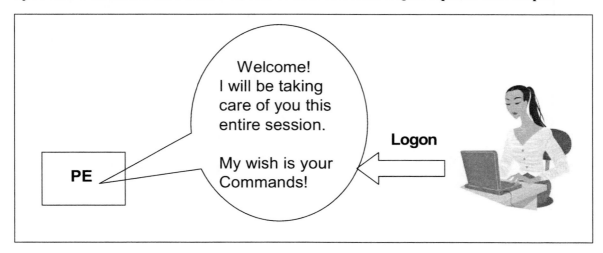

The Parsing Engine in Detail

"It's always been and always will be the same in the world: the horse does the work and the coachman is tipped."

– Anonymous

It's always been and always will be the same in the world: The AMPs do most of the work and the PE gets the credit. The PE will go through six steps to come up with a plan. The plan allows the PE to guide the AMPs like a coachman.

 USER Writes SQL and a Request Parcel is generated to the Parsing Engine (PE).

| PE | Is this SQL in my Plan Library (RTS Cache)? If Yes, check Security and APPLY the same plan as last time! |

Syntaxer – Check the Syntax and build the initial Parse Tree.

Resolver – Use the DD Cache and Resolve up to 64 Views/Macros with the real Table IDs. Build Annotated Parse Tree.

Security - Is the user allowed to access the tables?

Optimizer – Use Collect Statistics to build the plan and EXPLAIN. Will the AMPs use an index or a full table scan?

Generator – Place any hard-coded literals in the plan to generate Plastic Steps. Place plan in Plan Library (RTS Cache).

Apply – Apply Data Parcels (parameters) and create Concrete Steps. Call Dispatcher to pass Plan to the proper AMPs.

The Parsing Engine Knows All

"Never mistake knowledge for wisdom. One helps you make a living; the other helps you make a life."

– Sandra Carey

The above quote should be discarded because Teradata knowledge will help you make such an incredible living that everyone will know you must have great wisdom. You had the wisdom to invest in one of the most exciting technologies of the 21st century. My job is to make it easy to understand and fun so you will hunger for more knowledge. I want you to be like the Parsing Engine and understand everything about a Teradata system. The Parsing Engine knows the system hardware and software, the data demographics, and from that information can come up with the best access path.

The Teradata Parsing Engine Knows All		
System Information	**Data Demographics**	**Access Path Decisions**
Number of Nodes Number of AMPs Type of CPUs Disk Array Information BYNET Information Amount of Memory	Number of Rows Column Information Row Size Skew Values Rows Per Value Index Demographics	What Access Path? What Type of Join? Join Redistribution of Duplication? What Order of the Table Joins? Should a Bitmap be used? Can a Cover Query be Used?

The Access Module Processors (AMPs)

"A true friend is one who walks in when the rest of the world walks out."

– Anonymous

The AMPs are truly mans best friend because they will work like a dog to read and write the data. (Their bark is worse then their byte). An AMP never walks out on a friend. The AMPs are the worker bees of the Teradata system because the AMPs read and write the data to their assigned disks. The Parsing Engine is the boss and the AMPs are the workers. The AMPs merely follow the PE's plan and read or write the data.

The **AMPs** are always connected to a **singe virtual disk or Vdisk**. The philosophy of parallel processing revolves around the AMPs. Teradata takes each table and spreads the rows evenly among all the AMPs. When data is requested from a particular table each AMP retrieves the rows for the table that they hold on their disk. If the data is spread evenly then each AMP should retrieve their rows simultaneously with the other AMPs. That is what we mean when we say Teradata was born to be parallel.

The AMPs will also **perform output conversion** while the PE performs **input conversion**. The AMPs do the **physical work** associated with **retrieving an answer set**.

The PE is the boss and the AMPs are the workers. **Could** you have a **Teradata system** without **AMPs**? No – who would **retrieve the data**? Could you have a **Teradata system** without **PEs**? Of course not – could you get along **without your boss**?!!!

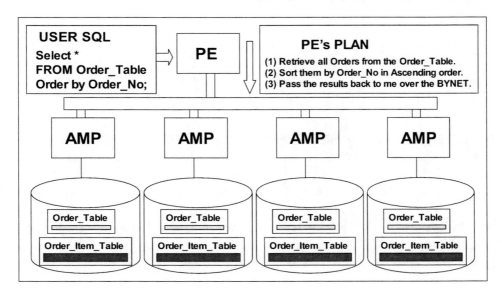

The BYNET

"Not all who wander are lost."

– J. R. R. Tolkien

The BYNET is the communication network between AMPs and PE's. Data and communication never wanders and is never lost. How well does the BYNET know communication? It is the lord of the things! How often does the PE pass the plan to the AMPs over the BYNET? Every time – it makes it a hobbit!

The PE passes the PLAN to the AMPs over the BYNET. The AMPs then retrieve the data from their disks and pass it to the PE over the BYNET.

The BYNET gets its name from the Banyan tree. The Banyan tree has the ability to continually plant new roots to grow forever. Likewise, the BYNET scales as the Teradata system grows in size. The BYNET is scalable.

There are always two BYNETs for redundancy and extra bandwidth. AMPs and PEs can use both BYNETs to send and retrieve data simultaneously. What a network!

- The PE checks the user's SQL Syntax;
- The PE checks the user's security rights;
- The PE comes up with a plan for the AMPs to follow;
- The PE passes the plan along to the AMPs over the BYNET;
- The AMPs follow the plan and retrieve the data requested;
- The AMPs pass the data to the PE over the BYNET; and
- The PE then passes the final data to the user.

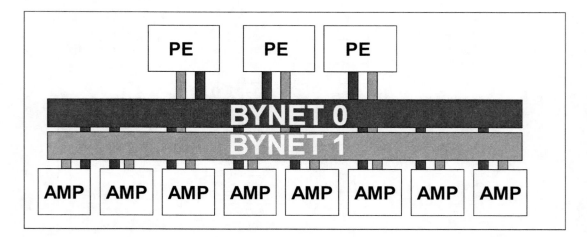

A Visual for Data Layout

"I saw the angel in the marble and carved until I set him free."

--Michelangelo

Teradata saw the users in the warehouse and parallel processed until it set them free. Free to ask any question at any time on any data. The Sistine Chapel wasn't painted in a day and a true data warehouse takes time to carve. Sculpt your warehouse with love and caring and you will build something that will allow your company to have limits that go well beyond the ceiling. Below is a logical view of data on AMPs. Each AMP holds a portion of a table. Each AMP keeps the tables in their own separate drawers.

AMP 1	AMP 2	AMP 3	AMP 4
Employee Table	Employee Table	Employee Table	Employee Table
Order Table	Order Table	Order Table	Order Table
Customer Table	Customer Table	Customer Table	Customer Table
Student Table	Student Table	Student Table	Student Table

How Teradata handles Data Access

- The **PE** handles **session control** functions

- The **AMPs** retrieve and **perform database functions** on their requested rows

- The **BYNET** sends **communications between** the nodes

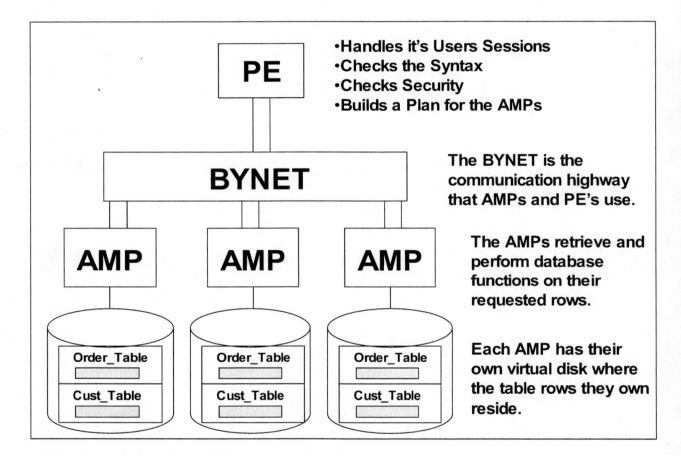

These statements are true about session control responsible for load balancing across the Bynet?

- **The Parser checks statements for proper syntax.**

- **The Optimizer (PE) develops a new and separate plan to determine the best response**

- **The Dispatcher takes steps from the parser and transmits them over the BYNET.**

The PE uses Statistics to come up with the Plan

COLLECT STATISTICS is remarkable. Here is how it works. Let's say you have an employee table with 1,000,000 employees. You decide to collect statistics on the column Last_name.

The AMPs will now either do a full table scan or a percentage COLLECT STATISTICS based on which option you choose.

The system will sort the last_name values in the employee table and place the names in 100 intervals. Because the last_name values are sorted and statistics are gathered about all 100 intervals the Parsing Engine can estimate the rows it will need to have the AMPs retrieve.

Interval 1	Interval 2	Interval 3	Interval 4	
Arden	Brubaker	Davis	Grace	
Allen	Bell	Davis	Fryer	
55	40	90	44	
100	120	100	75	
800	790	900	750	

Statistics Kept in interval

Highest Value in Interval:
Most Frequent Value in Interval:
Rows with Most Frequent Value:
Other Values in the Interval:
Number of Rows of Other Values:

COLLECT STATISTICS sorts the values and places them in 100 different intervals. The PE can interrogate the intervals to Estimate ranges of values as well as frequent values.

When there are NO Statistics Collected on a Table

When statistics are not collected on a table, the optimizer will state in the explain that it has low confidence. This is because it is not confident with exactly what is going on with the table. To come up with a plan, Teradata must perform dynamic AMP sampling. To perform dynamic sampling, the optimizer will choose an AMP to represent an estimation of population demographics. It will instruct the AMP to choose a random block from a random cylinder and count the rows in that cylinder.

The optimizer knows how many AMPs are in the configuration, the number of cylinders, the number of data blocks inside a cylinder, and the number of rows per block in the sampled cylinder. It then does the math and estimates (with low confidence) the statistics to come up with a plan.

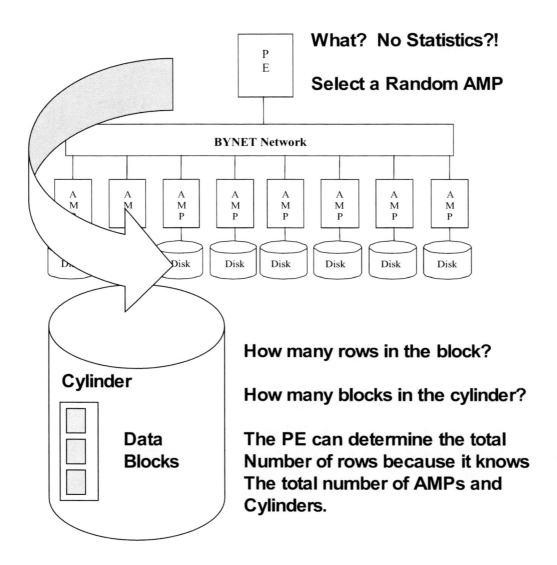

What? No Statistics?!

Select a Random AMP

How many rows in the block?

How many blocks in the cylinder?

The PE can determine the total Number of rows because it knows The total number of AMPs and Cylinders.

Teradata Cabinets, Nodes, Vprocs, and Disks

"The best way to predict the future is to create it."

- Sophia Bedford-Pierce

Teradata predicted data warehousing 20 years before its time by creating it. Who could have imagined 100 Terabyte systems back in the 1970's? Teradata did and created an architecture that can scale indefinitely.

In the picture below we see a Teradata cabinet with four nodes. Each node has two Intel processors of lightning speed. Inside each nodes memory are the AMPs and PEs which are referred to as Virtual Processor of VPROCs. Each node is attached to both BYNETs and each node is attached directly to a set of disks. Each AMP then has one virtual disk where it stores its tables and rows. If you want to expand your system merely buy another Node Cabinet and another Disk Cabinet.

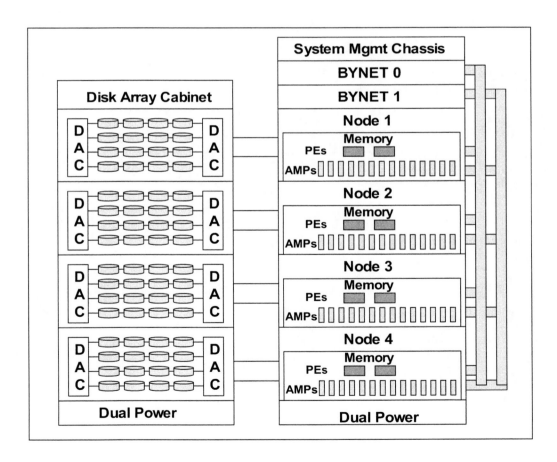

Teradata Understands SQL

The Teradata database responds to Structured Query Language (SQL) requests. SQL can be entered in many ways. It can come from applications or directly from power users. Below are the many ways to submit SQL to Teradata:

- **Queryman or SQL Assistant**
- **BTEQ (Interactive mode)**
- **BTEQ (Batch mode)**
- **Embedded in a stored procedure**
- **Embedded in a client application (written in a procedural language)**
- **Cliv2**
- **ODBC**
- **JDBC**

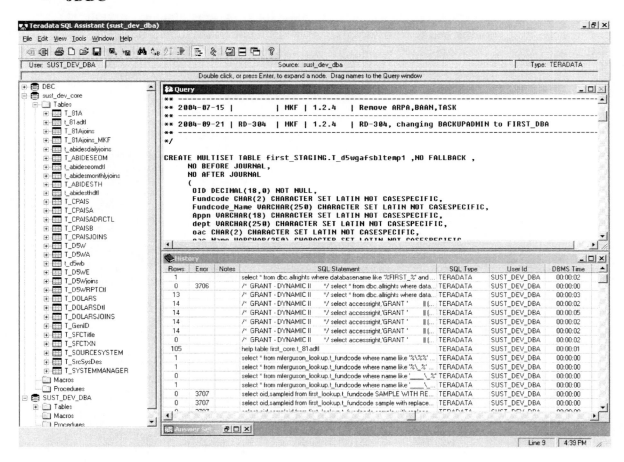

Teradata Maximums

Below are the current **system maximums**.

System Parameter	Value
Total Data Capacity	120 GB per AMP
Maximum number of sectors per data block	255
Maximum data block size	130,560 bytes
Max columns per table or view	2048
Max columns over table or view lifetime	2560
Maximum row size	64,000 bytes
Max columns per index	64
Max SQL request size	1 MB
Max columns per ORDER BY clause	16
Max Partitions for PPI Table	65,535
Max secondary and join indexes per table	32
Max columns/indexes statistics collected	512 per table
Max tables joined per query	64
Max number of nested subqueries	64
Max global temporary tables per session	2000
Max Volatile tables per session	1000

Teradata Maximums per Release

Below are the current **system maximums for Release V2R4, V2R5, and V2R6**.

Teradata Limitations	V2R4	V2R5	V2R6
Columns in a Table	256	2048	2048
Columns in an index	16	16	64
Columns in Collect Stats	40	512	512
Max Vdisk Size per AMP	112 GB	1.2 GB	1.2 GB
Max Block Size in Sectors	127	255	255
Max Table Header Size	64K	64K	128K
Spool Table for a Query	2048	2048	2048
Total Databases and Users	4.2 Billion	4.2 Billion	4.2 Billion

Primary Index (PI)

"Acting is all about honesty.. If you can fake that, you've got it made"

- George Burns

To store the data, the value(s) in the PI are hashed though a calculation to determine which AMP will possess the data. The same data values always hash the same row hash and therefore are always associated with the same AMP. The PI is what makes or breaks the system. The PI is responsible for all of the systems data distribution.

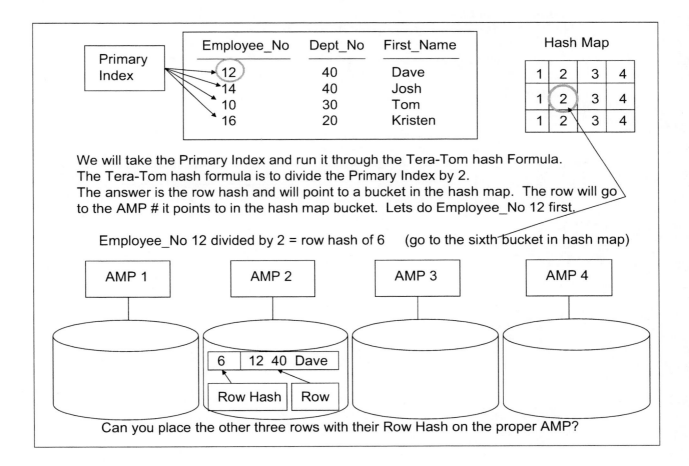

We will take the Primary Index and run it through the Tera-Tom hash Formula.
The Tera-Tom hash formula is to divide the Primary Index by 2.
The answer is the row hash and will point to a bucket in the hash map. The row will go to the AMP # it points to in the hash map bucket. Lets do Employee_No 12 first.

Employee_No 12 divided by 2 = row hash of 6   (go to the sixth bucket in hash map)

Can you place the other three rows with their Row Hash on the proper AMP?

Primary Index cont.

Here the data is spread evenly across all AMPs based on their hash value.

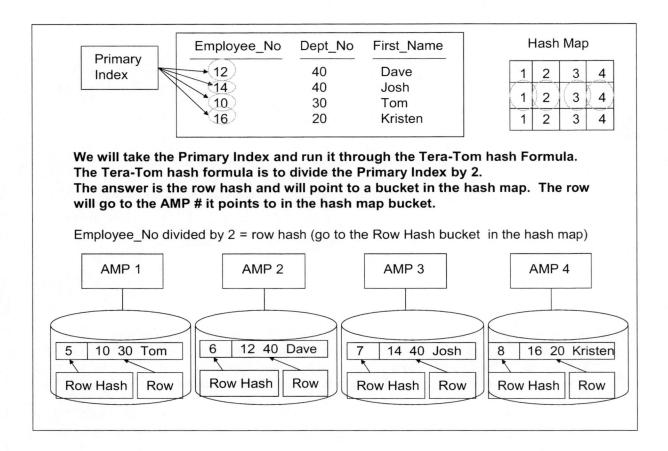

We will take the Primary Index and run it through the Tera-Tom hash Formula.
The Tera-Tom hash formula is to divide the Primary Index by 2.
The answer is the row hash and will point to a bucket in the hash map. The row will go to the AMP # it points to in the hash map bucket.

Employee_No divided by 2 = row hash (go to the Row Hash bucket in the hash map)

Primary Index cont.

Spread evenly

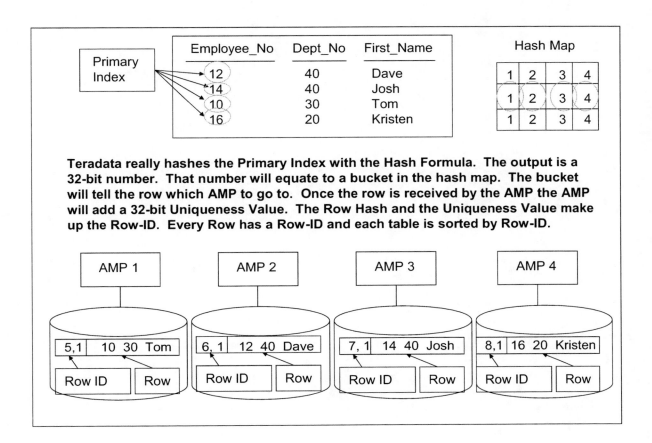

Teradata really hashes the Primary Index with the Hash Formula. The output is a
32-bit number. That number will equate to a bucket in the hash map. The bucket
will tell the row which AMP to go to. Once the row is received by the AMP the AMP
will add a 32-bit Uniqueness Value. The Row Hash and the Uniqueness Value make
up the Row-ID. Every Row has a Row-ID and each table is sorted by Row-ID.

Chapter 2 — SQL Basics

"The difference between genius and stupidity is that genius has its limits"

Anonymous

Rows and Columns

Structured Query Language is the language to retrieve data from tables. We shall start with the very basics in case you are new. Below is a table called the Employee_Table. The Employee_Table below has 12 rows of data. Each row contains 5 columns.

Employee_Table

Employee_No	Dept_No	First_Name	Last_Name	Salary
1	10	Tom	Coffing	50000.00
2	10	Leona	Coffing	75000.50
3	20	Steve	Wilmes	95054.30
4	20	Gareth	Walter	94986.35
5	30	Robert	Hines	120987.45
6	30	Mark	Ferguson	97087.67
7	30	Scott	Smith	143987.94
8	40	Marsha	Lewis	98453.88
9	40	Sara	Wilson	97450.75
10	50	Mike	Larkins	245098.00
11	999	Arfy	Coffing	NULL
12	999	Spot	Coffing	NULL

Teradata stores its information inside Tables. A table consists of rows and columns. A **row** is one instance **of all columns**. According to relational concepts **column positions are arbitrary** and a column always **contains like data**.

Column	Column	Column	Column	Column
Employee_No	Dept_No	First_Name	Last_Name	Salary
2	10	Leona	Coffing	75000.50

Row

The SELECT Command

The first command we will learn is the SELECT Command. We will SELECT Columns from Tables. After the word SELECT will be the Columns that we want to see on the report. Each Column name will be separated by a comma. We will then list the table to pull the columns FROM.

```
SELECT     Employee_No
           ,Dept_No
           ,First_Name
           ,Last_Name
FROM       Employee_Table ;
```

12 Rows Returned

Employee_No	Dept_No	First_Name	Last_Name
1	10	Tom	Coffing
2	10	Leona	Coffing
3	20	Steve	Wilmes
4	20	Gareth	Walter
5	30	Robert	Hines
6	30	Mark	Ferguson
7	30	Scott	Smith
8	40	Marsha	Lewis
9	40	Sara	Wilson
10	50	Mike	Larkins
11	999	Arfy	Coffing
12	999	Spot	Coffing

The SELECT Command with *

When you use the **SELECT** * in your SQL the system will **SELECT ALL Columns** in the table. Below is an example.

```
SELECT    *
FROM      Employee_Table ;
```

12 Rows Returned

Employee_No	Dept_No	First_Name	Last_Name	Salary
1	10	Tom	Coffing	50000.00
2	10	Leona	Coffing	75000.50
3	20	Steve	Wilmes	95054.30
4	20	Gareth	Walter	94986.35
5	30	Robert	Hines	120987.45
6	30	Mark	Ferguson	97087.67
7	30	Scott	Smith	143987.94
8	40	Marsha	Lewis	98453.88
9	40	Sara	Wilson	97450.75
10	50	Mike	Larkins	245098.00
11	999	Arfy	Coffing	NULL
12	999	Spot	Coffing	NULL

As you can see in our example above our SELECT * query brought back every column. It also brought back every row. The SELECT * has nothing to do with bringing back every row. It only brings back every column. We actually brought back every row because we did not have a WHERE Clause.

The WHERE Clause

When you use the SELECT * in your SQL the system will SELECT ALL Columns in the table. When you place a **WHERE clause in your SQL** it will **limit the number of rows retrieved**. In our example we will SELECT ALL Columns, but only for rows with a Dept_No of 999. Only Arfy Coffing and Spot Coffing should return.

Employee_Table

Employee_No	Dept_No	First_Name	Last_Name	Salary
1	10	Tom	Coffing	50000.00
2	10	Leona	Coffing	75000.50
3	20	Steve	Wilmes	95054.30
4	20	Gareth	Walter	94986.35
5	30	Robert	Hines	120987.45
6	30	Mark	Ferguson	97087.67
7	30	Scott	Smith	143987.94
8	40	Marsha	Lewis	98453.88
9	40	Sara	Wilson	97450.75
10	50	Mike	Larkins	245098.00
11	999	Arfy	Coffing	NULL
12	999	Spot	Coffing	NULL

```
SELECT    *
FROM      Employee_Table
WHERE     Dept_No = 999 ;
```

2 Rows Returned

Employee_No	Dept_No	First_Name	Last_Name	Salary
11	999	Arfy	Coffing	NULL
12	999	Spot	Coffing	NULL

The Order BY Clause

When Teradata brings back an answer set it will be unsorted **unless you use the ORDER BY statement**. The ORDER BY statement will sort the data based on the column(s) listed. The default Order is Ascending. Here are two examples of the ORDER BY statement. The first example uses the **column name** and the **second uses a number**. The 4 represents the 4th column being retrieved. **Both queries bring back the same results**.

```
SELECT      *
FROM        Employee_Table
ORDER BY    Last_Name ;
```

```
SELECT      *
FROM        Employee_Table
ORDER BY    4 ;
```

12 Rows Returned

Employee_No	Dept_No	First_Name	Last_Name	Salary
1	10	Tom	Coffing	50000.00
2	10	Leona	Coffing	75000.50
11	999	Arfy	Coffing	NULL
12	999	Spot	Coffing	NULL
6	30	Mark	Ferguson	97087.67
5	30	Robert	Hines	120987.45
10	50	Mike	Larkins	245098.00
8	40	Marsha	Lewis	98453.88
7	30	Scott	Smith	143987.94
4	20	Gareth	Walter	94986.35
3	20	Steve	Wilmes	95054.30
9	40	Sara	Wilson	97450.75

Sorting by Multiple Columns

You can sort by multiple columns as in our example below by **separating the ORDER BY list with commas.**

```
SELECT        *
FROM          Employee_Table
ORDER BY      Last_Name, First_Name ;
```

12 Rows Returned

Employee_No	Dept_No	First_Name	Last_Name	Salary
11	999	Arfy	Coffing	NULL
2	10	Leona	Coffing	75000.50
12	999	Spot	Coffing	NULL
1	10	Tom	Coffing	50000.00
6	30	Mark	Ferguson	97087.67
5	30	Robert	Hines	120987.45
10	50	Mike	Larkins	245098.00
8	40	Marsha	Lewis	98453.88
7	30	Scott	Smith	143987.94
4	20	Gareth	Walter	94986.35
3	20	Steve	Wilmes	95054.30
9	40	Sara	Wilson	97450.75

Sorting In Descending Order

You can sort in **Descending Order** by using the keyword **DESC** in your SQL.

```
SELECT       *
FROM         Employee_Table
ORDER BY     Last_Name DESC ;
```

12 Rows Returned

Employee_No	Dept_No	First_Name	Last_Name	Salary
9	40	Sara	Wilson	97450.75
3	20	Steve	Wilmes	95054.30
4	20	Gareth	Walter	94986.35
7	30	Scott	Smith	143987.94
8	40	Marsha	Lewis	98453.88
10	50	Mike	Larkins	245098.00
5	30	Robert	Hines	120987.45
6	30	Mark	Ferguson	97087.67
11	999	Arfy	Coffing	NULL
2	10	Leona	Coffing	75000.50
12	999	Spot	Coffing	NULL
1	10	Tom	Coffing	50000.00

"My son has taken up meditation - at least it's better than sitting doing nothing."

Max Kauffmann

Valid Teradata Names

Teradata has the following rules when naming a Teradata object.

Teradata Object Names

Each object name consists from 1 to 30 characters.
A name can consist of upper or lower case letters from a – z or A – Z.
A name can consist of special characters of $, #, or _
A name can NOT begin with a digit or be a keyword

Teradata Name Rules

Databases must have unique names throughout the system.
Objects such as tables, views, macros, stored procedures, and triggers must have unique names WITHIN A DATABASE.
All COLUMNS must have unique names inside a table or view.

YOU ARE NOT ANSI SQL – 99 Compliant if your names contain
Contains lower case letters
Has more than 18 characters
Contains either a $ or #

Punctuation (Period .)

The **Period (.)** is used to distinguish between a **database, an object or a column**. Our example below shows exactly how the period is used. To **qualify** an object means to include the table or database it is from.

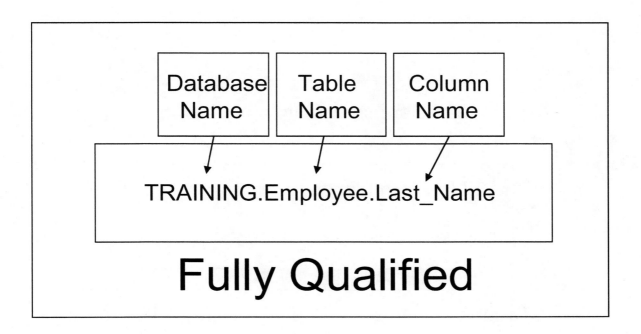

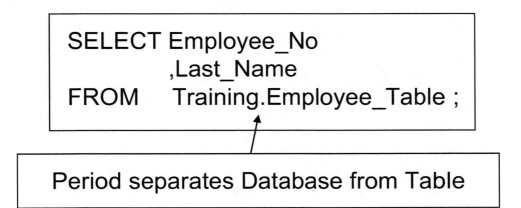

How to SET your Default Database

You can use the DATABASE command to tell Teradata that you want to currently point to a database as a default.

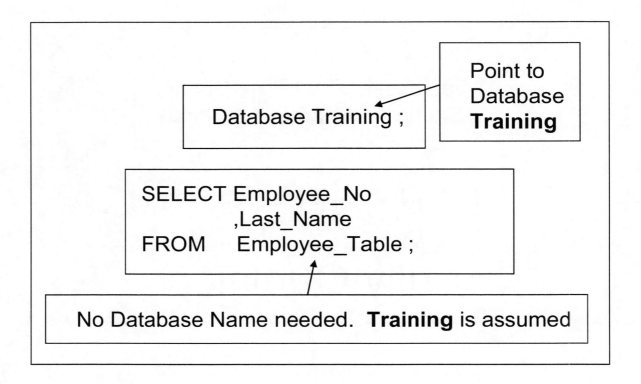

Punctuation (Comma ,)

The **comma** is used to separate **columns in a SELECT list**. A comma is also used to **separate table names** using Teradata **join syntax**. A comma is also used to **separate columns** in an **ORDER BY statement**. Our next example will utilize commas in all three places.

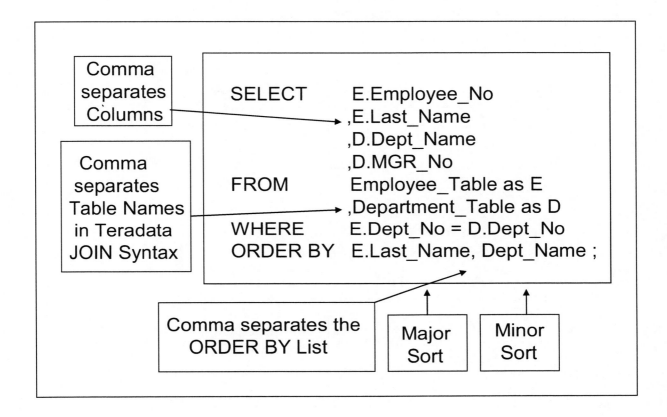

Punctuation (Single Quotes '   ')

Single Quotes are used on all **Character String literals**.   Below are some excellent examples.

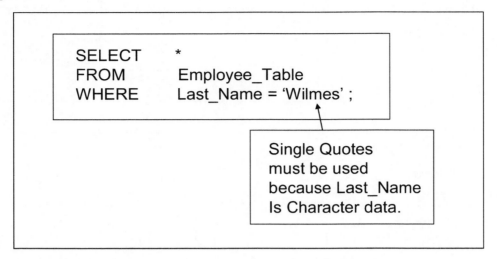

```
SELECT        *
FROM          Employee_Table
WHERE         Last_Name = 'Wilmes' ;
```

Single Quotes must be used because Last_Name Is Character data.

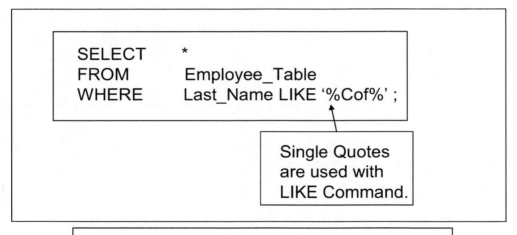

```
SELECT        *
FROM          Employee_Table
WHERE         Last_Name LIKE '%Cof%' ;
```

Single Quotes are used with LIKE Command.

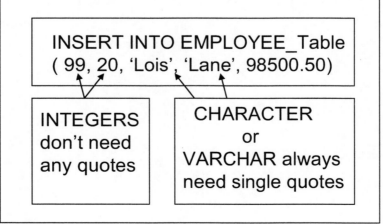

```
INSERT INTO EMPLOYEE_Table
( 99, 20, 'Lois', 'Lane', 98500.50)
```

INTEGERS don't need any quotes

CHARACTER or VARCHAR always need single quotes

34

Punctuation (Double Quotes " ")

Double Quotes are used when **aliasing a column** that has **multiple words and spaces separating them**. You will also use **double quotes** on all aliases that are **reserved words**.

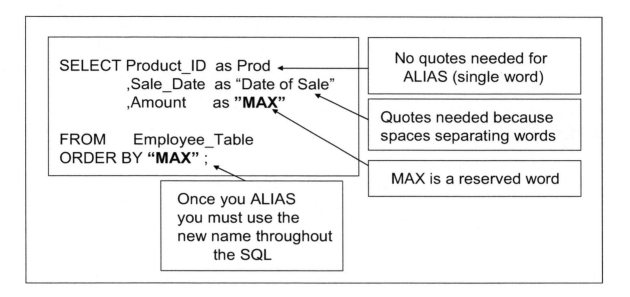

10 Rows Returned

Prod	Date of Sale	MAX
10	2004-01-03	2000.00
10	2004-01-02	3000.00
20	2004-01-05	4000.00
10	2004-01-01	5000.00
10	2004-01-05	5000.00
10	2004-01-04	6000.00
20	2004-01-01	12000.00
20	2004-01-02	13000.00
20	2004-01-03	15000.00
20	2004-01-04	20000.00

Punctuation - Placing Comments inside the SQL

Teradata gives you two options for placing comments inside your SQL. The **ANSI way** of commenting is by placing **two double dashes** (--) at the beginning of a line. Any other words after the double dashes on the same line are considered comments.

The **Teradata form** of doing this is to place a **/* to start a comment and */ to end the comment**. This allows you to span your comments among multiple lines easily.

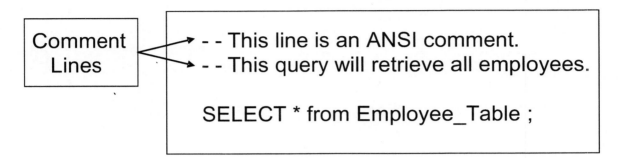

Comment Lines

- - This line is an ANSI comment.
- - This query will retrieve all employees.

SELECT * from Employee_Table ;

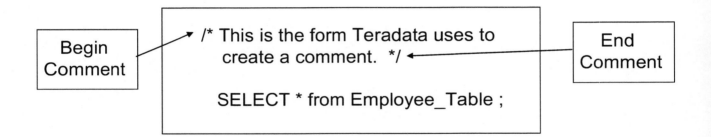

Begin Comment

/* This is the form Teradata uses to create a comment. */

End Comment

SELECT * from Employee_Table ;

-- **Below are reserved words used by Teradata**

SELECT database, session, account, USER, date, time ;

One Row Returned

Database	Session	Account	USER	Date	Time
Training	1000	$M	DBC	2004-06-05	21:07:32

Chapter 4 - Help, Show, and Explain

"Be the change that you want to see in the world."

Mahatma Gandhi

The HELP Command

Users can use the HELP command for many purposes. Two HELP commands to get you started are HELP Database *Databasename* and HELP TABLE *Tablename*.

The first HELP command you should utilize is the **HELP Database command**. This will tell you **all the objects in a particular database**.

```
HELP Database Training;
```

4 rows processed

Table/View/Macro name	Kind	Comment	Protection	Creator Name
Department_Table	T	?	F	DBC
Employee_table	T	?	F	DBC
Emp_Dept_Macro	M	?	F	DBC
Emp_View	V	?	F	DBC

```
HELP Table Employee_Table ;
```

5 rows processed

Column name	Type	Comment	Nullable	Format
Employee_no	I	Emp Number	Y	-(10)9
Dept_no	I	Department Number	Y	-(10)9
First_name	CV	?	Y	X(20)
Last_name	CF	?	Y	X(20)
Salary	D	?	Y	-------.99

Help Table will give you the **Column names, data types**, and **comments**.

The HELP Command continued

You can utilize the HELP command to get information about your session.

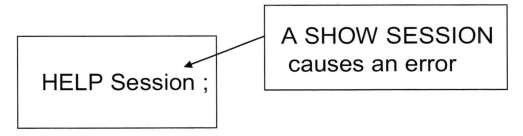

HELP Session ;

A SHOW SESSION causes an error

	User Name	Account Name	Logon Date	Logon Time	Current Database
1 row returned	DBC	DBC	04/10/24	20:08:29	Training

You can also find out if a table has collected statistics with the HELP Statistics command. The command will show you the Date, Time, Unique Values, and Column Names for all columns or indexes in which statistics were collected.

HELP Statistics Employee_table;

Date	Time	Unique Values	Column Names
3 rows returned			
04/10/24	20:50:01	12	employee_no
04/10/24	20:50:09	4	dept_no
04/10/24	20:51:00	12	first_name, last_name

The SHOW Command

The **SHOW Command will display the DDL of certain objects**. This includes the original **CREATE statement** plus any **additional changes or indexes made after the original CREATE**. The SHOW command includes tables, views, macros, triggers, and stored procedures.

> Show Table Employee_table;

```
CREATE SET TABLE TRAINING.Employee_Table, FALLBACK,
NO BEFORE JOURNAL,
NO AFTER JOURNAL
(
employee_no      INTEGER,
dept_no          INTEGER,
first_name       VARCHAR(20) CHARACTER SET LATIN NOT CASESPECIFIC,
last_name        CHAR(20) CHARACTER SET LATIN NOT CASESPECIFIC,
salary           DECIMAL(10,2))
UNIQUE PRIMARY INDEX(employee_no)
UNIQUE INDEX (first_name, last_name);
```

> Show View emp_view ;

```
CREATE View emp_view
AS
SELECT   employee_no
         ,dept_no
         ,first_name
         ,last_name
FROM     employee_table ;
```

The EXPLAIN Command

If you type the word **EXPLAIN** in front of your SQL you will see the **Parsing Engines (PE) plan**. The SQL will not execute with the EXPLAIN keyword in the front. It merely allows you to see the plan the AMPs will take to satisfy the query.

```
EXPLAIN SEL *
        FROM    Employee_Table
        WHERE first_name = 'Leona'
        AND     last_name = 'Coffing';
```

1) First, we do a two-AMP RETRIEVE step from TRAINING.employee_table by way of unique index #4 "TRAINING.employee_table.first_name = 'Leona', TRAINING.employee_table.last_name = 'Coffing'" with no residual conditions. The estimated time for this step is 0.02 seconds.
-> The row is sent directly back to the user as the result of statement 1. The total estimated time is 0.02 seconds.

```
EXPLAIN SEL *
          FROM    Emp_View ;
```

1) First, we lock a distinct TRAINING."psuedo table" for read on a RowHash to prevent global deadlock for TRAINING.Employee_table.
2) Next, we lock TRAINING.Employee_table for read.
3) We do an all-AMPs RETRIEVE step from TRAINING.Employee_table by way of an all-rows scan with no residual conditions into spool 1 (group_amps), which is built locally on the AMPs. The size of Spool 1 is estimated with high confidence to be 1 row. The estimated time for this step is 0.03 seconds.
4) Finally, we send out an END TRANSACTION step to all AMPs involved in processing the request.
-> The contents of Spool 1 are sent back to the user as the result of statement 1. The total estimated time is 0.03 seconds.

Chapter 5 — SELECTING Rows

"It is the mark of an educated mind to be able to entertain a thought without accepting it."

Aristotle

Checking for NULL Values with IS NULL

Some columns will contain NULL values. These will usually be represented by a question mark question mark (?) in SQL Assistant or QueryMan. A NULL value is an unknown value. Therefore you cannot use an equality or equal sign in your SQL WHERE clause to check for NULLs. There are only two commands that check for NULL values. **Those key words are**:

IS NULL

IS NOT NULL

Here is an example of **using equality** and receiving **an error**.

```
SELECT        *
FROM          Employee_Table
WHERE         Salary = NULL ;
```

ERROR: Equality not valid; must use IS NULL

Here is an example of the **IS NULL** statement.

```
SELECT        *
FROM          Employee_Table
WHERE         Salary IS NULL ;
```

2 Rows Returned

Employee_No	Dept_No	First_Name	Last_Name	Salary
11	999	Arfy	Coffing	NULL
12	999	Spot	Coffing	NULL

Checking for NULL Values with IS NOT NULL

Some columns will contain NULL values. These will usually be represented by a question mark (?) in SQL Assistant or QueryMan. A NULL value is an unknown value. Therefore you cannot use an equality or equal sign in your SQL WHERE clause to check for NULLs. There are only two commands that check for NULL values. Those key words are:

IS NULL

IS NOT NULL

Here is an example of the **IS NOT NULL** statement.

```
SELECT        *
FROM          Employee_Table
WHERE         Salary IS NOT NULL ;
```

10 Rows Returned

Employee_No	Dept_No	First_Name	Last_Name	Salary
1	10	Tom	Coffing	50000.00
2	10	Leona	Coffing	75000.50
3	20	Steve	Wilmes	95054.30
4	20	Gareth	Walter	94986.35
5	30	Robert	Hines	120987.45
6	30	Mark	Ferguson	97087.67
7	30	Scott	Smith	143987.94
8	40	Marsha	Lewis	98453.88
9	40	Sara	Wilson	97450.75
10	50	Mike	Larkins	245098.00

How will NULL Values Sort?

When you use the ORDER BY statement on a column with NULL values the **NULL values will come back first**. Remember, **NULL values in ASC mode** will come back **first**. NULL values will **even come back first** over odd possibilities such as **spaces, blanks, or zeros**.

The same concept goes for **DESC mode**. If you sort in **descending order** then the **NULL values** will come back **last.** They will even come back in **DESC mode** after odd possibilities such as **spaces, blanks, or zeros**.

12 Rows Returned

Employee_No	Dept_No	First_Name	Last_Name	Salary
11	999	Arfy	Coffing	**NULL**
12	999	Spot	Coffing	**NULL**
1	10	Tom	Coffing	50000.00
2	10	Leona	Coffing	75000.50
4	20	Gareth	Walter	94986.35
3	20	Steve	Wilmes	95054.30
6	30	Mark	Ferguson	97087.67
9	40	Sara	Wilson	97450.75
8	40	Marsha	Lewis	98453.88
5	30	Robert	Hines	120987.45
7	30	Scott	Smith	143987.94
10	50	Mike	Larkins	245098.00

The DISTINCT Command

Sometimes it is only necessary to see the values in a column without seeing multiple values that are the same. You might want to know the different departments in the Employee_Table. The **DISTINCT** command can be used to accomplish this goal. Remember, we had 12 employees in six different departments. Notice that **all duplicates are eliminated**.

```
SELECT      Distinct Dept_No
FROM        Employee_Table
ORDER BY  1 ;
```

6 rows returned

Dept_No
10
20
30
40
50
999

The DISTINCT Command with Multiple Columns

Our next example will show the **DISTINCT command** with **multiple columns**. The DISTINCT command with multiple columns will **put the columns together** and **eliminate duplicate values if all columns requested are identical**. Remember that we had two people in Dept_No 10 named Coffing and who could ever forget that we also had Arfy and Spot in Dept_No 999. Notice that only one Coffing came back for Dept_No 10 and the same with Dept_No 999. For a row to be eliminated in our example the Dept_No and the Last_Name combined had to have a duplicate.

```
SELECT      Distinct Dept_No
                     ,Last_Name
FROM        Employee_Table
ORDER BY  1 ;
```

10 Rows Returned

Dept_No	Last_Name
10	Coffing
20	Wilmes
20	Walter
30	Hines
30	Ferguson
30	Smith
40	Lewis
40	Wilson
50	Larkins
999	Coffing

Multiple DISTINCT statements in the same SQL

Our next example will show the multiple DISTINCT statements in the same SQL. Notice that our aggregate gets different answers for our Employee_Table for employees, departments, and last names.

Employee_Table

Employee_No	Dept_No	First_Name	Last_Name	Salary
1	10	Tom	Coffing	50000.00
2	10	Leona	Coffing	75000.50
3	20	Steve	Wilmes	95054.30
4	20	Gareth	Walter	94986.35
5	30	Robert	Hines	120987.45
6	30	Mark	Ferguson	97087.67
7	30	Scott	Smith	143987.94
8	40	Marsha	Lewis	98453.88
9	40	Sara	Wilson	97450.75
10	50	Mike	Larkins	245098.00
11	999	Arfy	Coffing	NULL
12	999	Spot	Coffing	NULL

```
SELECT          COUNT(DISTINCT employee_no) as Employees
                ,COUNT(DISTINCT dept_no)     as Departments
                ,COUNT(DISTINCT last_name)   as Distinct_Name
FROM Employee_table;
```

One Row Returned

Employees	Departments	Distinct_Name
12	6	9

The AND Operator

If you don't want every row to return, but instead just one or more then the WHERE clause is utilized. You can use the AND operator in conjunction with the WHERE clause to further limit the number of rows returning. Our example will use the WHERE clause and the AND operator. Both requirements will need to be met for a row to return.

Employee_Table

Employee_No	Dept_No	First_Name	Last_Name	Salary
1	10	Tom	Coffing	50000.00
2	10	Leona	Coffing	75000.50
3	20	Steve	Wilmes	95054.30
4	20	Gareth	Walter	94986.35
5	30	Robert	Hines	120987.45
6	30	Mark	Ferguson	97087.67
7	30	Scott	Smith	143987.94
8	40	Marsha	Lewis	98453.88
9	40	Sara	Wilson	97450.75
10	50	Mike	Larkins	245098.00
11	999	Arfy	Coffing	NULL
12	999	Spot	Coffing	NULL

```
SELECT    *
FROM      Employee_Table
WHERE     Dept_No = 10
AND       Salary > 60000.00 ;
```

1 Row Returned

Employee_No	Dept_No	First_Name	Last_Name	Salary
2	10	Leona	Coffing	75000.50

The OR Operator

Sometimes you will need to bring back rows that meet one value OR another value. Either value brings back the row. Here is an example:

Employee_Table

Employee_No	Dept_No	First_Name	Last_Name	Salary
1	10	Tom	Coffing	50000.00
2	10	Leona	Coffing	75000.50
3	20	Steve	Wilmes	95054.30
4	20	Gareth	Walter	94986.35
5	30	Robert	Hines	120987.45
6	30	Mark	Ferguson	97087.67
7	30	Scott	Smith	143987.94
8	40	Marsha	Lewis	98453.88
9	40	Sara	Wilson	97450.75
10	50	Mike	Larkins	245098.00
11	999	Arfy	Coffing	NULL
12	999	Spot	Coffing	NULL

```
SELECT     *
FROM       Employee_Table
WHERE      Dept_No = 10
OR         Dept_No = 20 ;
```

4 Rows Returned

Employee_No	Dept_No	First_Name	Last_Name	Salary
1	10	Tom	Coffing	50000.00
2	10	Leona	Coffing	75000.50
3	20	Steve	Wilmes	95054.30
4	20	Gareth	Walter	94986.35

The NOT Operator   *Ne, Not eq*

The NOT operator will bring back rows NOT =, >, < to a particular column. Here is an example:

Employee_Table				
Employee_No	**Dept_No**	**First_Name**	**Last_Name**	**Salary**
1	10	Tom	Coffing	50000.00
2	10	Leona	Coffing	75000.50
3	20	Steve	Wilmes	95054.30
4	20	Gareth	Walter	94986.35
5	30	Robert	Hines	120987.45
6	30	Mark	Ferguson	97087.67
7	30	Scott	Smith	143987.94
8	40	Marsha	Lewis	98453.88
9	40	Sara	Wilson	97450.75
10	50	Mike	Larkins	245098.00
11	999	Arfy	Coffing	NULL
12	999	Spot	Coffing	NULL

```
SELECT    *
FROM      Employee_Table
WHERE     Salary NOT < 100000 ;
```

3 Rows Returned				
Employee_No	**Dept_No**	**First_Name**	**Last_Name**	**Salary**
5	30	Robert	Hines	120987.45
7	30	Scott	Smith	143987.94
10	50	Mike	Larkins	245098.00

Order of Precedence for (), NOT, AND, or OR

Teradata will always evaluate **Parenthesis first and then NOT, AND an OR is last**. Remember that the **order of precedence** is **( )**, **NOT**, **AND**, and finally **OR**. It is best to place parenthesis in your SQL to be sure. Here is a mistake. Let's assume we want to find anyone in Dept_No 10 OR Dept_No 20 who is making more then 90000. The first example below will not work. Why? Because without the Parenthesis the SQL below is evaluated as SELECT * FROM Employee_Table where Dept_No = 20 AND Salary > 90000 or pick anyone in Dept_No 10. Notice the Parenthesis in our second example.

```
SELECT     *
FROM       Employee_Table
WHERE      Dept_No = 10
OR         Dept_No = 20
AND        Salary    > 90000 ;
```

4 Rows Returned

Employee_No	Dept_No	First_Name	Last_Name	Salary
1	10	Tom	Coffing	50000.00
2	10	Leona	Coffing	75000.50
3	20	Steve	Wilmes	95054.30
4	20	Gareth	Walter	94986.35

```
SELECT     *
FROM       Employee_Table
WHERE      ( Dept_No = 10
OR           Dept_No = 20 )
AND          Salary    > 90000 ;
```

2 Rows Returned

Employee_No	Dept_No	First_Name	Last_Name	Salary
3	20	Steve	Wilmes	95054.30
4	20	Gareth	Walter	94986.35

USING an IN List instead of OR

Instead of using an **OR operator** you can use an **IN List**. Our first example will use the OR operator and our second example will return the exact same results because it is essentially the same query.

```
SELECT     *
FROM       Employee_Table
WHERE      Dept_No = 10
OR         Dept_No = 20 ;
```

4 Rows Returned

Employee_No	Dept_No	First_Name	Last_Name	Salary
1	10	Tom	Coffing	50000.00
2	10	Leona	Coffing	75000.50
3	20	Steve	Wilmes	95054.30
4	20	Gareth	Walter	94986.35

```
SELECT     *
FROM       Employee_Table
WHERE      Dept_No IN (10,20) ;
```

4 Rows Returned

Employee_No	Dept_No	First_Name	Last_Name	Salary
1	10	Tom	Coffing	50000.00
2	10	Leona	Coffing	75000.50
3	20	Steve	Wilmes	95054.30
4	20	Gareth	Walter	94986.35

The BETWEEN Operator

The Between Operator will bring back a range of values. It is said to be **inclusive** because it brings back all rows with the starting and ending values and everything in BETWEEN. Another way to express the **BETWEEN statement** would be:

Column >= A and Column <= B

Employee_Table

Employee_No	Dept_No	First_Name	Last_Name	Salary
1	10	Tom	Coffing	50000.00
2	10	Leona	Coffing	75000.50
3	20	Steve	Wilmes	95054.30
4	20	Gareth	Walter	94986.35
5	30	Robert	Hines	120987.45
6	30	Mark	Ferguson	97087.67
7	30	Scott	Smith	143987.94
8	40	Marsha	Lewis	98453.88
9	40	Sara	Wilson	97450.75
10	50	Mike	Larkins	245098.00
11	999	Arfy	Coffing	NULL
12	999	Spot	Coffing	NULL

```
SELECT    *
FROM      Employee_Table
WHERE     Employee_No Between 8 AND 10 ;
```

3 Rows Returned

Employee_No	Dept_No	First_Name	Last_Name	Salary
8	40	Marsha	Lewis	98453.88
9	40	Sara	Wilson	97450.75
10	50	Mike	Larkins	245098.00

Notice that 8 and 10 were included in the answer set! Inclusive means included.

The LIKE Operator and Percent Wildcard

When you use the WHERE clause and an EQUAL sign then a column must be completely equal to the value if the row is to be returned. When you use the WHERE with the LIKE operator only portions have to be EQUAL for the row to be returned. There are **two wildcards with LIKE** and they are **percent (%) and the Underscore (_)**. If you use a percent **%** it is a wildcard for **any number of characters**. If you use an **underscore _** it is a wildcard for **only one character**.

Here is an example of the % wildcard used with the LIKE command.

Employee_Table

Employee_No	Dept_No	First_Name	Last_Name	Salary
1	10	Tom	Coffing	50000.00
2	10	Leona	Coffing	75000.50
3	20	Steve	Wilmes	95054.30
4	20	Gareth	Walter	94986.35
5	30	Robert	Hines	120987.45
6	30	Mark	Ferguson	97087.67
7	30	Scott	Smith	143987.94
8	40	Marsha	Lewis	98453.88
9	40	Sara	Wilson	97450.75
10	50	Mike	Larkins	245098.00
11	999	Arfy	Coffing	NULL
12	999	Spot	Coffing	NULL

```
SELECT    *
FROM      Employee_Table
WHERE     Last_Name LIKE 'L%' ;
```

2 Rows Returned

Employee_No	Dept_No	First_Name	Last_Name	Salary
8	40	Marsha	Lewis	98453.88
10	50	Mike	Larkins	245098.00

The LIKE Operator - Underscore Wildcard _

Here is an example of the _ wildcard used with the LIKE command. The Underscore is only a wildcard for a single character. Our SQL example will look for anyone who has the first character of their last_name a 'W' and the third character an 'L' and the fifth character an 'E'.

Employee_Table

Employee_No	Dept_No	First_Name	Last_Name	Salary
1	10	Tom	Coffing	50000.00
2	10	Leona	Coffing	75000.50
3	20	Steve	Wilmes	95054.30
4	20	Gareth	Walter	94986.35
5	30	Robert	Hines	120987.45
6	30	Mark	Ferguson	97087.67
7	30	Scott	Smith	143987.94
8	40	Marsha	Lewis	98453.88
9	40	Sara	Wilson	97450.75
10	50	Mike	Larkins	245098.00
11	999	Arfy	Coffing	NULL
12	999	Spot	Coffing	NULL

```
SELECT    *
FROM      Employee_Table
WHERE     Last_Name LIKE 'W_L_E%' ;
```

2 Rows Returned

Employee_No	Dept_No	First_Name	Last_Name	Salary
3	20	Steve	Wilmes	95054.30
4	20	Gareth	Walter	94986.35

LIKE Operator

"All human actions have on or more of these seven causes: chance, nature, compulsion, habit, reason, passion, and desire."

--Aristotle

In a situation when we want to find all employees who have a first name ending in 'E', we will use the LIKE Operator to do this. Remember the '%' wildcard is used to find all names with any amount of characters preceding our known value of 'E'.

This example illustrates how to find all names ending in 'E' using the LIKE operator.

```
SEL *
FROM Employee_Table
WHERE First_Name LIKE '%E';
```

Employee_no	dept_no	first_name	Last_name	Salary
3	20	Steve	Wilmes	95054.30
10	50	Mike	Larkins	245098.00

LIKE Operator with TRIM Function

When looking for all Last Names ending in 'S' we will use the TRIM Function to eliminate all trailing spaces from the letter of each name. We use this function because our last name column is a CHAR(20) meaning that all last names will take up 20 bytes. So, the last name of 'Polen' will take up five spaces leaving 15 spaces trailing. The TRIM will eliminate those 15 spaces and show the last letter of that name as 'N'.

This example illustrates how to find all last names ending in 'E' using the LIKE operator. However, considering that the Last_Name is a CHAR the TRIM Function will eliminate all trailing spaces.

```
SEL *
FROM Employee_Table
WHERE TRIM(Last_Name) LIKE '%S';
```

Employee_no	dept_no	first_name	Last_name	Salary
1	30	Robert	Hines	120987.45
10	50	Mike	Larkins	245098.00
3	20	Steve	Wilmes	95054.30
8	40	Marsha	Lewis	98453.88

LIKE ANY Operator

The LIKE ANY Operator will show multiple searches within one query. Here we are looking for any name having either an 'A' or an 'E' in it.

This example illustrates how to find all names containing a character string of either characters 'A' or 'E', in either order is returned.

```
SEL *
FROM Employee_Table
WHERE First_Name LIKE ANY ('%A%', '%E%');
```

Employee_no	dept_no	first_name	Last_name	Salary
9	40	Sara	Wilson	97450.75
11	999	Arfy	Coffing	?
5	30	Robert	Hines	120987.45
10	50	Mike	Larkins	245098.00
3	20	Steve	Wilmes	95054.30
8	40	Marsha	Lewis	98453.88
6	30	Mark	Ferguson	97087.67
4	20	Gareth	Walter	94986.35
2	10	Leona	Coffing	75000.50

LIKE ALL Operator

The LIKE ALL Operator shows all values containing multiple constraints. In this example we are looking for all names that have both an 'A' as well as an 'E' in them.

This example illustrates how to find all names containing a character string of both characters 'A' and 'E', this is returned in either order.

```
SEL *
FROM Employee_Table
WHERE First_Name LIKE ALL ('%A%', '%E%');
```

Employee_no	dept_no	first_name	Last_name	Salary
2	10	Leona	Coffing	75000.50
4	20	Gareth	Walter	94986.35

LIKE ESCAPE '\' Command

This LIKE Command uses the ESCAPE '\' to show all names with a "_" after the word Teradata. If for example we have a word with an "_" in it and we wanted to locate that, we will enter in either the text such as LIKE (Teradata_%')ESCAPE'\' or if we knew how many spaces we needed to cover before we fount the "_" (8 in this case for example), but did not know what the letters were we could type in something like this: LIKE ('_ _ _ _ _ _ _ __%')ESCAPE'\'.

This example illustrates how to find all names containing a "_" in the 9th position of the certification column.

```
SEL *
FROM cert_table
WHERE certification LIKE ('Teradata\_%') ESCAPE'\';
```

Certification	Test_No
Teradata_DBA	NR-0014
Teradata_Application_Development	NR-0016
Teradata_SQL	NR-0013
Teradata_Physical_Implementation	NR-0012
Teradata_Basics	NR-0011
Teradata_Designer	NR-0015

SQL that causes a Full Table Scan (FTS)

The chart below shows SQL that will cause Teradata to perform a Full Table Scan (FTS). This means that every AMP reads each of its rows for a table so every row in the table was read. The great news is that **Teradata performs in parallel** so each row is **read only once** by the owning AMP.

SQL that always causes a Full Table Scan (FTS)
Nonequality comparisons
Column_name IS NOT NULL
All **NOT** Conditions
SUBSTR(column_name)
Column_name **BETWEEN** .. AND ..
Condition 1 OR Condition 2
All Aggregates – **SUM, MAX, MIN, AVG, COUNT**
DISTINCT
ANY
ALL
INDEX (column_name)
Column_1 || Column_2 = value
Column_name LIKE
Missing WHERE Clause

Chapter 6 — Aggregates

"I went to a restaurant that serves 'breakfast any time.' So I ordered French toast during the Renaissance."

Steven Wright

The Five Aggregates

This chapter will focus on five aggregates. Those aggregates are SUM, AVG, MIN, MAX, and COUNT.

Here are some simple rules to follow with aggregates:

- Aggregates produce a **single line answer set.**

- Aggregates **ignore NULL values** in their calculations.

- You can't mix **normal columns** with **aggregates** unless you use the **GROUP BY** statement.

Employee_Table

Employee_No	Dept_No	First_Name	Last_Name	Salary
1	10	Tom	Coffing	50000.00
2	10	Leona	Coffing	75000.50
3	20	Steve	Wilmes	95054.30
4	20	Gareth	Walter	94986.35
5	30	Robert	Hines	120987.45
6	30	Mark	Ferguson	97087.67
7	30	Scott	Smith	143987.94
8	40	Marsha	Lewis	98453.88
9	40	Sara	Wilson	97450.75
10	50	Mike	Larkins	245098.00
11	999	Arfy	Coffing	NULL
12	999	Spot	Coffing	NULL

Select Max(Salary), Min(Salary) from Employee_Table;

One row returned

Max(Salary)	Min(Salary)
245098.00	50000.00

Aggregate Example with NULL Values

We will look at a table called Small_Table with merely the Employee_No and their salary.

Small_Table	
Employee_No	Salary
1	50000
2	50000
3	NULL

Your job is to provide the answers for the next three queries.

SELECT AVG(SALARY) FROM Small_Table ;

Query 1 answer _____

SELECT COUNT(SALARY) FROM Small_Table ;

Query 2 answer _____

SELECT COUNT(*) FROM Small_Table ;

Query 3 answer _____

Aggregate Example Answers

Small_Table	
Employee_No	Salary
1	50000
2	50000
3	NULL

Query 1

```
SELECT AVG(SALARY) FROM Small_Table ;
```

The answer for Query 1 is **50000**.   This is because employee_no 3 has a **salary of NULL**. The **NULL** is **completely ignored** in the calculation.

Query 2

```
SELECT COUNT(SALARY) FROM Small_Table ;
```

The answer for Query 2 is **2**. This again is because employee_no 3 has a **salary of NULL** so it is **completely ignored** in the calculation.

Query 3

```
SELECT COUNT(*) FROM Small_Table ;
```

The answer for Query 3 is **3**. This is because **Count(*)** counts the **entire row**. Since the **entire row isn't NULL** it **is counted** in the equation.

Aggregates and the GROUP BY Statement

If you utilize an aggregate in your select list and include a **non-aggregate (normal column)** you must use a **GROUP BY statement** or you will receive an error. A GROUP BY statement will allow the aggregates to be broken into groups.

Employee_Table

Employee_No	Dept_No	First_Name	Last_Name	Salary
1	10	Tom	Coffing	50000.00
2	10	Leona	Coffing	75000.50
3	20	Steve	Wilmes	95054.30
4	20	Gareth	Walter	94986.35
5	30	Robert	Hines	120987.45
6	30	Mark	Ferguson	97087.67
7	30	Scott	Smith	143987.94
8	40	Marsha	Lewis	98453.88
9	40	Sara	Wilson	97450.75
10	50	Mike	Larkins	245098.00
11	999	Arfy	Coffing	NULL
12	999	Spot	Coffing	NULL

```
SELECT Dept_no, SUM (Salary)
FROM    Employee_Table
GROUP BY Dept_No ;
```

6 rows returned

Dept_no	SUM(Salary)
10	125000.50
20	190040.65
30	362063.06
40	195904.63
50	245098.00
999	NULL

Non-Aggregates must be Grouped

Anytime you mix aggregates (SUM, MAX, MIN, AVG, and COUNT) with non-aggregates (normal columns) you must use the **group by** statement. Why does the following example fail?

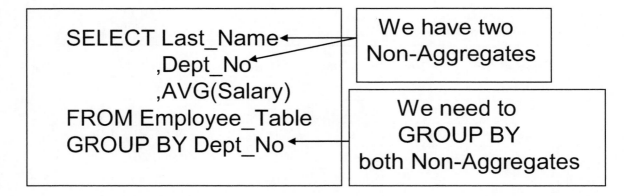

FAILURE: WHY?

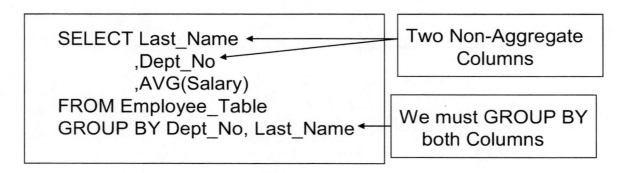

SUCCESS:

Aggregates and the HAVING Statement

The WHERE Clause is used to limit the rows selected and when aggregates are involved the non-selected rows are not part of the calculating process. The HAVING Clause is used to limit the GROUPS coming back by evaluating the GROUP Totals. In other words, a HAVING statement evaluates the group totals and eliminates groups not meeting the requirements. **WHERE evaluates the base rows** and **HAVING evaluates the GROUP totals**. **Having is to Aggregates** what **Qualify is to OLAP functions**.

Our first example shows a standard GROUP BY Statement and the results.

```
SELECT Dept_no, SUM (Salary)
FROM    Employee_Table
GROUP BY Dept_No ;
```

6 rows returned

Dept_no	SUM(Salary)
10	125000.50
20	190040.65
30	362063.06
40	195904.63
50	245098.00
999	NULL

Our next example shows a standard GROUP BY Statement with the HAVING statement.

```
SELECT Dept_no, SUM(Salary)
FROM    Employee_Table
GROUP BY Dept_no
Having Sum(Salary) >= 200000.00 ;
```

2 rows returned

Dept_no	SUM(Salary)
30	362063.06
50	245098.00

GROUP BY and HAVING Together

...use eliminates rows from the base table before any calculations begin.

...sed with aggregates and non-aggregates and its purpose is to calculate ~~aggregates in g~~ ~~.~~ oupings.

The HAVING statement evaluates group totals and eliminates groups that don't qualify.

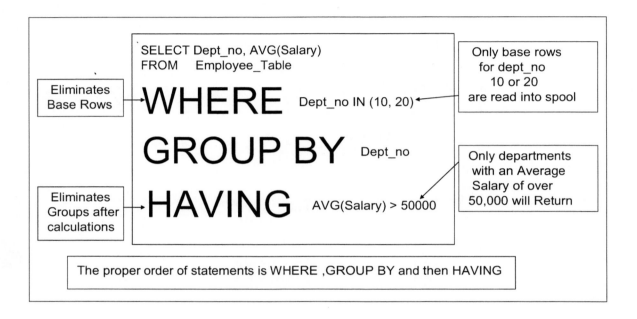

Aggregates need an ALIAS in Views or Macros

Anytime you utilize an **Aggregate** in a **view** or a **macro** you must give the aggregate an **ALIAS name**. If you don't you will receive an error during the CREATE VIEW or CREATE MACRO statement so don't forget to ALIAS.

Here is an example of creating a view using aggregates and aliasing the aggregates.

```
CREATE VIEW Employee_Salary_View
AS
SELECT Dept_no
        ,SUM(Salary) as SUMMY
        ,Max (Salary) as "MAX"
FROM    Employee_Table
GROUP BY Dept_no ;
```

Now that the view has been created and the aggregates have been aliased you can SELECT any columns you need in your query from the view.

```
SELECT Dept_no
        ,"MAX"
FROM    Employee_Salary_View ;
```

6 rows returned

Dept_no	"MAX"
10	75000.50
20	95054.30
30	143987.94
40	98453.88
50	245098.00
999	?

Query Results when a Table is Empty

When you run an **aggregate query** against an **empty table** you will get a **NULL** for the answer set. If you run a query that SELECTS * from an empty table it will show you the columns, but have no data present.

```
CREATE Table Empty_Table
(
 Employee_no            Integer
,Salary                 Decimal(10,2)
) Unique Primary Index(Employee_no);
```

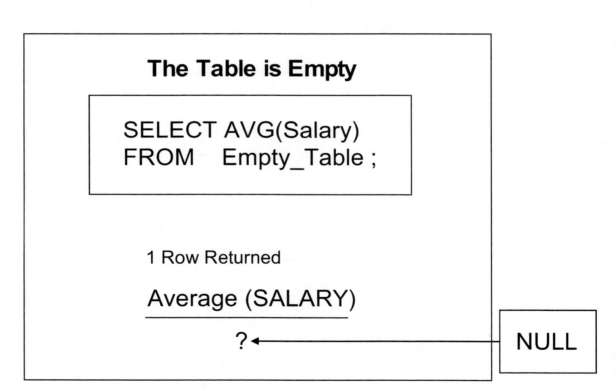

Chapter 7 — Subqueries *(No where clause)*

"It is a sin to be silent when it is your duty to protest."

Abraham Lincoln

The IN Statement (for review)

This chapter will focus on subqueries. Subqueries involve multiple queries that work together to bring back an answer set. We will discuss two types of subqueries in this chapter. They are normal subqueries and Correlated subqueries.

Subqueries are often confusing to students so let me explain them in their simplest form. Do you remember the IN List? Here is an example to refresh your memory.

Employee_Table

Employee_No	Dept_No	First_Name	Last_Name	Salary
1	10	Tom	Coffing	50000.00
2	10	Leona	Coffing	75000.50
3	20	Steve	Wilmes	95054.30
4	20	Gareth	Walter	94986.35
5	30	Robert	Hines	120987.45
6	30	Mark	Ferguson	97087.67
7	30	Scott	Smith	143987.94
8	40	Marsha	Lewis	98453.88
9	40	Sara	Wilson	97450.75
10	50	Mike	Larkins	245098.00
11	999	Arfy	Coffing	NULL
12	999	Spot	Coffing	NULL

```
SELECT    *
FROM      Employee_Table
WHERE     Dept_No IN (10,20) ;
```

4 Rows Returned

Employee_No	Dept_No	First_Name	Last_Name	Salary
1	10	Tom	Coffing	50000.00
2	10	Leona	Coffing	75000.50
3	20	Steve	Wilmes	95054.30
4	20	Gareth	Walter	94986.35

Normal Subqueries

A Subquery is SQL that involves multiple queries where one query provides input to another query. A **normal subquery** will have at least two queries. A top query and a bottom query. The **bottom query runs first** producing an answer set. The **bottom query distinct answer set is passed to the top query**, which uses the answer set as **input** to **it's IN List**.

Look at the next two examples below. The first is the same query as the page before using an IN List. The second will produce the exact same results utilizing a Subquery.

```
SELECT    *
FROM      Employee_Table
WHERE     Dept_No IN (10,20) ;
```

```
SELECT        *
FROM          Employee_Table
WHERE         Dept_No IN
      (SELECT Dept_No from Employee_Table
        WHERE Dept_No = 10
          OR    Dept_No = 20);
```

4 Rows Returned

Employee_No	Dept_No	First_Name	Last_Name	Salary
1	10	Tom	Coffing	50000.00
2	10	Leona	Coffing	75000.50
3	20	Steve	Wilmes	95054.30
4	20	Gareth	Walter	94986.35

The bottom query runs first producing an answer set of 10 and 20. The 10 and 20 is passed to the top query and evaluated as an IN (10,20) statement. Remember some fundamental rules. The bottom query runs first. It passes a distinct answer set to the top query. The answer set is utilized by the top query. The bottom query result answer is NOT in the final answer set, but instead is utilized by the top query as input.

Normal Subqueries using Multiple Tables

Our next example will be more real world. It involves multiple tables. The two tables being utilized are the Employee_table and the Department_Table. Each is listed below.

Employee_Table

Employee_No	Dept_No	First_Name	Last_Name	Salary
1	10	Tom	Coffing	50000.00
2	10	Leona	Coffing	75000.50
3	20	Steve	Wilmes	95054.30
4	20	Gareth	Walter	94986.35
5	30	Robert	Hines	120987.45
6	30	Mark	Ferguson	97087.67
7	30	Scott	Smith	143987.94
8	40	Marsha	Lewis	98453.88
9	40	Sara	Wilson	97450.75
10	50	Mike	Larkins	245098.00
11	999	Arfy	Coffing	NULL
12	999	Spot	Coffing	NULL

Department_Table

Dept_No	Dept_name	MGR_No	Budget
10	Sales	2	266000
20	Marketing	4	356000
30	HR	6	200000
40	Development	9	126000
50	IT	10	25000000

Subqueries using Multiple Tables Continued

Using the two tables on the previous page we will show an example of a subquery involving multiple tables.

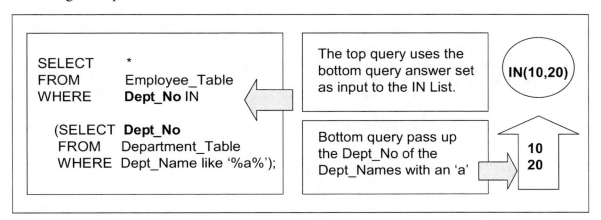

The bottom query runs first and evaluates the Department_Table. The bottom query will capture the Dept_No values for all departments that have an 'a' in their Dept_Name. The only Dept_Name values with an 'a' in them are dept 10 and 20. The values of 10 and 20 are passed to the top query to be used as input to the IN list. The top query then executes delivering the final answer set.

Department_Table

Dept_No	Dept_name	MGR_No	Budget
10	Sales	2	266000
20	Marketing	4	356000
30	HR	6	200000
40	Development	9	126000
50	IT	10	25000000

4 Rows Returned

Employee_No	Dept_No	First_Name	Last_Name	Salary
1	10	Tom	Coffing	50000.00
2	10	Leona	Coffing	75000.50
3	20	Steve	Wilmes	95054.30
4	20	Gareth	Walter	94986.35

Subqueries use values from the same Domain

Subqueries have a top and bottom query. The bottom query runs first and then passes a distinct answer set to the top query. The top query uses the answer set as input and usually does so in an IN List. The SELECT column or columns from the bottom query must be from the same domain as the IN List column or columns in the top query. Please match apples to apples! Here is another example of a subquery involving the Employee_Table and the Department_Table. This query is different. In our next query we want to find all information from the Employee_Table if the employee is a manager of a valid department.

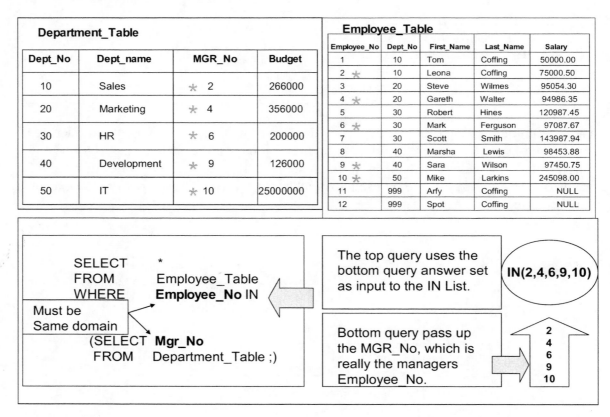

Department_Table

Dept_No	Dept_name	MGR_No	Budget
10	Sales	* 2	266000
20	Marketing	* 4	356000
30	HR	* 6	200000
40	Development	* 9	126000
50	IT	* 10	25000000

Employee_Table

Employee_No	Dept_No	First_Name	Last_Name	Salary
1	10	Tom	Coffing	50000.00
2 *	10	Leona	Coffing	75000.50
3	20	Steve	Wilmes	95054.30
4 *	20	Gareth	Walter	94986.35
5	30	Robert	Hines	120987.45
6 *	30	Mark	Ferguson	97087.67
7	30	Scott	Smith	143987.94
8	40	Marsha	Lewis	98453.88
9 *	40	Sara	Wilson	97450.75
10 *	50	Mike	Larkins	245098.00
11	999	Arfy	Coffing	NULL
12	999	Spot	Coffing	NULL

```
SELECT          *
FROM            Employee_Table
WHERE           Employee_No IN
Must be
Same domain
                (SELECT  Mgr_No
FROM            Department_Table ;)
```

The top query uses the bottom query answer set as input to the IN List.

IN(2,4,6,9,10)

Bottom query pass up the MGR_No, which is really the managers Employee_No.

2
4
6
9
10

5 rows returned

Employee_no	Dept_No	First_Name	Last_Name	Salary
2	10	Leona	Coffing	75000.50
4	20	Gareth	Walter	94986.35
6	30	Mark	Ferguson	97087.67
9	40	Sara	Wilson	97450.75
10	50	Mike	Larkins	245098.00

Using Subqueries with Aggregates

Subqueries can use aggregates in the subquery and these aggregates can be passed to the top query for comparison. Below is an example of finding all employees who make more than the average company salary.

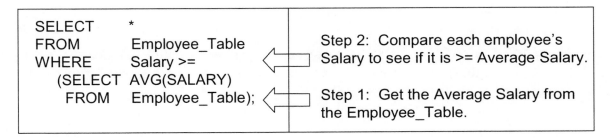

The next query (below) will find the employee(s) who make the maximum salary within the company.

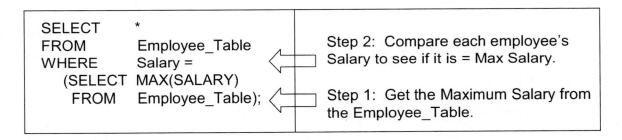

Notice that our domains are consistent. We are comparing salary with either the Average or Max Salary in both our examples.

Multi-column Subquery

"Advice is what we ask for when we already know the answer but wish we didn't."

- Erica Jong

Although this works well for MIN and MAX type of values (equalities), it does not work well for finding values greater than or less than comparisons. For this type of processing, a Correlated subquery is the best solution.

Notice we have two columns in our WHERE clause. They have parenthesis around both columns. There are also two columns in our subquery.

```
SEL *
FROM Order_Table
WHERE (Cust_Num, Order_Total) IN
      (SEL Cust_num, MAX(Order_Total) FROM Order_Table
      GROUP BY 1);
```

Cust_Num	Order_no	Order_Date	Order_Total
1	100	6/6/2004	5000.00
2	200	6/7/2004	4000.00
3	300	6/8/2004	2000.00
5	400	6/9/2004	1000000.00

Correlated Subquery

A Correlated Subquery is extremely powerful in Teradata. Our previous pages showed examples of normal subqueries. On the previous page we saw an example of a subquery that brought back all employees who make greater than or equal to the company's average salary. What if you were asked to write a query that would display all employees who make >= average salary **in their department**? Use a Correlated Subquery.

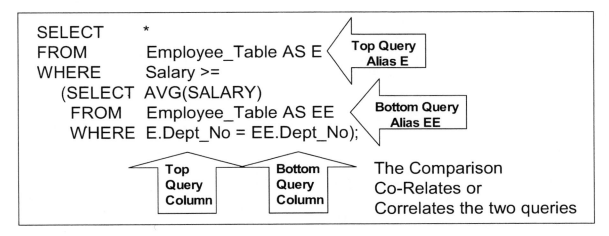

```
SELECT       *
FROM         Employee_Table AS E          Top Query
                                          Alias E
WHERE        Salary >=
   (SELECT  AVG(SALARY)
    FROM    Employee_Table AS EE          Bottom Query
                                          Alias EE
    WHERE   E.Dept_No = EE.Dept_No);
```

Top Query Column   Bottom Query Column   The Comparison Co-Relates or Correlates the two queries

How a Correlated Subquery runs

- The **top query runs first** placing output in spool **(Outer Query).**

- The **outer query** processes **one row** and then **compares it to one row in the subquery.**

- The **bottom query** will run **one time** for **each distinct department** in the table. If there are four distinct departments then the bottom query will run only 4 times.

Instead of comparing the selected subquery values against all the rows in the main query, the correlated subquery works backward. It first reads a row in the main query, and then goes into the subquery to find all the rows that match the specified column value. Then, it gets the next row in the main query and retrieves all the subquery rows that match the next value in this row. This processing continues until all the qualifying rows from the main SELECT are satisfied.

EXISTS

The **EXISTS statement** tests to see if a row has been found. It is either **true** or **false**. This can be used in normal or correlated subqueries. If a row is found, the EXISTS test is true, and conversely, if a row is not found, the result is false. When a **true condition is determined,** the value in the SELECT is **returned** from the main query. When the condition is determined to be **false, no rows are selected**. As a matter of fact this is the purpose of EXISTS. To test the existence of specified rows in a subquery. We will use the tables below to test our EXISTS statement.

In this series of pages we will show you the tables used and four different queries. So you can get a feel for how EXISTS, NOT EXISTS, IN, and NOT IN are used.

Pet_Table

Species	**Category**	Name	Vitamins
Dog	**10**	Moose	K9
Cat	**20**	Crackers	B4
Hamster	**30**	Hammy	C4
Gold Fish	**40**	Finnegan	Zinc

Pet_History_Table

Category	Pet_Store	Buy_Date	Price
10	AnimalsRus	2002-02-25	249.00
20	Exotic Pets	2001-03-14	110.00
30	Jungle Jims	2003-01-15	49.95
NULL	Sunshine Fish	2004-01-01	19.99

Estimate the Number of Rows for each Query

SELECT * from Pet_Table
Where **category IN** ← [**Normal Subquery**]
  (**Sel category** from Pet_Table_History)
ORDER BY 1;

Rows
_____

SELECT * from Pet_Table ← [**NOT IN Subquery**]
Where **category NOT IN**
  (**Sel category** from Pet_Table_History)
ORDER BY 1;

Rows
_____

SELECT * **from Pet_Table as P** ← [**Correlated Exists**]
Where exists
  (**Sel * from Pet_Table_History as H**
WHERE **P**.category = **H**.category
)
ORDER BY 1 ;

Rows
_____

SELECT * from Pet_Table as **P**   [**NOT Exists**]
Where **NOT exists** ←
  (Sel * from Pet_Table_History as **H**
WHERE **P**.category = **H**.category
)
ORDER BY 1 ;

Rows
_____

Number of Rows Returned Quiz answers

Below are the answer sets to all four queries on the previous page.

3 Rows Returned

Species	Category	Name	Vitamin
Cat	20	Crackers	B4
Dog	10	Moose	K9
Hamster	30	Hammy	Zinc

3 rows

0 Rows Returned

Species	Category	Name	Vitamin

0 rows returned because of NULL

3 Rows Returned

Species	Category	Name	Vitamin
Cat	20	Crackers	B4
Dog	10	Moose	K9
Hamster	30	Hammy	Zinc

3 rows

1 Row Returned

Species	Category	Name	Vitamin
Gold Fish	40	Finnegan	Zinc

1 row

NOT IN Returns Nothing when NULLS are Present

A **NOT IN query** will return no rows if a **NULL value** is in the **subquery or IN list**. This is because a NULL is unknown data. First, let's look at the NOT IN query that returned no rows. Then we will bold the second query to show how we took care of NULL values. Our queries are attempting to find all pets in the Pet_Table that do not have a valid category in the Pet_History_Table.

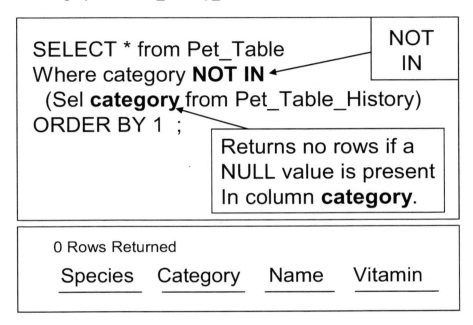

SELECT * from Pet_Table
Where category **NOT IN**
  (Sel **category** from Pet_Table_History)
ORDER BY 1 ;

NOT IN

Returns no rows if a NULL value is present In column **category**.

0 Rows Returned			
Species	Category	Name	Vitamin

SELECT * from Pet_Table
Where category **NOT IN**
  (Sel **category** from Pet_Table_History
    WHERE category IS NOT NULL)
ORDER BY 1 ;

This is a technique to handle NULL values In a NOT IN subquery.

1 Row Returned			
Species	Category	Name	Vitamin
Gold Fish	40	Finnegan	Zinc

NOT EXISTS Vs NOT IN

What is interesting about **EXISTS** and **NOT EXISTS** is that they can easily handle **evaluating NULL values**. A NOT IN query will return nothing if there is a NULL value in the subquery or IN list. Use the NOT EXISTS instead of NOT IN if:

- Any column of the NOT IN condition allows NULL values.

- Any rows from the main query have a null in any column of the NOT IN condition that you want to always be returned.

- Any NULL values returned in the SELECT list of the subquery prevent rows from the main query from being returned.

```
SELECT * from Pet_Table as P          Correlated
Where exists                             Exists
  (Sel * from Pet_Table_History as H
WHERE P.category = H.category
)
ORDER BY 1 ;
```

3 Rows Returned

Species	Category	Name	Vitamin
Cat	20	Crackers	B4
Dog	10	Moose	K9
Hamster	30	Hammy	Zinc

Chapter 8 – Joins

"A life filled with love may have some thorns, but a life empty of love will have no roses."

Anonymous

Primary Key/Foreign Key Relationships

Tables are usually joined together based on a Primary Key/Foreign Key relationship. Each table is logically built around a Primary Key. A Primary Key must be unique, can't have NULL values, and should never be changed. A Foreign Key is a normal key in a table that has a relation with the Primary Key of another table.

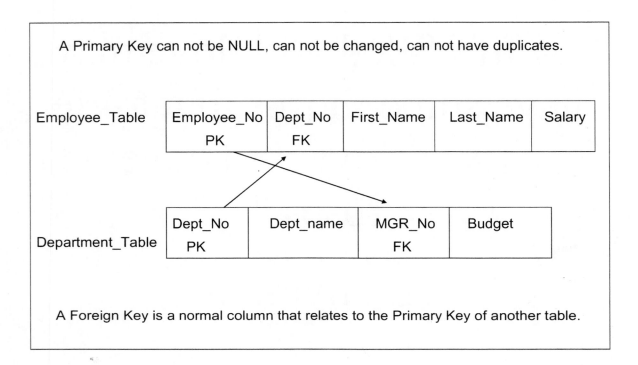

A Primary Key can not be NULL, can not be changed, can not have duplicates.

Employee_Table

| Employee_No PK | Dept_No FK | First_Name | Last_Name | Salary |

Department_Table

| Dept_No PK | Dept_name | MGR_No FK | Budget |

A Foreign Key is a normal column that relates to the Primary Key of another table.

Employee_Table

Employee_No	Dept_No	First_Name	Last_Name	Salary
1	10	Tom	Coffing	50000.00
2	10	Leona	Coffing	75000.50
3	20	Steve	Wilmes	95054.30
4	20	Gareth	Walter	94986.35
5	30	Robert	Hines	120987.45
6	30	Mark	Ferguson	97087.67
7	30	Scott	Smith	143987.94
8	40	Marsha	Lewis	98453.88
9	40	Sara	Wilson	97450.75
10	50	Mike	Larkins	245098.00
11	999	Arfy	Coffing	NULL
12	999	Spot	Coffing	NULL

Department_Table

Dept_No	Dept_name	MGR_No	Budget
10	Sales	2	266000
20	Marketing	4	356000
30	HR	6	200000
40	Development	9	200000
50	IT	10	25000000

A Join using Teradata Syntax

Tables are usually joined together based on a Primary Key/Foreign Key relationship. The following example will join the **Employee_Table** with the **Department_Table** providing us a report with **all employees in valid departments**.

Employee_Table

Employee_No	Dept_No	First_Name	Last_Name	Salary
1	10	Tom	Coffing	50000.00
2	10	Leona	Coffing	75000.50
3	20	Steve	Wilmes	95054.30
4	20	Gareth	Walter	94986.35
5	30	Robert	Hines	120987.45
6	30	Mark	Ferguson	97087.67
7	30	Scott	Smith	143987.94
8	40	Marsha	Lewis	98453.88
9	40	Sara	Wilson	97450.75
10	50	Mike	Larkins	245098.00
11	999	Arfy	Coffing	NULL
12	999	Spot	Coffing	NULL

Department_Table

Dept_No	Dept_name	MGR_No	Budget
10	Sales	2	266000
20	Marketing	4	356000
30	HR	6	200000
40	Development	9	200000
50	IT	10	25000000

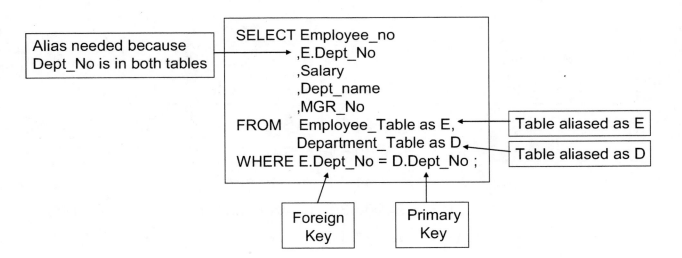

Alias needed because Dept_No is in both tables

```
SELECT Employee_no
      ,E.Dept_No
      ,Salary
      ,Dept_name
      ,MGR_No
FROM   Employee_Table as E,
       Department_Table as D
WHERE E.Dept_No = D.Dept_No ;
```

Table aliased as E
Table aliased as D
Foreign Key
Primary Key

The results are on the next page. You will notice in the result set that Arfy and Spot Coffing are not returned. That is because both are in invalid departments (Dept_no's that are not in the Department_Table).

A Join using ANSI Syntax

Tables are usually joined together based on a Primary Key/Foreign Key relationship. The following example will join the Employee_Table with the Department_Table providing us **all employees in valid departments**. This example is done with ANSI join syntax.

The difference between the ANSI and Teradata syntax is that the Teradata syntax separates both joining tables with a comma. The ANSI syntax uses the Keywords INNER JOIN in place of the comma. When INNER JOIN is used you must replace the WHERE clause with an ON clause.

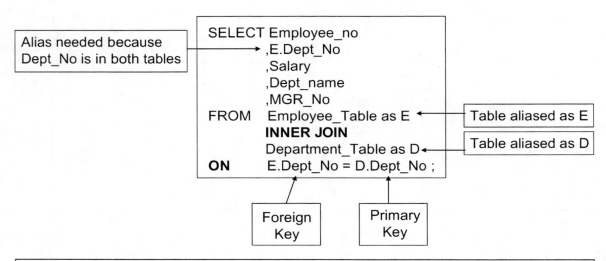

```
SELECT Employee_no
      ,E.Dept_No
      ,Salary
      ,Dept_name
      ,MGR_No
FROM   Employee_Table as E
       INNER JOIN
       Department_Table as D
ON     E.Dept_No = D.Dept_No ;
```

Alias needed because Dept_No is in both tables

Table aliased as E

Table aliased as D

Foreign Key

Primary Key

10 Rows Returned

Employee_No	Dept_No	Salary	Dept_name	MGR_No
1	10	50000.00	Sales	2
2	10	75000.50	Sales	2
3	20	95054.30	Marketing	4
4	20	94986.35	Marketing	4
5	30	120987.45	HR	6
6	30	97087.67	HR	6
7	30	143987.94	HR	6
8	40	98453.88	Development	9
9	40	97450.75	Development	9
10	50	245098.00	IT	10

A LEFT OUTER JOIN

In our previous examples we saw an inner join between the Employee_Table and the Department_Table returning all employees in valid departments. We also noticed in our previous query that Arfy Coffing and Spot Coffing did not return in the result set. This is because Arfy and Spot were in Dept_No 999 in the Employee_Table and there was no Dept_No 999 in the Department_Table. Inner Joins join matching rows. Outer Joins join matching rows just like an inner join, but in a left outer join all rows from the left table that did not have a match bring back the left table column requests and fill the columns requested from the Right Table with NULL values.

Employee_Table

Employee_No	Dept_No	First_Name	Last_Name	Salary
1	10	Tom	Coffing	50000.00
2	10	Leona	Coffing	75000.50
3	20	Steve	Wilmes	95054.30
4	20	Gareth	Walter	94986.35
5	30	Robert	Hines	120987.45
6	30	Mark	Ferguson	97087.67
7	30	Scott	Smith	143987.94
8	40	Marsha	Lewis	98453.88
9	40	Sara	Wilson	97450.75
10	50	Mike	Larkins	245098.00
11	999	Arfy	Coffing	NULL
12	999	Spot	Coffing	NULL

Department_Table

Dept_No	Dept_name	MGR_No	Budget
10	Sales	2	266000
20	Marketing	4	356000
30	HR	6	200000
40	Development	9	200000
50	IT	10	25000000

Notice that Arfy and Spot are in Dept_No 999 and that there is no Dept_No 999 in the Department_Table

```
SELECT     E.Employee_no
           ,E.Dept_No
           ,E.Salary
           ,D.Dept_name
           ,D.MGR_No
FROM   Employee_Table as E
LEFT OUTER JOIN
       Department_Table as D
ON     E.Dept_No = D.Dept_No
ORDER BY 1;
```

The Left Table is always the first table after the FROM Clause.

The Left Table will return every row whether it has a match or doesn't

A LEFT OUTER JOIN (Continued)

Here is our answer set. Notice that there were ten rows that had matches. Employees 11 and 12 did not have a match because they are in Dept_No 999 and there is no corresponding Dept_No 999 in the Department_Table. All Columns requested by the LEFT Table will be filled even if the row does not have a match. For non-matches, Teradata will place NULL values for all columns requested by the RIGHT Table.

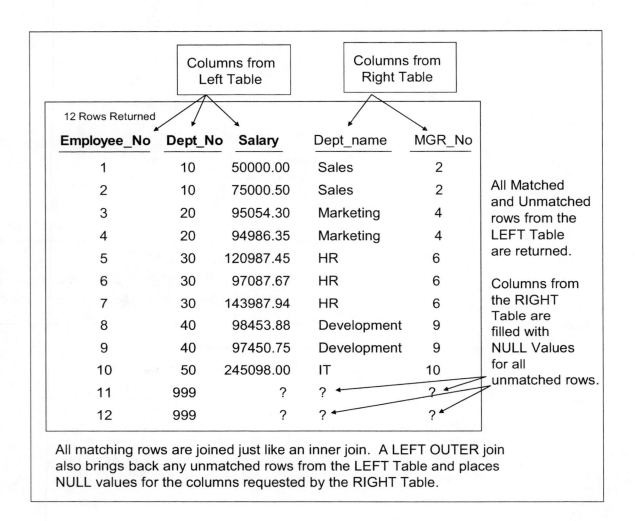

Columns from Left Table			Columns from Right Table	
Employee_No	**Dept_No**	**Salary**	Dept_name	MGR_No
1	10	50000.00	Sales	2
2	10	75000.50	Sales	2
3	20	95054.30	Marketing	4
4	20	94986.35	Marketing	4
5	30	120987.45	HR	6
6	30	97087.67	HR	6
7	30	143987.94	HR	6
8	40	98453.88	Development	9
9	40	97450.75	Development	9
10	50	245098.00	IT	10
11	999	?	?	?
12	999	?	?	?

12 Rows Returned

All Matched and Unmatched rows from the LEFT Table are returned.

Columns from the RIGHT Table are filled with NULL Values for all unmatched rows.

All matching rows are joined just like an inner join. A LEFT OUTER join also brings back any unmatched rows from the LEFT Table and places NULL values for the columns requested by the RIGHT Table.

This outer join shows us that we have ten employees in valid departments and that there are also two employees who are in invalid departments. NULL values have been placed for Dept_name and MGR_No because they are columns from the RIGHT Table.

A Series of Joins (Inner)

An INNER JOIN will bring back all matching rows in the WHERE or ON Clause. In our example below we had 3 matches.

Customer_Table

Cust_Name	Phone	Cust_Num
ABC Consulting	937 855-4838	1
TempHelpers	513 300-0346	2
CPUDoctor	816 140-3423	3
Fergie's	456 334-1543	4

Order_Table

Cust_Num	Order_No	Order_Date	Order_Total
1	100	06-06-2004	5000.00
2	200	06-07-2004	4000.00
3	300	06-08-2004	2000.00
5	400	06-09-2004	1000000.00

We have a customer (Fergie's) who has not placed an order.
We have an order ($1,000,000) without a valid customer.

```
SELECT C.Cust_Name, C.Cust_Phone
       ,O.Order_Date, O.Order_Total
FROM   Customer_Table as C
INNER  JOIN
       Order_Table as O
ON     C.Cust_Num = O.Cust_Num
ORDER BY Order_Date ;
```

3 Rows Returned

Cust_Name	Cust_Phone	Order_Date	Order_Total
ABC Consulting	937 855-4838	06-06-2004	5000.00
TempHelpers	513 300-0346	06-07-2004	4000.00
CPUDoctor	816 140-3423	06-08-2004	2000.00

A Series of Joins (LEFT OUTER)

A LEFT OUTER JOIN will bring back all rows from the LEFT Table. If a LEFT Row does not have a matching RIGHT row then the LEFT table will place the LEFT column requests on the report and place NULL Values for the RIGHT columns requests.

Customer_Table

Cust_Name	Phone	Cust_Num
ABC Consulting	937 855-4838	1
TempHelpers	513 300-0346	2
CPUDoctor	816 140-3423	3
Fergie's	456 334-1543	4

Order_Table

Cust_Num	Order_No	Order_Date	Order_Total
1	100	06-06-2004	5000.00
2	200	06-07-2004	4000.00
3	300	06-08-2004	2000.00
5	400	06-09-2004	1000000.00

We have a customer (Fergie's) who has not placed an order.
We have an order ($1,000,000) without a valid customer.

```
SELECT C.Cust_Name, C.Cust_Phone
       ,O.Order_Date, O.Order_Total
FROM   Customer_Table as C
LEFT OUTER JOIN
       Order_Table as O
ON     C.Cust_Num = O.Cust_Num
ORDER BY Order_Date ;
```

4 Rows Returned

Cust_Name	Cust_Phone	Order_Date	Order_Total
Fergie's	456 334-1543	?	?
ABC Consulting	937 855-4838	06-06-2004	5000.00
TempHelpers	513 300-0346	06-07-2004	4000.00
CPUDoctor	816 140-3423	06-08-2004	2000.00

A Series of Joins (RIGHT OUTER)

A RIGHT OUTER JOIN will bring back all rows from the RIGHT Table. If a RIGHT Row does not have a matching LEFT row then the RIGHT table will place the RIGHT column requests on the report and place NULL Values for the LEFT columns requests.

Customer_Table

Cust_Name	Phone	Cust_Num
ABC Consulting	937 855-4838	1
TempHelpers	513 300-0346	2
CPUDoctor	816 140-3423	3
Fergie's	456 334-1543	4

Order_Table

Cust_Num	Order_No	Order_Date	Order_Total
1	100	06-06-2004	5000.00
2	200	06-07-2004	4000.00
3	300	06-08-2004	2000.00
5	400	06-09-2004	1000000.00

We have a customer (Fergie's) who has not placed an order.
We have an order ($1,000,000) without a valid customer.

```
SELECT C.Cust_Name, C.Cust_Phone
        ,O.Order_Date, O.Order_Total
FROM    Customer_Table as C
RIGHT OUTER JOIN
        Order_Table as O
ON      C.Cust_Num = O.Cust_Num
ORDER BY Order_Date ;
```

4 Rows Returned

Cust_Name	Cust_Phone	Order_Date	Order_Total
ABC Consulting	937 855-4838	06-06-2004	5000.00
TempHelpers	513 300-0346	06-07-2004	4000.00
CPUDoctor	816 140-3423	06-08-2004	2000.00
?	?	06-09-2004	1000000.00

A Series of Joins (FULL OUTER)

A FULL OUTER JOIN will bring back all rows from both tables. The matching rows are brought back as well as any non-matching rows. You can recognize unmatched rows because NULL values will be put in columns where matches can't be found.

Customer_Table

Cust_Name	Phone	Cust_Num
ABC Consulting	937 855-4838	1
TempHelpers	513 300-0346	2
CPUDoctor	816 140-3423	3
Fergie's	456 334-1543	4

Order_Table

Cust_Num	Order_No	Order_Date	Order_Total
1	100	06-06-2004	5000.00
2	200	06-07-2004	4000.00
3	300	06-08-2004	2000.00
5	400	06-09-2004	1000000.00

We have a customer (Fergie's) who has not placed an order.
We have an order ($1,000,000) without a valid customer.

```
SELECT C.Cust_Name, C.Cust_Phone
       ,O.Order_Date, O.Order_Total
FROM    Customer_Table as C
FULL OUTER JOIN
       Order_Table as O
ON      C.Cust_Num = O.Cust_Num
ORDER BY Order_Date ;
```

5 Rows Returned

Cust_Name	Cust_Phone	Order_Date	Order_Total
Fergie's	456 334-1543	?	?
ABC Consulting	937 855-4838	06-06-2004	5000.00
TempHelpers	513 300-0346	06-07-2004	4000.00
CPUDoctor	816 140-3423	06-08-2004	2000.00
?	?	06-09-2004	1000000.00

Join Types vs. Join Strategies

Teradata's Optimizer has the ability to interpret a user's join types and then make decisions on what is the best path or join strategy to take in order complete the query. Basically, joins are combining rows from two or more tables. The key here is that these two tables have a common trait, albeit a same column that both tables have. As we go through this chapter, examples will point to these join types. However, our main focus in this chapter is to analyze how Teradata determines the join strategy based on the user's input. This chapter will also make recommendations on how the user can influence the join strategy. Keep in mind that the optimizer will have the last say on all joins completed in Teradata. Teradata allows up to 64 tables to be joined in a single query. As discussed, some of the common join types are:

- **Inner (may be a self join)**
- **Outer (Left, Right, Full)**
- **Exclusion**
- **Cross (may be a Cartesian)**

When the user inputs a join type, Teradata will then utilize clever join plans, or strategies, to perform the joins. These join strategies are:

- **Merge (Exclusion)**
- **Nested**
- **Row Hash**
- **Product (including Cartesian Product joins)**

A Merge Join is the most **popular join plan** and is usually based on equality (not always). A **Merge Join** requires that the data from the **tables be sorted** before attempting the **join operation**. A Merge Join **always requires rows** from the two tables to **be on the same AMP**. It will take the joining columns in the WHERE or ON clause and either **redistribute them by row hash** into a spool file or duplicate them across all AMPs. The bottom line is that when **neither join column** is a **Primary Index** and the join is based on equality or non-equality in a **merge join** or **exclusion merge join**, the qualified rows from both tables must be **rehashed** and then **redistributed** or **duplicated** and then always **sorted**.

A **Nested Join** is only used when the user specifies a **constant value** in the WHERE clause. This is because a Nested Join always uses at least one **Unique Index**.

A **Row Hash** join always copies the **smaller table into memory**.

A **product or Cartesian Product Join** will **duplicate** the **smaller table** on **every AMP**

The Key Things about Teradata and Joins

Each AMP holds a portion of a table.

Teradata uses the Primary Index to distribute the rows among the AMPs.

Each AMP keeps their tables separated from other tables like someone might keep clothes in a dresser drawer.

Each AMP sorts their tables by Row ID.

For a JOIN to take place the two rows being joined must find a way to get to the same AMP.

If the rows to be joined are not on the same AMP, Teradata will either redistribute the data or duplicate the data in spool to make that happen.

Merge Join Strategies

A **Join** that has uses the **Primary Index** of both tables in the **WHERE clause** never uses a **SPOOL** File. If two tables being joined have the **same Primary Index** value and they are **joined on that value** then Teradata performs a **Merge Join** with a **row hash match scan**. A **Merge Join** could also make use of a **Primary Index** on each of two tables **with matching Partitioned Primary Indexes.**

Let's say you have a table with a **multi-column composite primary key**. You can minimize join costs by **minimizing row redistribution**. To **minimize row redistribution**, the table should be defined with a **NUPI** on the columns most **frequently joined**.

```
SELECT A.Column3, B.Column4
FROM           Table1   AS A
INNER JOIN
                Table2   AS B
ON  A.Column1 = B.Column1
```

Is one of the tables big and the other small?
Yes – Then duplicate the smaller table on all AMPS.

Are A.Column1 and B.Column1 the Primary Indexes of their tables?
Yes – Then the join is already prepared naturally.

Is Column1 the Primary Index of one of the tables only?
Yes – Then redistribute the other table by Column1 in Spool.

Are A.Column1 and B.Column1 both NOT the Primary Indexes of their tables?
Yes – Redistribute both tables in Spool by Column1.

Joins need the joined rows to be on the same AMP

This is an extremely important chapter because Teradata is brilliant at joins. If you can understand the upcoming pages you will have gained great knowledge. It is this type of knowledge that really separates the good ones from the great ones.

When **Teradata joins two tables** it must place the **joining rows** on the **same AMP**. If the rows are not naturally on the same AMP then Teradata will perform two strategies to get them placed together. **Teradata will redistribute one or both of the tables in spool** or it will **copy the smaller table to all of the AMPs**.

In our picture below we are joining the Customer table with the Order table. AMP 25 is ready for the join because the rows it holds are sorted and the matching rows are on the same AMP. This was accomplished by only three possibilities:

- The two tables had their Primary Index as Cust_Num so the rows naturally resided together.
- Teradata redistributed one or both tables by rehashing them by Cust_Num in spool.
- Teradata placed the smaller table on all AMPs

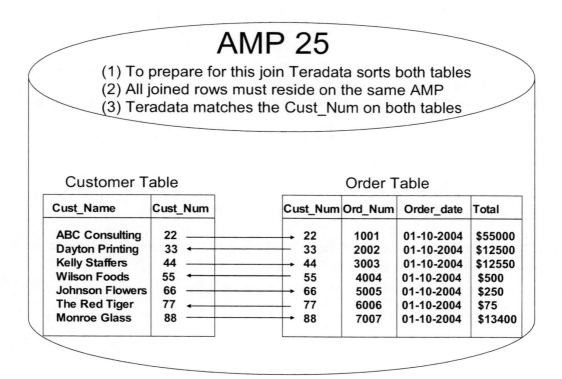

Another Great Join Picture

Our picture below shows AMP 25 again and we are joining the Department table with the Employee table. This is a one to many row join because one department holds many employees. Teradata was able to place the matching rows on the same AMP and did so by three different possibilities:

- The two tables had their Primary Index as Dept_No so the rows naturally resided together.

- Teradata redistributed one or both tables by rehashing them by Dept_No in spool.

- Teradata placed the smaller Department table on all AMPs.

```
SELECT E.Name, E.Salary, D.Department_Name
FROM    Employee as E
INNER JOIN
        Department as D
ON      E.Dept_No = D.Dept_No
```

AMP 25

(1) To prepare for this join Teradata sorts both tables
(2) All joined rows must reside on the same AMP
(3) Teradata matches the Dept_No on both tables

Department Table

Department_Name	Dept_No
Sales	10
Marketing	20
Finance	30
IT	40

Employee Table

Dept_No	Emp_No	Name	Salary
10	1	Joe Davis	$55000
10	88	Mark Weis	$72500
20	54	Kim Brewer	$82550
20	40	Kyle Lane	$88500
20	34	Sandy Cole	$67250
30	73	Lyle Smith	$15675
40	83	Ray Moon	$22400

Joining Tables with matching rows on different AMPs

Our picture below shows a 3 AMP system. Each AMP holds rows from both the Department Table and the Employee Table. We will join the two tables based on the equality WHERE E.Dept_No = D.Dept_No. Since the join syntax will join on the Dept_No column from both tables, Teradata will realize that the Dept_No column is the Primary Index of the Department Table, but not the Employee Table. Teradata will need to redistribute the Employee Table in spool and rehash it by Dept_No in order to get the rows on the same AMPs (We will show that picture on the next page).

AMP 1

Department Table			Employee Table		
Department_Name	Dept_No		Dept_No	Emp_No	Name	Salary
Sales	10		30	73	Lyle Smith	$15675
			40	83	Ray Moon	$22,400

AMP 2

Department Table			Employee Table		
Department_Name	Dept_No		Dept_No	Emp_No	Name	Salary
Marketing	20		20	34	Sandy Cole	$67250
			10	1	Joe Davis	$55000

AMP 3

Department Table			Employee Table		
Department_Name	Dept_No		Dept_No	Emp_No	Name	Salary
IT	40		20	40	Kyle Lane	$88500
Finance	30		10	88	Mark Weis	$72500
			20	54	Kim Brewer	$82550

Redistributing a Table for Join Purposes

Our picture below shows that Teradata has redistributed the Employee table into Spool and rehashed by Dept_No. Now the joining rows are on the AMP with their joining row partners.

```
SELECT E.Name, E.Salary, D.Department_Name
FROM    Employee as E
INNER JOIN
        Department as D
ON      E.Dept_No = D.Dept_No
```

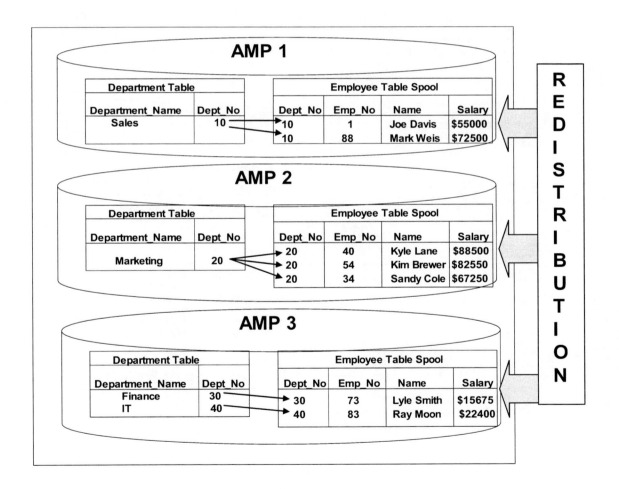

Big Table Small Table Join Strategy

Our picture below shows a 3 AMP system. Each AMP holds rows from both the Department Table and the Employee Table. We will join the two tables based on equality WHERE E.Dept_No = D.Dept_No. Let's pretend that the Department Table is small and that the Employee Table is extremely large. In the case of a big table small table join, Teradata will duplicate the smaller table on all AMPs. (We will show that Teradata places the Department table on each AMP in our next picture).

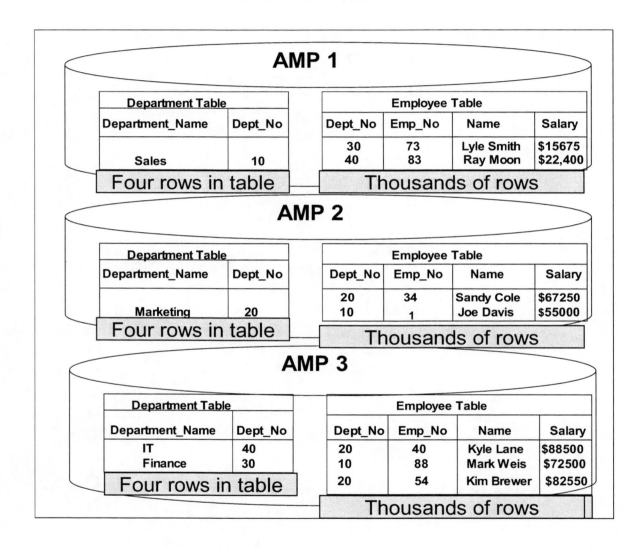

Big Table Small Table Duplication

Our picture below shows that Teradata will duplicate the Department table on all AMPs .

There are only **three join types** that will take the smaller table and **DUPLICATE ACROSS ALL AMPS** and they are a **merge** join, **hash** join, and it is always done on any **product join**. That is why **Merge, Hash,** and **Product joins** always require using **ALL AMPs**.

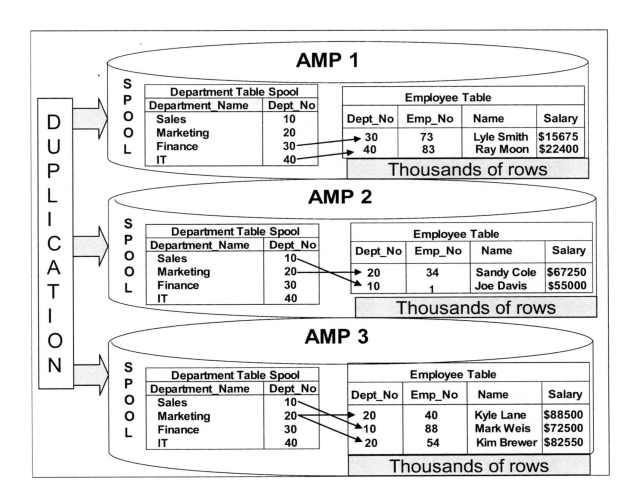

Nested Join

A nested join strategy is probably the most precise join available. The **Nested Join** is designed to utilize a **unique index** type (Either Unique Primary Index or Unique Secondary Index) from **one** of the tables in the join statement in order to retrieve a **single row**. It then matches that **row** to **one or more rows** on the other table being used in the join **using an index**.

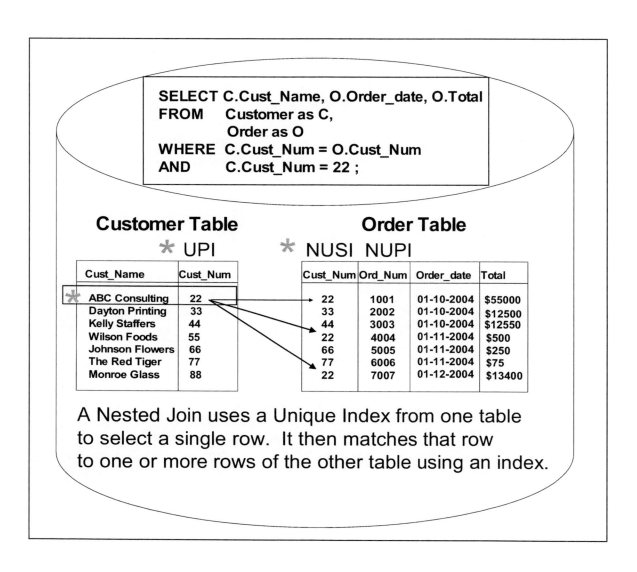

A Nested Join uses a Unique Index from one table to select a single row. It then matches that row to one or more rows of the other table using an index.

Hash Join

The Hash Join is part of the Merge Join Family. A Hash Join can only take place if one or both of the tables on each AMP can fit completely inside the AMP's memory.

A **Hash Join** uses **Memory** or **Cache** for one table and joins it by **hash** to an **unsorted spool** and does so quite quickly. Hash Joins are generally **faster** than Merge Joins because a **Hash Join** does not need to **sort** the **larger table**.

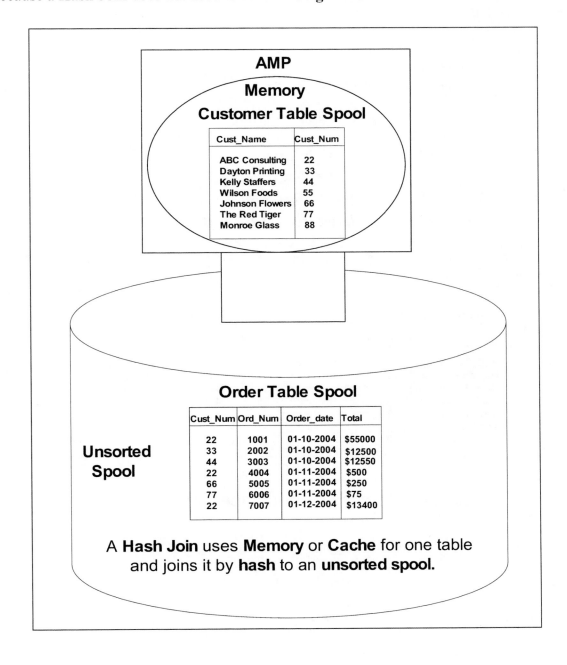

AMP

Memory

Customer Table Spool

Cust_Name	Cust_Num
ABC Consulting	22
Dayton Printing	33
Kelly Staffers	44
Wilson Foods	55
Johnson Flowers	66
The Red Tiger	77
Monroe Glass	88

Order Table Spool

Unsorted Spool

Cust_Num	Ord_Num	Order_date	Total
22	1001	01-10-2004	$55000
33	2002	01-10-2004	$12500
44	3003	01-10-2004	$12550
22	4004	01-11-2004	$500
66	5005	01-11-2004	$250
77	6006	01-11-2004	$75
22	7007	01-12-2004	$13400

A **Hash Join** uses **Memory** or **Cache** for one table and joins it by **hash** to an **unsorted spool.**

Exclusion Join

Exclusion Joins are only used on queries with the NOT IN, EXCEPT, or MINUS operators and are based on set subtractions. Anytime a NULL is used in a NOT IN list then the results will be nothing. An additional WHERE with an IS NOT NULL is common practice to avoid no results returning.

Here is the way that exclusion joins work. Teradata is looking for rows from one table that are NOT IN another table. There are 3 rules that apply to qualifying a row.

1. Any matches disqualifies a row
2. Any unknown disqualifies a row
3. Rows that don't have matches qualify

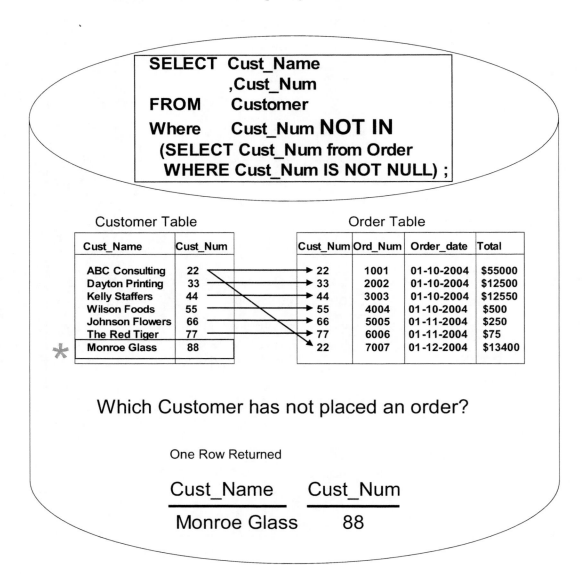

```
SELECT   Cust_Name
         ,Cust_Num
FROM     Customer
Where    Cust_Num NOT IN
  (SELECT Cust_Num from Order
   WHERE Cust_Num IS NOT NULL) ;
```

Customer Table

Cust_Name	Cust_Num
ABC Consulting	22
Dayton Printing	33
Kelly Staffers	44
Wilson Foods	55
Johnson Flowers	66
The Red Tiger	77
Monroe Glass	88

Order Table

Cust_Num	Ord_Num	Order_date	Total
22	1001	01-10-2004	$55000
33	2002	01-10-2004	$12500
44	3003	01-10-2004	$12550
55	4004	01-10-2004	$500
66	5005	01-11-2004	$250
77	6006	01-11-2004	$75
22	7007	01-12-2004	$13400

Which Customer has not placed an order?

One Row Returned

Cust_Name	Cust_Num
Monroe Glass	88

Product Joins

Product Joins compare every row of **one table** to **every row** of **another table**. They are called product joins because they are a product of the number of rows in table one multiplied by the number of rows in table two. For example, if one table has five rows and the other table has five rows, then the Product Join will compare 5 x 5 or 25 rows with a potential of 25 rows coming back.

To **avoid** a **product join**, check your syntax to ensure that the join is based on an **EQUALITY** condition. A **Product Join** always results when the join condition is based on **Inequality**. The reason the optimizer chooses **Product Joins** for join conditions other than equality is because **Hash Values** cannot be compared for **greater than** or **less then** comparisons.

A **Product Join**, **Merge Join**, and **Exclusion Merge** Join always requires **SPOOL** Files. **A Product Join** will usually be utilized when the **JOIN constraint** is **"OR"ed**.

A Product Join compares every row of one table to every row of another table.

Table_A
Row 1
Row 2
Row 3
Row 4
Row 5

Table_B
Row 1
Row 2
Row 3
Row 4
Row 5

The smaller table is always duplicated on all AMPs

Cartesian Product Join

"The superior man is modest in his speech, but exceeds in his actions."

– Confucius (551 BC – 479 BC)

A Cartesian Product join will always exceed in its actions because it **joins every row** from **one table** with **every row** in the **joining table**. It is usually a mistake and inferior coding.

Just as discussed with Product Joins above, a Cartesian Product Join is usually something you want to avoid. If we decided to run this query in Michigan this would be called the big "Mistake on the Lake". A Cartesian Product Join will join every row in one table to every row in another table. The only thing that decides the number of rows will be the total number of rows from both tables. If one table has 5 rows and another has 10 rows, then you will always get 50 rows returned. Imagine this situation – we have a table with 10 million rows and another with 25 million rows and a Cartesian product join is written (by accident) against these two tables. What will be the result? Well, based on the example above, you will get back about 250 Trillion Rows (250,000,000,000,000)! This is definitely NOT the correct answer this user would want. This is why spool space limitations are utilized.

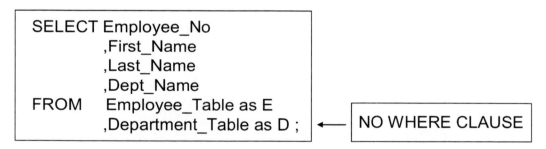

```
SELECT Employee_No
        ,First_Name
        ,Last_Name
        ,Dept_Name
FROM    Employee_Table as E
        ,Department_Table as D ;     ←— NO WHERE CLAUSE
```

So how do you avoid writing a Cartesian Product Join?

To avoid a Cartesian Product Join, check your syntax to ensure that the join is based on an EQUALITY condition. In the join syntax example above, the WHERE clause is missing. Because this clause is missing, a common domain condition between the two tables (i.e., e.dept = d.dept) does not exist, the result is a product join. Another cause of a product join is when aliases are not used after being established.

Cross Join

A Cross Join is another way to perform a Product Join or they can even perform what is called a Cartesian Product Join. A Cartesian Product join will always **join every row** from **one table** with **every row** in the **joining table**. It is usually a mistake and inferior coding. A product join will compare every row with every row and bring back the qualifying rows.

Below is an example of a two cross joins. One is a product join and the other is a Cartesian product join because it is missing the WHERE clause.

```
Select Employee_no
       ,Mgr_no
From   Employee_Table e
CROSS JOIN
       Department_Table d
WHERE e.dept_no = d.dept_no;
```

```
Select Employee_no
       ,Mgr_no
From   Employee_Table e
CROSS JOIN
       Department_Table d ;
```

Cross Joins only us a WHERE clause and **never an ON clause**.

Because there is NO WHERE clause this is a Cartesian Product.

Self Join

A Self Join is a join between a table and itself. The one table is defined twice using aliasing. Teradata places a copy of the table into spool and therefore it can join to itself.

You can easily recognize a SELF Join because one table will be used twice and aliasing is involved.

Normally, a self join requires some degree of de-normalization to allow for two columns in the same table to be part of the same domain. Since our Employee table does not contain the manager's employee number, the output cannot be shown. However, the concept is shown here.

Our Self-Join query will attempt to find all employees making more money then their manager.

> For example sake
> we have denormalized
> the Employee_Table2.
> We have added a column
> called **MGR**.

Employee_Table2

Employee_No	Dept_No	First_Name	Last_Name	Salary	MGR
1	10	Tom	Coffing	50000.00	N
2	10	Leona	Coffing	75000.50	Y
3	20	Steve	Wilmes	95054.30	N
4	20	Gareth	Walter	94986.35	Y
5	30	Robert	Hines	120987.45	N
6	30	Mark	Ferguson	97087.67	Y
7	30	Scott	Smith	143987.94	N
8	40	Marsha	Lewis	98453.88	N
9	40	Sara	Wilson	97450.75	Y
10	50	Mike	Larkins	245098.00	Y
11	999	Arfy	Coffing	NULL	N
12	999	Spot	Coffing	NULL	N

Self Join Cont.

```
SELECT Emps.Employee_no as Emp_no
        ,Emps.Dept_no
        ,Emps.Last_name
        ,Emps.Salary
        ,Mgrs.Employee_no as Manager_no
        ,Mgrs.Last_Name as Mgrs_Name
        ,Mgrs.Salary as Mgrs_Salary

FROM    Employee_Table as Emps
        ,Employee_Table as Mgrs

WHERE Emps.dept_no = Mgrs.dept_no
AND     Mgrs.MGR = 'Y'
AND     Emps.Salary > Mgrs.Salary ;
```

Same Table Aliased Twice

4 rows returned						
Emp_no	Dept_no	Last_name	Salary	Manager_No	Mgrs_Name	Mgrs_Salary
3	20	Wilmes	95054.30	4	Walter	94986.35
5	30	Hines	120987.45	6	Ferguson	97087.67
7	30	Smith	143987.94	6	Ferguson	97087.67
8	40	Lewis	98453.88	9	Wilson	97450.75

Adding Residual Conditions to a Join

Adding WHERE and AND clauses to Joins can limit the rows involved in a join. Teradata will also deliver different results on outer joins based on the WHERE or AND syntax. We will use the two tables below for our examples.

Movie_Star_Table

Dept_no	Name	Current_film
10	Will Smith	Men In Black II
20	Goldie Hawn	Laugh In – The Movie
30	Nicolas Cage	Matchstick Men
50	**Julia Roberts**	Pretty Woman

Movie_Star_Dept_Table

Dept_no	Dept_name	Budget
10	MIB Agency	10000000.00
20	Bold is Gold	20000000.00
30	A Perfect Match	5000000.00
40	**Roberts Assoc**	25000000.00

No Match

Adding Residual Conditions to a Join Cont.

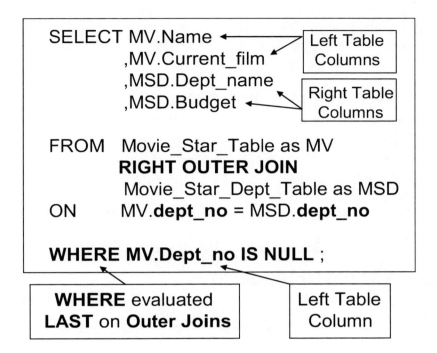

```
SELECT  MV.Name
        ,MV.Current_film
        ,MSD.Dept_name
        ,MSD.Budget

FROM    Movie_Star_Table as MV
        RIGHT OUTER JOIN
        Movie_Star_Dept_Table as MSD
ON      MV.dept_no = MSD.dept_no

WHERE MV.Dept_no IS NULL ;
```

Left Table Columns

Right Table Columns

WHERE evaluated LAST on Outer Joins

Left Table Column

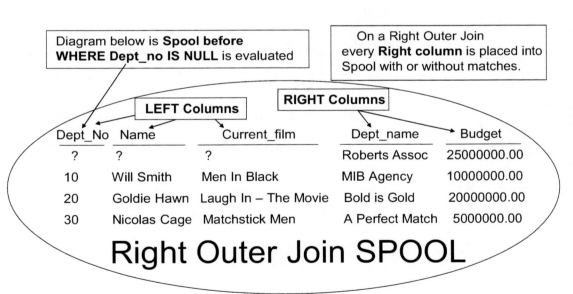

Diagram below is **Spool before WHERE Dept_no IS NULL** is evaluated

On a Right Outer Join every **Right column** is placed into Spool with or without matches.

LEFT Columns

RIGHT Columns

Dept_No	Name	Current_film	Dept_name	Budget
?	?	?	Roberts Assoc	25000000.00
10	Will Smith	Men In Black	MIB Agency	10000000.00
20	Goldie Hawn	Laugh In – The Movie	Bold is Gold	20000000.00
30	Nicolas Cage	Matchstick Men	A Perfect Match	5000000.00

Right Outer Join SPOOL

1 row returned

Name	Current_film	Dept_name	Budget
?	?	Roberts Assoc	25000000.00

Adding Residual Conditions to a Join (AND)

Our next query will be the same as the previous except we will use a different JOIN syntax. We will use the AND instead of the WHERE clause and on Outer Joins different results are delivered.

Movie_Star_Table

Dept_no	Name	Current_film
10	Will Smith	Men In Black II
20	Goldie Hawn	Laugh In – The Movie
30	Nicolas Cage	Matchstick Men
50	**Julia Roberts**	Pretty Woman

Movie_Star_Dept_Table

Dept_no	Dept_name	Budget
10	MIB Agency	10000000.00
20	Bold is Gold	20000000.00
30	A Perfect Match	5000000.00
40	**Roberts Assoc**	25000000.00

No Match

Adding Residual Conditions to a Join (AND) Cont.

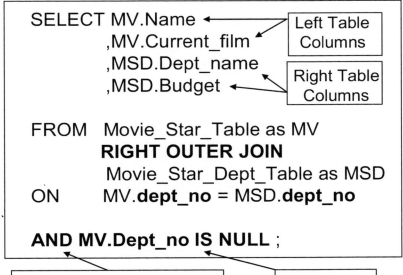

SELECT MV.Name

,MV.Current_film

,MSD.Dept_name

,MSD.Budget

Left Table Columns

Right Table Columns

FROM Movie_Star_Table as MV

RIGHT OUTER JOIN

Movie_Star_Dept_Table as MSD

ON MV.**dept_no** = MSD.**dept_no**

AND MV.Dept_no IS NULL ;

AND evaluated with **the ON Statement**

Left Table Column

All requested Left columns have nulls placed because all failed to meet both conditions. This resulted in no matches.

On a Right Outer Join every **Right column** is placed into Spool with or without matches.

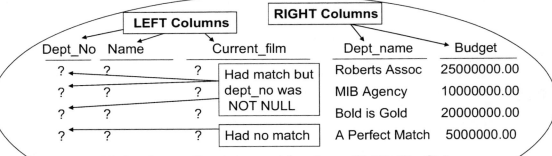

LEFT Columns   **RIGHT Columns**

Dept_No	Name	Current_film	Dept_name	Budget
?	?	?	Roberts Assoc	25000000.00
?	?	?	MIB Agency	10000000.00
?	?	?	Bold is Gold	20000000.00
?	?	?	A Perfect Match	5000000.00

Had match but dept_no was NOT NULL

Had no match

Right Outer Join SPOOL

NO LEFT rows meet both criteria
(1) Have a matching Dept_no AND
(2) Have a Dept_no that IS NULL

Because no rows met both criteria a RIGHT OUTER JOIN brings back all columns requested from the Right Table and places Null values for all non-matching Left Table requested columns.

Adding Residual Conditions to a Join (AND) Cont.

As you can see our result set below is much different then our previous result. Outer Joins are the only joins that will handle the WHERE and AND syntax differently.

4 rows returned

Name	Current_film	Dept_name	Budget
?	?	MIB Agency	10000000.00
?	?	Bold is Gold	20000000.00
?	?	A Perfect Match	5000000.00
?	?	Roberts Assoc	25000000.00

Joins using Teradata Syntax

When doing a Join using the Teradata Syntax we will not use the key word INNER JOIN to link the tables, but a comma instead. We can see that joining more than two tables is easily done. We separate each table by a comma implying a join is to take place. After the tables we are joining are listed, in the WHERE clause we will show our Primary Key Foreign Key relationship. When there are multiple relationships we will continue to show the remaining relationships with the AND operator. These will go in the order of the relationships of the tables being joined above. With the Teradata syntax, if we forget to put in the WHERE clause we will create a Cartesian Product Join. Not something you want to do by accident.

```
SEL E.Employee_No  AS EMP
       ,E.First_Name
       ,E.Last_Name
       ,D.Dept_Name
       ,J.Job_Desc
       ,J.Job_Start_Date
       ,J.Job_End_Date
FROM Department_Table AS D
     ,Employee_Table AS E
     ,Emp_Job_Table AS EJ
     ,Job_Table AS J
WHERE D.Dept_No = E.Dept_No
AND   E.Employee_No = EJ.Emp_No
AND   J.Job_No = EJ.Job_No
ORDER BY 1;
```

This is a four table join using Teradata Syntax.

EMP	First_Name	Last_Name	Dept_Name	Job_Desc	Job_Start_Date	Job_End_Date
1	Tom	Coffing	Sales	Software Maintenance	1/1/2006	12/31/2006
2	Leona	Coffing	Sales	New Development	1/1/2006	12/31/2006
3	Steve	Wilmes	Marketing	Financial Pilot	1/1/2006	12/31/2006
4	Gareth	Walter	Marketing	HR Benefits	1/1/2006	12/31/2006
5	Robert	Hines	HR	Backup and Recovery	1/1/2006	12/31/2006
6	Mark	Ferguson	HR	Installation	1/1/2006	12/31/2006
7	Scott	Smith	HR	Legal	1/1/2006	12/31/2006
9	Sara	Wilson	Development	Software Maintenance	1/1/2006	12/31/2006
10	Mike	Larkins	IT	New Development	1/1/2006	12/31/2006

Joins using ANSI Syntax

When joining tables using the ANSI syntax the same results will appear as if I did the join using Teradata syntax, however the ANSI way has a few features that are nice to have, and should be taken into account when deciding how to create your join. When using the ANSI syntax we will join each table with another by using the INNER JOIN command. After we join two tables we will use the ON clause to create our Primary Key, Foreign Key relationship. The nice thing about the ON clause is that if we forget to put it in, the query will not run. This is a nice safety to have. Now that we know how to join two tables using INNER JOIN, if we decide to add a third table we just write in INNER JOIN after the ON clause of the first join and continue with this pattern for up to 64 tables.

```
SEL E.Employee_No AS EMP
      ,E.First_Name
      ,E.Last_Name
      ,D.Dept_Name
      ,J.Job_Desc
      ,J.Job_Start_Date
      ,J.Job_End_Date
FROM Department_Table AS D
INNER JOIN
        Employee_Table AS E
ON D.Dept_No = E.Dept_No
INNER JOIN
        Emp_Job_Table AS EJ
ON E.Employee_No = EJ.Emp_No
INNER JOIN
        Job_Table AS J
ON J.Job_No = EJ.Job_No
ORDER BY 1;
```

This is a four table join using ANSI Syntax.

EMP	First_Name	Last_Name	Dept_Name	Job_Desc	Job_Start_Date	Job_End_Date
1	Tom	Coffing	Sales	Software Maintenance	1/1/2006	12/31/2006
2	Leona	Coffing	Sales	New Development	1/1/2006	12/31/2006
3	Steve	Wilmes	Marketing	Financial Pilot	1/1/2006	12/31/2006
4	Gareth	Walter	Marketing	HR Benefits	1/1/2006	12/31/2006
5	Robert	Hines	HR	Backup and Recovery	1/1/2006	12/31/2006
6	Mark	Ferguson	HR	Installation	1/1/2006	12/31/2006
7	Scott	Smith	HR	Legal	1/1/2006	12/31/2006
9	Sara	Wilson	Development	Software Maintenance	1/1/2006	12/31/2006
10	Mike	Larkins	IT	New Development	1/1/2006	12/31/2006

Another ANSI Join

This ANSI Join is a little different from the previous join. Here we will join each table using the INNER JOIN command, but will not put our ON clauses in our syntax until the end of our query. This is a similar format to the Teradata Join (doing all the joins first and then showing all of the Primary Key, Foreign Key relationships at the end), however we still are using ANSI syntax to make these joins so we will still use the ON clause to show all of our relationships.

When we show all of our relationships with our ON clause, we will do this from the last table relationship we show with our INNER JOINs and then go in the reverse order of how each of our tables are entered, putting them in the ON clause going in this order.

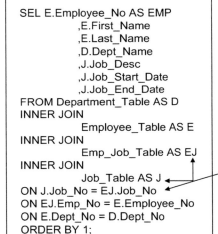

```
SEL E.Employee_No AS EMP
        ,E.First_Name
        ,E.Last_Name
        ,D.Dept_Name
        ,J.Job_Desc
        ,J.Job_Start_Date
        ,J.Job_End_Date
FROM Department_Table AS D
INNER JOIN
        Employee_Table AS E
INNER JOIN
        Emp_Job_Table AS EJ
INNER JOIN
        Job_Table AS J
ON J.Job_No = EJ.Job_No
ON EJ.Emp_No = E.Employee_No
ON E.Dept_No = D.Dept_No
ORDER BY 1;
```

This is another four table join using ANSI Syntax, but using a different method.

Notice all the ON clauses are at the end and the first ON represents the last two table relationship. The following ON clauses continue to work backwards until all relationships have been defined.

EMP	First_Name	Last_Name	Dept_Name	Job_Desc	Job_Start_Date	Job_End_Date
1	Tom	Coffing	Sales	Software Maintenance	1/1/2006	12/31/2006
2	Leona	Coffing	Sales	New Development	1/1/2006	12/31/2006
3	Steve	Wilmes	Marketing	Financial Pilot	1/1/2006	12/31/2006
4	Gareth	Walter	Marketing	HR Benefits	1/1/2006	12/31/2006
5	Robert	Hines	HR	Backup and Recovery	1/1/2006	12/31/2006
6	Mark	Ferguson	HR	Installation	1/1/2006	12/31/2006
7	Scott	Smith	HR	Legal	1/1/2006	12/31/2006
9	Sara	Wilson	Development	Software Maintenance	1/1/2006	12/31/2006
10	Mike	Larkins	IT	New Development	1/1/2006	12/31/2006

Chapter 9 — Join Indexes

"I have found the best way to give advice to your children is to find out what they want and then advise them to do it."

– Harry S. Truman (1884 - 1972)

Dewey have a great technique for you? Join Indexes are a relatively new feature that increases the efficiency and performance of queries containing joins. Teradata accesses the join index instead of resolving all the joins in the participating base tables.

A Join Index can have **repeating values** and Join Indexes are **automatically updated** when the **base tables change**. They actually create a new physical table. Users don't access the Join Index table, but the Teradata does when appropriate.

Think of join indexes as aggregates or summary tables that users don't have to maintain because Teradata automatically manages the entire process. In fact, a user cannot view the row contents of join indexes even if they wanted to. Their operation is entirely transparent to the user. After deleting a base table row, you will not have to update the aggregate or joined table – say goodbye to those pesky "temporary" tables that need manual refreshing on a daily basis or whenever the contributing table rows were changed.

A **Join Index** can have a **different Primary Index** then the base table.

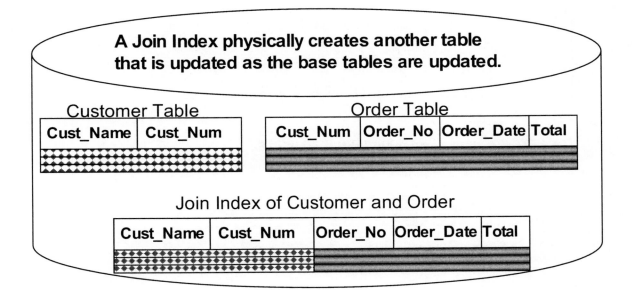

Three basic types of Join Indexes

Single Table Join Index – Distributes the rows of a single table on a foreign key hash value.

Multi-Table Join Index – Pre-Joins multiple tables and stores and maintains the results with the base tables.

Aggregate Join Index – Aggregates one or more columns into a summary table and maintains the results with the base tables.

Customer Table
UPI

Cust_Name	Cust_Num

Order Table
UPI

Cust_Num	Order_No	Order_Date	Total

Single Table Join Index
NUPI

Cust_Num	Order_No	Order_Date	Total

Multi-Table Join Index
NUPI

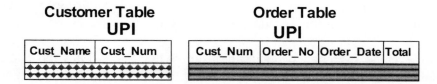

Cust_Name	Cust_Num	Order_No	Order_Date	Total

Aggregate Join Index
NUPI

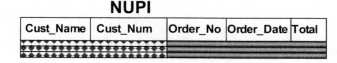

Cust_Num	Order_Date_Month	SUM (Total)

Join Index Fundamentals

Join Index drawbacks

Join index implementation must be thought out thoroughly. Simply throwing a solution at a problem without carefully weighing its costs and rewards is an invitation for trouble. While join indexes are truly useful, they do not enhance performance in every situation. It would be inefficient to create join indexes for 90% of all feasible joins – like denormalization, such a proposal would require exponential amounts of storage.

Space consumption poses one of the most important concerns when using Join Indexes. Although not directly available through a query, Teradata must still store every row of a Join Index on disk. This is done much like any table row is stored – hashed to an AMP. When a Join Index is defined you are looking at twice the amount of space needed per column. If the system is running low on physical disk storage, Join Indexes may do more harm than good.

Join Indexes also require a certain amount of overhead and upkeep. Teradata transparently maintains all join indexes so that the index rows are updated when the base rows change. This is beneficial from a human maintenance perspective because it limits the occurrence of update anomalies. However, the system overhead involved in this automatic maintenance is an important consideration.

When to use a Join Index

The benefits and drawbacks of a Join index are discussed in detail above. You should consider using a join index in the following circumstances:

- **Specific, large tables** are **frequently** and **consistently joined** in which the result set includes **a large number of joins** from joined tables.

- A table is consistently joined to other tables on a column other than its Primary Index.

- Queries all request a small, consistent subset of columns from joined tables containing many columns.

- The **retrieval benefits are greater** than the **cost of setting up, maintaining** and **storing the join index**.

Join Indexes versus other objects

Join Indexes versus Views

Join Index	View
Rows are physically stored on the disks.	Rows are compiled each time the view is referenced.
Ability to have a Primary Index.	Cannot have a Primary Index.
Uses up a Perm space.	Uses only Spool space, while the query is being executed.
Main function is to increase access speed to data.	Main function is to manipulate how data is seen in reports, and for security.
Rows are not accessible to users	Rows are accessible to users with the proper rights.

Join Indexes versus Summary Tables

Join Index	Summary Tables
Rows are physically stored on the disks.	Rows are physically stored on the disks.
Ability to have a Primary Index.	Ability to have Primary Index.
Uses up Perm space.	Uses up Perm Space
Main function is to increase access speed to data – maintained by RDBMS.	Main function is to increase access speed to data – users have to maintain.
Rows are not accessible to users	Rows are accessible to users with the proper rights.

Join Indexes versus Temporary Tables

Join Index	Temporary Tables
Rows are physically stored on the disks.	Rows are in Spool or Temp space.
Ability to have a Primary Index.	Ability to have Primary Index.
Uses up Perm space.	Does not use Perm Space.
Main function is to increase access speed to data.	Main function is to allow for a quick and disposable look at the data.
Rows are not accessible to users	Rows are accessible to users with the proper rights.

Multi-Table Join Index

"Beware of the young doctor and the old barber."

– Benjamin Franklin (1706 - 1790)

If you want to discover electricity in your warehouse place the right keys and string them together in a join index. A multi-table join index is defined as creating a join index that involves more than one table, generally for joins of known queries. The essence behind a multi-table join index is that Teradata stores an answer set of an often-used query on disk. For example, join indexes for an outer join have the ability to preserve the unmatched rows resulting from the join. This is beneficial because this allows the join index to optimize more queries that have few join conditions. When all columns required by a query are available via a **Join Index** this is an example of a **Cover Query**.

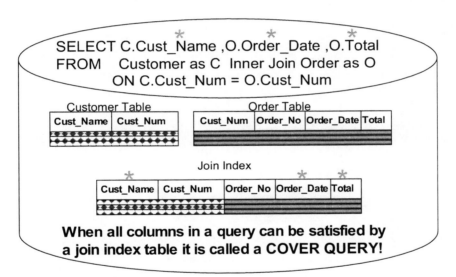

```
CREATE JOIN INDEX  Multi_Join_Index  AS
SELECT                 C.Cust_Name
                      ,C.Cust_Num
                      ,O.Order_no
                      ,O.Order_Date
                      ,O.Order_Total
FROM               Customer_Table as C
INNER JOIN         Order_Table as O
ON                    C.Cust_Num = O.Cust_Num
Primary Index(Cust_Num );
```

Multi-Table Join Index Cont.

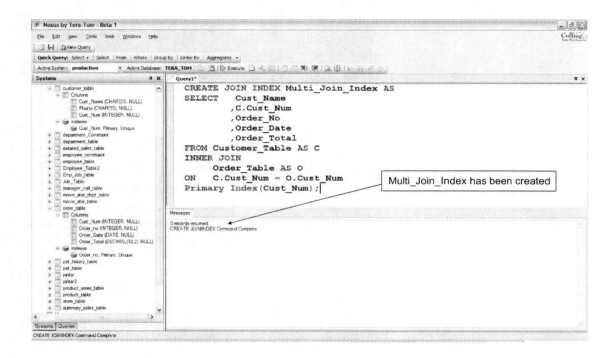

Single-Table Join Indexes

A Single-Table Join Index is defined on **all** or **some** of the columns of one table with the **primary index** generally being a **foreign key** in that table. A great reason for a Single-Table Join index is a base table that is joined often in queries, but with the Primary Index not being in the join criteria. The joins may also pull from only half the columns in that table as well. A single-table join index can be created including only the desired rows and the Primary Index that matches the join criteria.

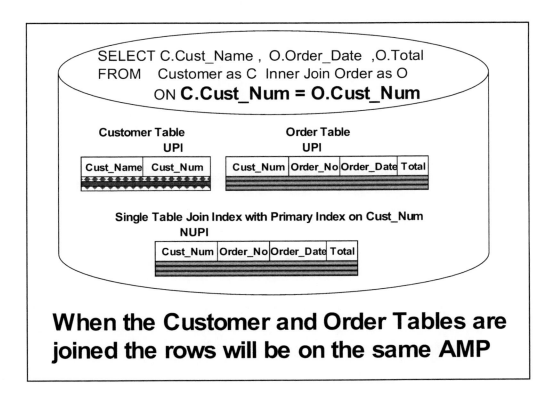

SELECT C.Cust_Name , O.Order_Date ,O.Total
FROM   Customer as C Inner Join Order as O
ON **C.Cust_Num = O.Cust_Num**

Customer Table
UPI

Cust_Name	Cust_Num

Order Table
UPI

Cust_Num	Order_No	Order_Date	Total

Single Table Join Index with Primary Index on Cust_Num
NUPI

Cust_Num	Order_No	Order_Date	Total

When the Customer and Order Tables are joined the rows will be on the same AMP

```
CREATE JOIN INDEX Single_Join_Index AS
SELECT              Cust_Num
                    ,Order_no
                    ,Order_Date
                    ,Order_Total
FROM        Order_Table
Primary Index (Cust_Num);
```

Single-Table Join Indexes *Continued*

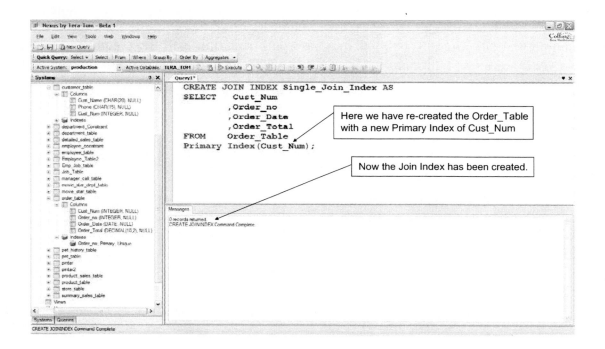

Aggregate Join Index

Aggregate join indexes literally **pre-join and** summarize **aggregated tables** without requiring any physical summary tables. Summary tables often possess inaccurate data due to being merely a snapshot of the base tables. If the base table rows change, the summary table won't reflect this change without human intervention from a DBA or user. And even if such tables are frequently refreshed, human error can cause for anomalies to be overlooked. The following restrictions apply to aggregate join indexes:

- COUNT and SUM are only permitted.
- The DISTINCT command is not permitted.
- Resulting COUNT and SUM columns should be stored as type FLOAT to avoid overflow:

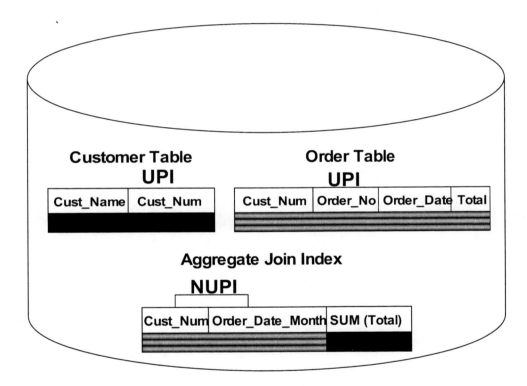

```
CREATE JOIN INDEX Agg_Join_Index AS
SELECT   Cust_Num
         ,Extract (Month from Order_Date)
                   AS MON
         ,Sum (Order_Total)
  FROM    Order_Table
  GROUP BY 1, 2
```

Aggregate Join Index Cont

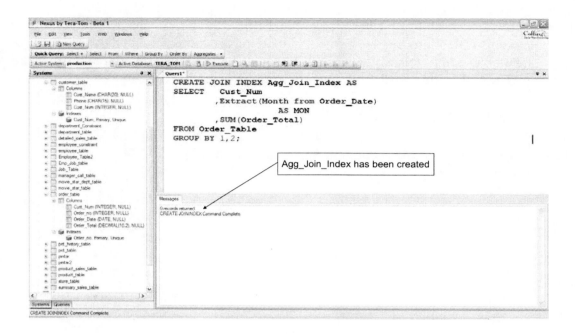

```
CREATE JOIN INDEX Agg_Join_Index AS
SELECT    Cust_Num
          ,Extract(Month from Order_Date)
                   AS MON
          ,SUM(Order_Total)
FROM Order_Table
GROUP BY 1,2;
```

Agg_Join_Index has been created

Sparse Index

A **Sparse Index** is a **join index** with a **WHERE Clause**. If V2R4 when you created a join index of two tables they were joined in their entirety. If you had a yearly table joined to another yearly table you had two twelve month tables physically joined together. The good news was that when queries joined the two tables the queries ran fast. The bad news was that even if you only ran queries asking for the most recent quarter of information you still had to maintain all twelve months in the join index table. Now, with Teradata V2R5 you can join index only the rows you want and do so with a WHERE Clause. A Sparse Index:

- Will have a WHERE clause in the Join Index
- Can have a Non-Unique Primary Index named in the join index

Create Join Index Cust_Ord_SPI
  AS
SELECT O.Order_No
       ,O.Cust_Num
       ,O.Order_Total
       ,O.Order_Date
       ,C. Cust_Name
FROM   Order_Table as O
INNER JOIN
       Customer_Table as C
ON   O.Cust_Num
=   C.Cust_Num
Where Extract (Month from Order_Date)
      IN (10, 11, 12)
Primary Index(Cust_Num)

Sparse Index Cont.

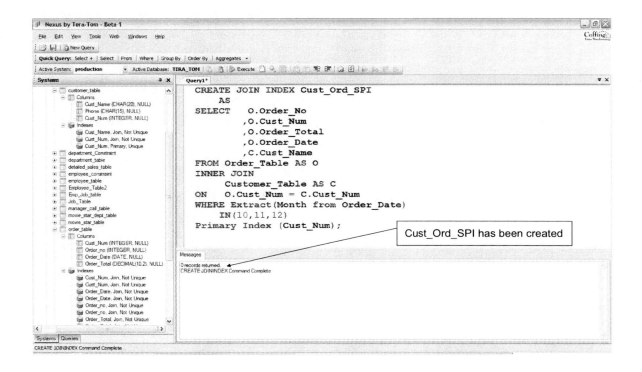

Sparse Index Picture

- Less maintenance and overhead because they are smaller

- Queries run faster because the Join Index table is smaller

- Create for queries with high volumes

- Sparse Indexes take up less space than Join Indexes

- Always collect statistics on the index even if only a single column is indexed

- You can redefine the WHERE clause

- You will get better UPDATE performance on the base tables if the index is strongly selective.

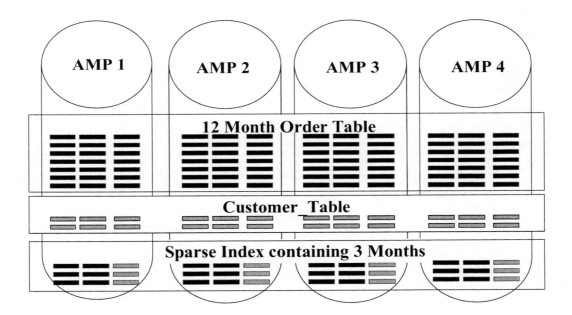

Global Join Index

Teradata is by nature born to be parallel. Generally, when you are accessing multiple rows you usually utilize All-AMPs. The Global Join Index allows you to minimize the number of AMPs you use because Global Join indexes are like Hashed NUSI's. Here is how it works!

A Global Join Index:

- Uses a single-table Join Index as an access path to a base table

- Creates a global index on a single table or a set of joined tables

- Hashes rows by an indexed column or set of columns

- Each Index row points back to the real base row in the real base table

- Will have rows hashed to a different AMP then the rows on the base table

- Is very similar to a hashed NUSI but most likely won't access all the AMPs

- Is also similar to a hashed USI, but most likely will be more than a 2-AMP operation

- Is outstanding for ODS queries with an equality condition on a strongly selective column because it changes two things:

    1. Table-level locks change to row hash locks
    2. All-AMP queries are now Group-AMP queries

Global Join Index Picture

A Global Join index was created on the Last_Name of the Employee_Table. The Join Index table will hash the last name and store it in a separate sub-table. The sub-table will contain the Last_Name, Last_Name Row-ID, and Base Row-IDs for every base row with that name. In the example below the name Mills hashes to the sub-table on AMP2. The Sub-table row contains the Base Table Row-IDs for all rows that have the Last_Name of Mills.

SELECT * FROM Employee_Table
WHERE   Last_Name = 'Mills';

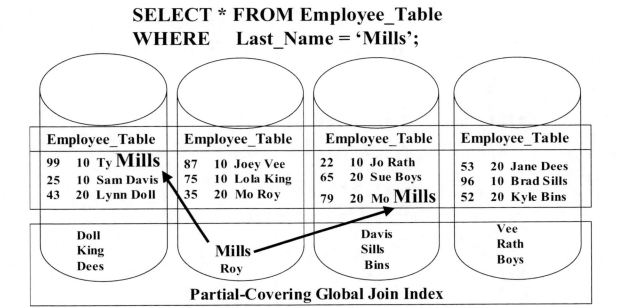

Partial-Covering Global Join Index

Global Join Index – Multi-Table Join Back

In the previous slides we saw a single table Global Join Index. A single table approach could not be used to fully cover joins. Multi-table join indexes can be used for join back. Join Back means the join index includes the base Row-ID where additional columns can be found quickly. Because they involve multiple columns from both tables and retain the base tables Row-IDs they can cover queries and join back to the Base Table for any remaining columns needed. Here is an example of the syntax. Notice that Row-IDs are also asked for in the syntax.

```
Create Join Index Emp_Dept_JI
    AS
SELECT Employee_No
        ,E.Dept_No
        ,E.Last_name
        ,E.First_name
        ,E.Salary
        ,D.Dept_Name
        ,E.ROWID as emp_row_id
        ,D.ROWID as dept_row_id
FROM    Employee_Table as E
INNER JOIN
        Department_Table as D
ON      E.Dept_No = D.Dept_No ;
```

Global Join Index – Multi-Table Join Back Cont.

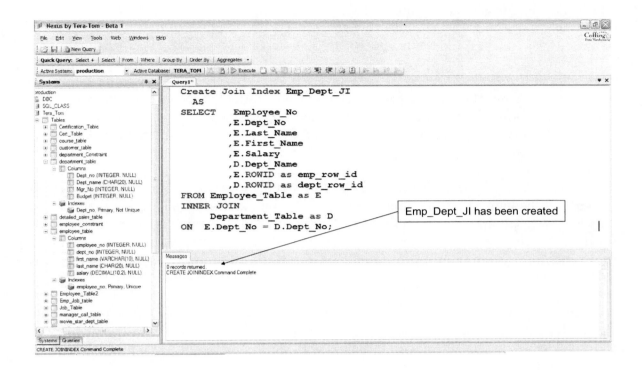

Hash Indexes

Hash indexes are similar to single-table simple join indexes in that they are used for denormalizing a single table by storing rows in a separate physical object from the base table. Hash indexes are limited to a SINGLE table and are beneficial in improving efficiency.

Like join indexes, Hash index rows are stored in a different object than the base table rows. This allows for faster access without needing access to the underlying rows. Also like their relative, they function as an alternative to the base rows instead of providing a different access path.

Like join indexes, hash indexes are known as "covered queries" because they are utilized when they contain all the columns requested by the query. If all of the columns are covered, the optimizer will usually choose to access the rows via the hash index instead of the base table rows. In a situation where the hash index partially covers the query, the optimizer may use the Row ID included with the Hash Index to access the other columns in the data row.

Join indexes and hash indexes are both transparently maintained by Teradata. When the base table changes, the Hash Index table is automatically updated. This automatic task is referred to as an update burden. Being that Hash Indexes are strikingly similar in functionality to secondary indexes, they should be carefully considered because they carry this update burden.

Hash indexes however, can offer marginal performance gains over a secondary index when certain columns are frequently needed from one table to join with many others. In these situations, the Hash index partially covers the query, but fully covers the rows from the base table, effectively eliminating any need to access the base table.

Hash Indexes:

- Can be ordered by hash or by values to facilitate range queries.

- Automatically has the Row ID of the base table row included in the Hash Index which the RDBMS software can use to access columns not included in a "covered query"

Hash Indexes vs. Single-Table Join Indexes

Hash indexes are nearly identical to single-table join indexes in the way they function and behave. By defining either index on a set of table columns, one can reduce the amount of columns and rows that participate in a join. See the previous section for a more detailed description on how such indexing can be used to redistribute table columns among AMPs to improve join performance.

The big difference between Hash and Single-Table Join Indexes is how they are defined:

CREATE HASH INDEX ([column1],[column2]...)
ON [tablename];

This is much simpler syntax than defining a single-table simple join index and thus one of the reasons one would chose a hash-index over a join index.

The following list summarizes the similarities of hash and single-table join indexes.

- Both improve query performance
- Both are ways to achieve denormalized results without physically doing so.
- Both are maintained automatically by Teradata and transparent to the user.
- Both are physical objects that comprise their own table in PERM.
- Neither can be explicitly queried or directly updated.
- Both can be FALLBACK protected.
- The following commands can be used on either:
  - SHOW HASH/JOIN INDEX
  - COLLECT STATISTICS
  - DROP STATISTICS
  - HELP INDEX
- Both are not permitted in MultiLoad and FastLoad utilities.
- Both can be compressed

However, Hash Indexes provide two additional capabilities which are:

- Can be ordered by hash or by values to facilitate range queries.

- Automatically has the Row ID of the base table row included in the Hash Index which the RDBMS software can use to access columns not included in a "covered query"

143

Chapter 10 – Aliasing, Title, Cast, and Format

"You can tell whether a man is clever by his answers. You can tell whether a man is wise by his questions."

Naguib Mahfouz

Title Function

The **TITLE function** allows for a specific title in the **output heading** for a column. **ALIAS** and **TITLE** are **different**. An **alias** is used to change the **name of a column** and **that new name** is to be **used throughout the SQL**. **ALIAS** will also **change the Title** for the column. A **title** does **not change a name** that can be used throughout the SQL. A Title merely changes the **output header** for the column. When Title and an alias are used together the alias takes over the heading for a column.

Order_Table

Cust_Num	Order_No	Order_Date	Order_Total
1	100	2004-06-06	5000.00
2	200	2004-06-07	4000.00
3	300	2004-06-08	2000.00
5	400	2004-06-09	1000000.00

```
SEL cust_num (Title 'Customer #')
    ,Order_no (Title 'Ord_no')
    ,Order_date (Title 'Date of Order')
FROM order_table
ORDER BY 1  ;
```

```
4 Rows Returned

Customer #      Ord_no      Date of Order
------------------   -----------   --------------------
            1       100      2004-01-01
            2       100      2004-01-02
            3       100      2004-01-03
            4       100      2004-01-04
```

Title Function in BTEQ adds functionality

BTEQ works differently then Queryman or SQL Assistant. **BTEQ** is designed to be a **report writer** where Queryman or SQL Assistant is designed more like a **spread sheet**. BTEQ allows more functionality as seen in our examples below.

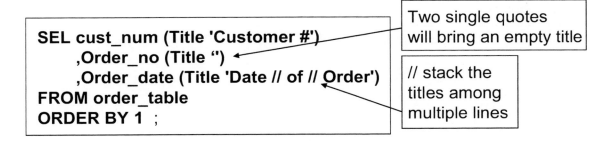

```
SEL cust_num (Title 'Customer #')
    ,Order_no (Title '')
    ,Order_date (Title 'Date // of // Order')
FROM order_table
ORDER BY 1  ;
```

Two single quotes will bring an empty title

// stack the titles among multiple lines

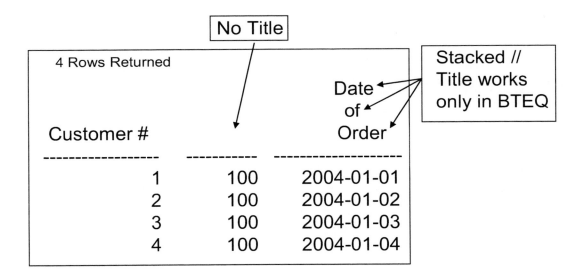

No Title

Stacked // Title works only in BTEQ

```
4 Rows Returned


                                          Date
                                           of
  Customer #                              Order
------------------    -----------    --------------------
                 1            100     2004-01-01
                 2            100     2004-01-02
                 3            100     2004-01-03
                 4            100     2004-01-04
```

147

Title Function used with Distinct

How about this next example? The Distinct will only bring back one row and the row is actually the word Order_No. If the word Distinct is removed the table will bring back the word Order_no one time for each row in the table.

Order_Table

Cust_Num	Order_No	Order_Date	Order_Total
1	100	2004-06-06	5000.00
2	200	2004-06-07	4000.00
3	300	2004-06-08	2000.00
5	400	2004-06-09	1000000.00

select distinct ((title (Order_No))) from Order_table;

One Row Returned

Title(order_no)

----

order_no

Teradata Data Types

Below is a chart that describes the data types used with columns in Teradata.

Data Type	Comments	Description
BYTEINT	**One Byte Integer**	-128 to 127
SMALLINT	**Two Byte Integer**	-32768 to 32767
INTEGER	**Four Byte Integer**	-2,147,483,648 to 2,147,483,647
DATE	**Four Byte Integer**	Stored as **YYYMMDD**
CHAR(X)	**CHARACTER Data**	X Number of Fixed Bytes
VARCHAR(X)	**Variable Character Data**	X Number of Variable Length Bytes
DECIMAL(X,Y)	X = Decimal Y = Places	Either **Decimal (18,Y)** or **(15,Y)**
FLOAT	Floating Point Format	<value>x10 to 307th power to -308th
TIME	Hours, Minutes & Seconds	
TIMESTAMP	**Year, Month, Day, Hour, Minute & Seconds**	
PRECISION	Stored Internally as FLOAT	
DOUBLE PRECISIOIN	Stored Internally as FLOAT	
BYTE(X)	Binary	1 to 64,000 Bytes
VARBYTE(X) Bytes	Variable Length Binary	1 to 64,000
GRAPHIC(X) KANJI Chars	Fixed Length 16-bit bytes	1 – 32,000
VARGRAPHIC(X)	Variable Length 16-bit bytes	1 – 32,000 Characters
LONG VARCHAR(X)	Variable Length string	64,000 characters max.

CAST Function

CAST stands for **Covert And STore**. CAST converts data from one data type to another for the life of the query.

```
SELECT CAST ('12345' AS Char(3))
```

```
One row Returned

'12345'

-------

123
```

```
SELECT CAST ('bb12345bbbbb' AS Char(3))
```

```
One Row Returned

'bb12345bbbb'

-------

bb1
```

CAST Examples

Cast is the Convert and Store option. Below are some outstanding examples of how to change a column or literal from one data type to another.

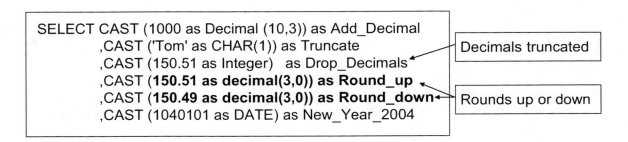

```
SELECT CAST (1000 as Decimal (10,3)) as Add_Decimal
      ,CAST ('Tom' as CHAR(1)) as Truncate
      ,CAST (150.51 as Integer)  as Drop_Decimals
      ,CAST (150.51 as decimal(3,0)) as Round_up
      ,CAST (150.49 as decimal(3,0)) as Round_down
      ,CAST (1040101 as DATE) as New_Year_2004
```

| Decimals truncated |

| Rounds up or down |

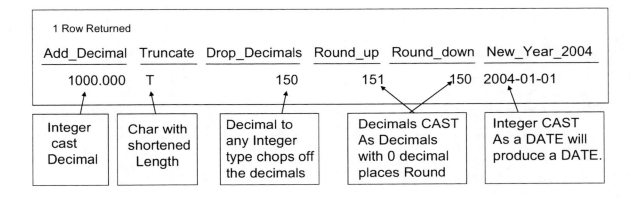

1 Row Returned

Add_Decimal	Truncate	Drop_Decimals	Round_up	Round_down	New_Year_2004
1000.000	T	150	151	150	2004-01-01

| Integer cast Decimal | Char with shortened Length | Decimal to any Integer type chops off the decimals | Decimals CAST As Decimals with 0 decimal places Round | Integer CAST As a DATE will produce a DATE. |

CAST Examples that FAIL

Cast is the Convert and Store option. Below are some outstanding examples of how to fail. One of the key things to remember is that you can't **convert data** that is **too large** for a **data type**.

The first example works perfectly, but each numeric value is at the highest level. Any higher numbers and you begin to receive OVERFLOW ERRORS.

```
SELECT  CAST(2147483647.9 as INTEGER) as Highest_Integer
       ,CAST(32767.9 as SMALLINT)      as Highest_Smallint
       ,CAST (127.9 as BYTEINT)        as Highest_Byteint
```

1 row returned	Decimals Truncated	
Highest_Integer	Highest_Smallint	Highest_Byteint
2147483647	32767	127

The **second example does NOT work**. Each received an **OVERFLOW ERROR**.

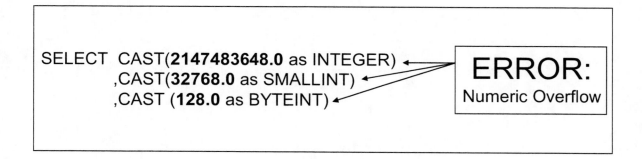

```
SELECT  CAST(2147483648.0 as INTEGER)
       ,CAST(32768.0 as SMALLINT)
       ,CAST (128.0 as BYTEINT)
```

ERROR:
Numeric Overflow

Derived Columns

Although most columns are retrieved from actual tables it is also advantageous that values can be calculated on the fly.

Order of Precedence of Math Operations

Operator	Operation	Comment / Example
()	Parentheses	enforce all math in **parentheses done first**
**	Exponentiation	$10**12$ is a Trillion (DBC 1012)
*	Multiplication	$5 * 5 = 25$
/	Division	**3 / 4 derives 0** since **both are integers** and **truncation** of **decimals occurs**
+	Addition	$5 + 5 = 10$
-	Subtraction	$5 - 6 = -1$ since negatives are allowed

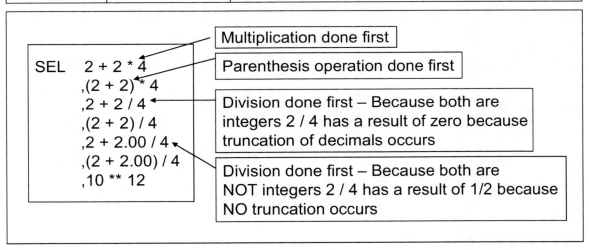

```
SEL   2 + 2 * 4          Multiplication done first
     ,(2 + 2) * 4        Parenthesis operation done first
     ,2 + 2 / 4          Division done first – Because both are
     ,(2 + 2) / 4        integers 2 / 4 has a result of zero because
     ,2 + 2.00 / 4       truncation of decimals occurs
     ,(2 + 2.00) / 4
     ,10 ** 12           Division done first – Because both are
                         NOT integers 2 / 4 has a result of 1/2 because
                         NO truncation occurs
```

One Row Returned

(2+(2*4))	((2+2)*4)	(2+(2/4))	((2+2)/4)	(2+(2.00)/4))	((2+2.00)/4)	(10**12)
10	16	2	1	2.50	1.00	1000000000000.00

Using and ALIAS on a Column

There are multiple ways to alias a column. Once you alias a column that column now has a new name through out the SQL.

Order_Table

Cust_Num	Order_No	Order_Date	Order_Total
1	100	2004-06-06	5000.00
2	200	2004-06-07	4000.00
3	300	2004-06-08	2000.00
5	400	2004-06-09	1000000.00

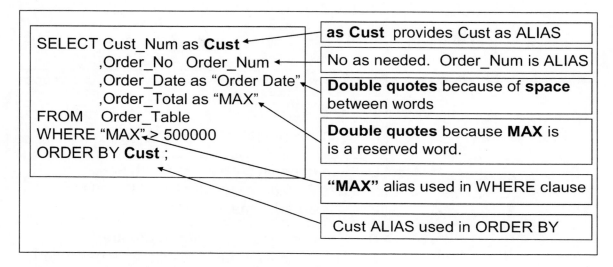

```
SELECT Cust_Num as Cust
      ,Order_No   Order_Num
      ,Order_Date as "Order Date"
      ,Order_Total as "MAX"
FROM    Order_Table
WHERE "MAX" > 500000
ORDER BY Cust ;
```

as Cust provides Cust as ALIAS

No as needed. Order_Num is ALIAS

Double quotes because of **space** between words

Double quotes because **MAX** is is a reserved word.

"MAX" alias used in WHERE clause

Cust ALIAS used in ORDER BY

One Row Returned

Cust	Order_Num	Order Date	MAX
5	400	2004-06-09	1000000.00

Formatting a Column

You can use the FORMAT command to format your output. The output below was run in BTEQ. Queryman and SQL Assistant use ODBC and there are options in ODBC that if they are not set then ODBC will not FORMAT. BTEQ always formats when asked.

Order_Table

Cust_Num	Order_No	Order_Date	Order_Total
1	100	2004-06-06	5000.00
2	200	2004-06-07	4000.00
3	300	2004-06-08	2000.00
5	400	2004-06-09	1000000.00

```
SEL    cust_num
       ,order_total (format '$$,$$$,$$$.99')
       ,order_date (format 'MMMbDDbYYYY')
       ,order_date (format 'MM-DD-YY')
       ,order_date (format 'YYYY-MM-DD')
FROM  order_table
WHERE Cust_num = 5 ;
```

One Row Returned

Cust_num	Order_total	Order_date	Order_date	Order_date
5	$1,000,000.00	JUN 09 2004	06-09-04	2004-06-09

Trick to make ODBC use the FORMAT command

You can use the FORMAT command to format your output. The output below was run in BTEQ. Queryman and SQL Assistant use ODBC and there are options in ODBC that if they are not set then ODBC will not FORMAT. BTEQ always formats when asked.

One of the tricks of the trade is to use the CAST (Convert And Store) command to CAST the output to CHARACTER data. Then all formatting works because ODBC thinks it is CHARACTER data. In our format examples we CAST each to CHAR.

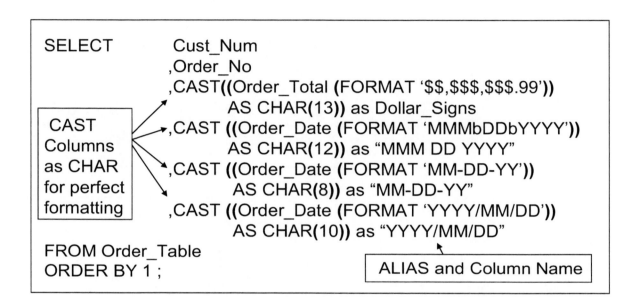

```
SELECT          Cust_Num
                ,Order_No
                ,CAST((Order_Total (FORMAT '$$,$$$,$$$.99'))
                        AS CHAR(13)) as Dollar_Signs
  CAST         ,CAST ((Order_Date (FORMAT 'MMMbDDbYYYY'))
  Columns              AS CHAR(12)) as "MMM DD YYYY"
  as CHAR      ,CAST ((Order_Date (FORMAT 'MM-DD-YY'))
  for perfect          AS CHAR(8)) as "MM-DD-YY"
  formatting   ,CAST ((Order_Date (FORMAT 'YYYY/MM/DD'))
                        AS CHAR(10)) as "YYYY/MM/DD"
FROM Order_Table
ORDER BY 1 ;                              ALIAS and Column Name
```

4 Rows Returned

Cust_Num	Order_No	Dollar_Signs	MMM DD YYYY	MM-DD-YY	YYYY/MM/DD
1	100	$5,000.00	Jun 06 2004	06-06-04	2004/06/06
2	200	$4,000.00	Jun 07 2004	06-07-04	2004/06/07
3	300	$2,000.00	Jun 08 2004	06-08-04	2004/06/08
5	400	$1,000,000.00	Jun 09 2004	06-09-04	2004/06/09

FORMAT Options for Dates

You can use the FORMAT command to format your output and below are options for date representation.

Date Format Symbols	Date Format Symbol Representation
MM	Month as two numeric digits
MMM or M3	Month as abbreviated 3 char (APR represents APRIL)
MMMM or M4	Month as full name (November)
DD	Day of Month as two numeric digits
DDD or D3	Day of Month as Day of Year (Feb 1 = 032)
YY	Year as two numeric digits
YYYY or Y4	Year as four numeric digits
EEE or E3	Day of Week abbreviated (Mon) for Monday
EEEE or E4	Day of Week using full name (Monday)

FORMAT Separators

You can use the FORMAT command to format your output and below are options for placing additional separators.

Separator Symbols	Separator Description
/	Slash Separator (default for dates)
b or B	Blank Separator (Provides a blank or a space)
,	Comma Separator
:	Colon Separator
.	Period Separator
'	Apostrophe Separator
-	Dash Separator (ANSI default)
9	Nine Separator
h	Hour Separator – The h formatting character must follow the HH.
m	Minute Separator – m formatting character must follow the MI.
s	Second Separator – s formatting character must follow SS formatting.

TIME FORMAT Options

You can use the FORMAT command to format your output and below are options for formatting the TIME.

Time Format Symbols	Time Format Symbol Representation
HH	Hour as two numeric digits
MI	Minute as two numeric digits
SS	Seconds as two numeric digits
S(n)	Replace n with number between 0 an 6 for fraction of a second
S(f)	Number of fractional seconds
T	Time in 12 hour formats (AM/PM)
Z	Z controls placement of Timezone (Must be either at the beginning or the end of the time formatting chars)

Date, Time, and Timestamp FORMAT Examples

Below are some excellent examples of formatting.

January 10, 1959	
FORMAT	**Result**
FORMAT 'YY/MM/DD'	59/01/10
FORMAT 'DD-MM-YY'	10-01-59
FORMAT 'YYYY/MM/DD'	1959/01/10
FORMAT 'YYYY-MM-DD'	1959-01-10
FORMAT 'DDBMMMBYYYY'	01 Jan 1959
FORMAT 'EEE,BM4BDD,BYYYY'	Sat, January 10, 1959

10:30:00	
FORMAT	**Result**
FORMAT 'HH:MIBT'	10:30 AM
FORMAT 'HHhMImSSs'	10h30m00s
FORMAT 'HH:MI:SSBT'	10:30:00 AM
FORMAT 'HH:MI'	10:30
FORMAT 'HH:MI:SSDS(F)'	10:30:00.000000
FORMAT 'HH:MI:SSDS(F)Z'	10:30:00.000000

January 10, 1959 at 10:30:00 AM	
Timestamp FORMAT	**Result**
FORMAT 'MMMBDD,BYYBHH:MI:SS'	Jan 10, 59 10:30:00
FORMAT 'MM-DD-YYBHH:MIBT'	01-10-59 10:30:00 AM
FORMAT 'YYYY/MM/DDBHH:MI:SS'	1959/01/10 10:30:00
FORMAT 'E3,BM4BDD,BY4BHH:MI:SS'	Sat, January 10, 1959 10:30:00

Chapter 11 – Interrogating Data

"The man who doesn't read good books has no advantage over the man who can't read them."

Mark Twain

SUBSTRING

The SUBSTRING function is used to retrieve portions of data stored in a column. When using SUBSTRING, the name of the column is passed to the function along with the starting character location for the retrieval and lastly, the number of characters to retrieve (length). Our example below will use the Department_Table to extract the first two characters in the Dept_name column.

Department_Table			
Dept_No	**Dept_name**	**MGR_No**	**Budget**
10	Sales	2	266000
20	Marketing	4	356000
30	HR	6	200000
40	Development	9	126000
50	IT	10	25000000

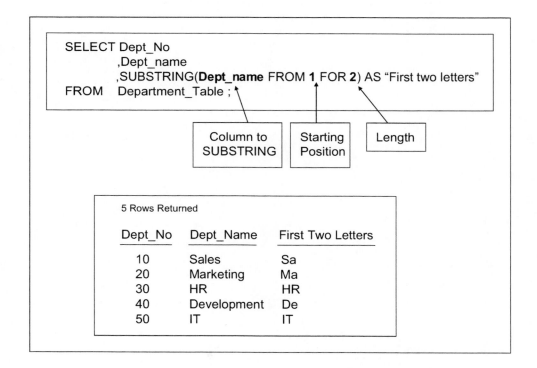

SUBSTR

The SUBSTR function is used to retrieve portions of data stored in a column. This was the original substring operation used by Teradata. When using SUBSTR, the name of the column is passed to the function along with the starting character location for the retrieval and lastly, the number of characters to retrieve (length). The main difference between SUBSTRING and SUBSTR is that SUBSTR uses commas instead of the keywords FROM and FOR. Our example below will use the Department_Table to extract the first two characters in the Dept_name column.

Department_Table			
Dept_No	**Dept_name**	**MGR_No**	**Budget**
10	Sales	2	266000
20	Marketing	4	356000
30	HR	6	200000
40	Development	9	126000
50	IT	10	25000000

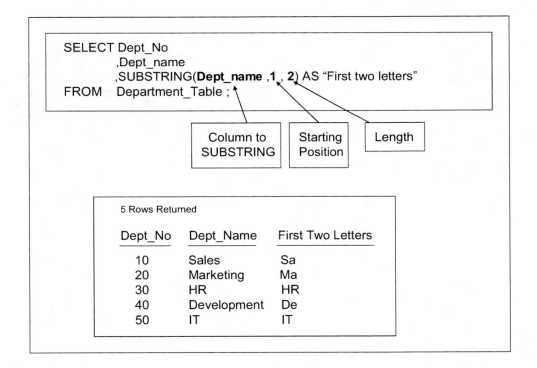

Concatenation of Character Strings

Concatenation is the process of taking two or more columns or literals and combining them into a single column. Below we will combine the First_name and Last_name columns into one single column for all people in Dept_No 10.

Employee_Table

Employee_No	Dept_No	First_Name	Last_Name	Salary
1	10	Tom	Coffing	50000.00
2	10	Leona	Coffing	75000.50
3	20	Steve	Wilmes	95054.30
4	20	Gareth	Walter	94986.35
5	30	Robert	Hines	120987.45
6	30	Mark	Ferguson	97087.67
7	30	Scott	Smith	143987.94
8	40	Marsha	Lewis	98453.88
9	40	Sara	Wilson	97450.75
10	50	Mike	Larkins	245098.00
11	999	Arfy	Coffing	NULL
12	999	Spot	Coffing	NULL

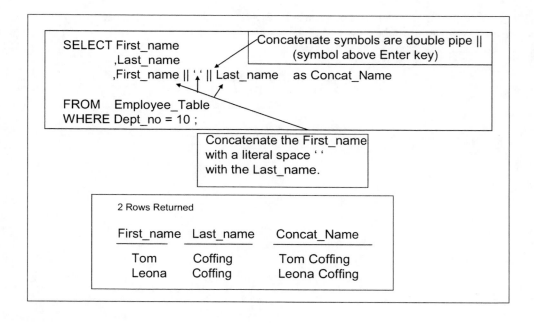

```
SELECT First_name
      ,Last_name
      ,First_name || ' ' || Last_name    as Concat_Name

FROM   Employee_Table
WHERE Dept_no = 10 ;
```

Concatenate symbols are double pipe ||
(symbol above Enter key)

Concatenate the First_name
with a literal space ' '
with the Last_name.

2 Rows Returned

First_name	Last_name	Concat_Name
Tom	Coffing	Tom Coffing
Leona	Coffing	Leona Coffing

Using SUBSTRING and Concatenation Together

Our next example will use the SUBSTRING command in conjunction with concatenation to bring us the first initial of employees First_name followed by a period and a space followed by the Last_name.

Employee_Table

Employee_No	Dept_No	First_Name	Last_Name	Salary
1	10	Tom	Coffing	50000.00
2	10	Leona	Coffing	75000.50
3	20	Steve	Wilmes	95054.30
4	20	Gareth	Walter	94986.35
5	30	Robert	Hines	120987.45
6	30	Mark	Ferguson	97087.67
7	30	Scott	Smith	143987.94
8	40	Marsha	Lewis	98453.88
9	40	Sara	Wilson	97450.75
10	50	Mike	Larkins	245098.00
11	999	Arfy	Coffing	NULL
12	999	Spot	Coffing	NULL

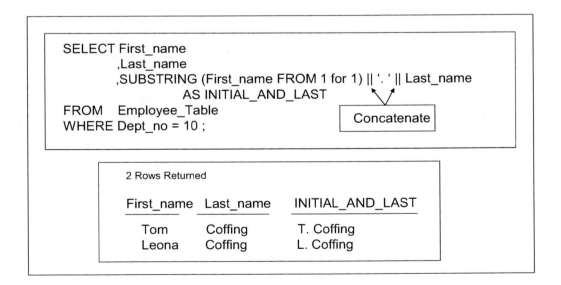

```
SELECT First_name
       ,Last_name
       ,SUBSTRING (First_name FROM 1 for 1) || '. ' || Last_name
              AS INITIAL_AND_LAST
FROM   Employee_Table
WHERE Dept_no = 10 ;
```

Concatenate

2 Rows Returned

First_name	Last_name	INITIAL_AND_LAST
Tom	Coffing	T. Coffing
Leona	Coffing	L. Coffing

CHARACTER Vs VARCHAR

Our Employee_Table was created with the First_name column as a VARCHAR(20). The Last_name column was created as a CHAR(20) data type. A CHAR data type will reserve the number of bytes you ask for so a CHAR (20) will reserve 20 bytes. If a person has a name of Wilmes then the system recognizes this as Wilmes and 14 spaces. Here is an example of Wilmes followed by 14 spaces. 'Wilmes   '.

A VARCHAR (20) is different because a **VARCHAR will eliminate trailing spaces**. A VARCHAR will add two bytes to each VARCHAR column called a Variable Length Indicator (VLI). If you had the name "Gareth" on a VARCHAR(20) column the system would recognize that Gareth has only 6 letters. It would store 6 in the VLI so the total length to store Gareth is only 8 bytes.

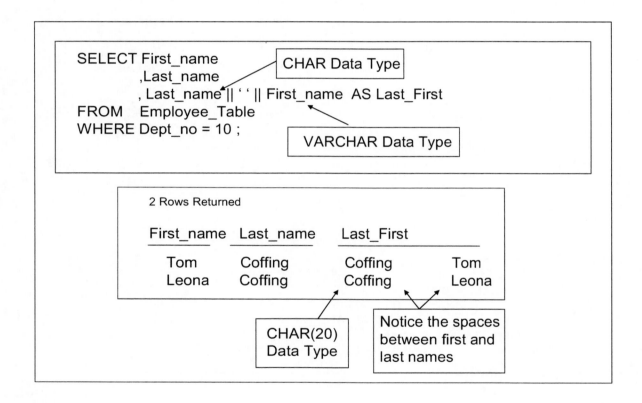

The TRIM Function

TRIM is used to eliminate space characters from fixed length data values. TRIM can eliminate the trailing spaces, leading spaces or both leading and trailing spaces.

In our example below we TRIM the Last_name column before we concatenate it with a literal space and then the First_name column.

TRIM Syntax

TRIM (TRAILING FROM <Column-name>)
/* Trims only spaces stored after all text characters */

TRIM (LEADING FROM <Column-name>)
/* Trims only spaces stored before all text characters */

TRIM (BOTH FROM <Column-name>)
/* Trims all spaces stored before and after all text characters */

TRIM(<Column-name>) /* Defaults to BOTH */

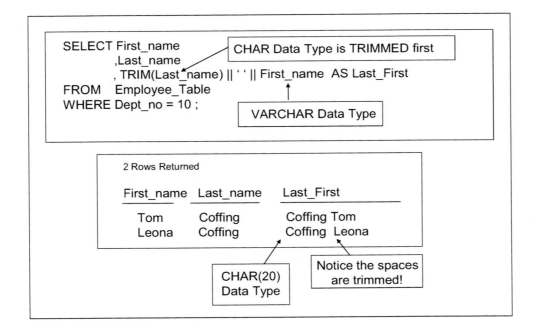

CHARACTERS Command

The **CHARACTERS** command counts the **number of bytes** in a **VARCHAR column** and returns the total.

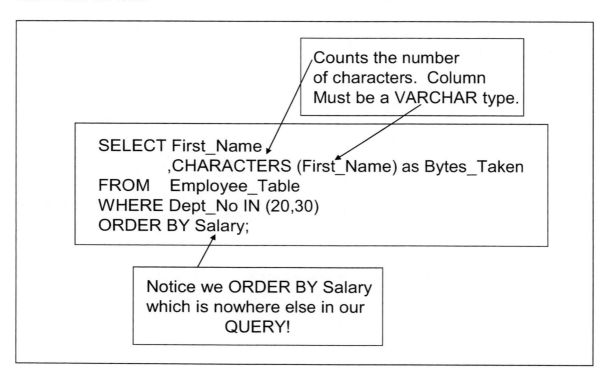

```
SELECT First_Name
        ,CHARACTERS (First_Name) as Bytes_Taken
FROM    Employee_Table
WHERE Dept_No IN (20,30)
ORDER BY Salary;
```

Counts the number of characters. Column Must be a VARCHAR type.

Notice we ORDER BY Salary which is nowhere else in our QUERY!

5 rows returned

First_Name	Bytes_Taken
Scott	5
Robert	6
Mark	4
Steve	5
Gareth	6

COUNT THAT VARCHAR

1 2 3 4 (5)

SCOTT

Output Results for Multiple Commands Mixed

When you have multiple commands working on a column remember that Teradata starts working from inward to out. Here are some examples to prepare you for the unexpected.

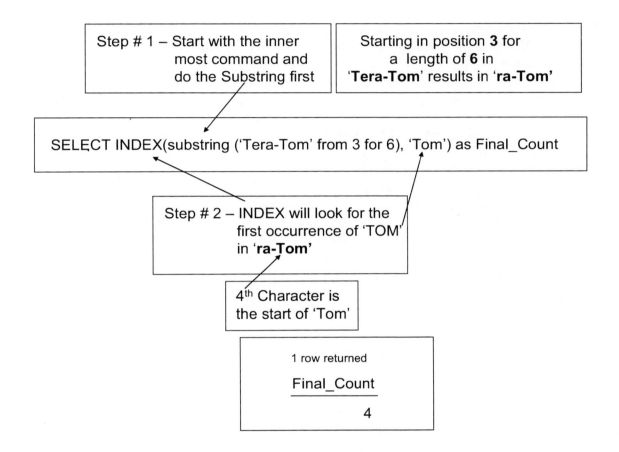

Step # 1 – Start with the inner most command and do the Substring first

Starting in position **3** for a length of **6** in '**Tera-Tom**' results in '**ra-Tom**'

SELECT INDEX(substring ('Tera-Tom' from 3 for 6), 'Tom') as Final_Count

Step # 2 – INDEX will look for the first occurrence of 'TOM' in '**ra-Tom**'

4th Character is the start of 'Tom'

1 row returned

Final_Count

4

The POSITION Function

The **POSITION function** is used to return a number that represents the starting location of a **specified character string** with character data. The POSITION function expects to be passed two pieces of information. First, pass it the name of the column containing the data to examine and second, the character string that it should look for within the data.

The POSITION function returns a single numeric value that points to the location of the first occurrence of the character string in the data. If the character string is not found a zero is returned.

Department_Table

Dept_No	Dept_name	MGR_No	Budget
10	Sales	2	266000
20	Marketing	4	356000
30	HR	6	200000
40	Development	9	126000
50	IT	10	25000000

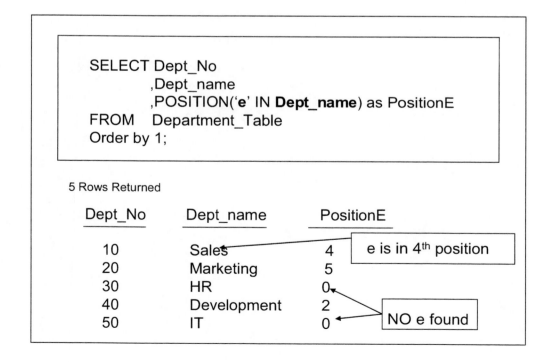

```
SELECT Dept_No
       ,Dept_name
       ,POSITION('e' IN Dept_name) as PositionE
FROM   Department_Table
Order by 1;
```

5 Rows Returned

Dept_No	Dept_name	PositionE
10	Sales	4
20	Marketing	5
30	HR	0
40	Development	2
50	IT	0

e is in 4th position

NO e found

The INDEX Function

We just learned about the **POSITION function** and now we will **learn of its equivalent** called the **INDEX function**. INDEX is the original way Teradata brought back a position, but POSITION is the ANSI standard. The INDEX function is used to return a number that represents the starting location of a specified character string with character data. The INDEX function expects to be passed two pieces of information. First, pass it the name of the column containing the data to examine and second, the character string that it should look for within the data.

The INDEX function returns a single numeric value that points to the location of the first occurrence of the character string in the data. If the character string is not found a zero is returned.

Department_Table			
Dept_No	**Dept_name**	**MGR_No**	**Budget**
10	Sales	2	266000
20	Marketing	4	356000
30	HR	6	200000
40	Development	9	126000
50	IT	10	25000000

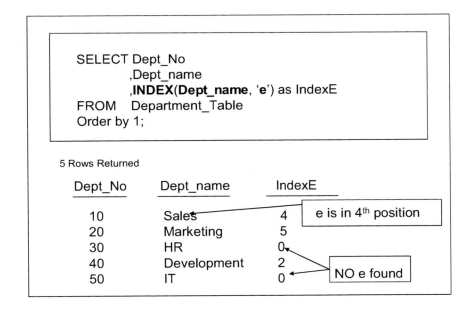

```
SELECT Dept_No
       ,Dept_name
       ,INDEX(Dept_name, 'e') as IndexE
FROM   Department_Table
Order by 1;
```

5 Rows Returned

Dept_No	Dept_name	IndexE	
10	Sales	4	e is in 4th position
20	Marketing	5	
30	HR	0	
40	Development	2	NO e found
50	IT	0	

SUBSTRING and POSITION Together

The SUBSTRING and POSITION commands can be used together. The SUBSTRING syntax asks for the column name to perform the SUBSTRING, the starting position to begin the SUBSTRING and the length of characters.

The example below will use the Course_Table to exclude the first word in the Course_Name.

Course_Table

Course_ID	Course_Name	Credits	Seats
1	Teradata Basics	3	100
2	Teradata Database Design	3	25
3	Teradata SQL	3	20
4	Teradata DBA	4	12
5	Teradata Appl Dev	3	16

```
SELECT Course_ID
       ,Course_Name
       ,SUBSTRING (Course_Name FROM
           POSITION(' ' IN Course_Name) +1) as Second_Word_On
FROM    Course_Table
Order by 1;
```

Starting Position of SUBSTRING | No Ending Position of SUBSTRING

5 Rows Returned

Course_ID	Course_Name	Second_Word_On
1	Teradata Basics	Basics
2	Teradata Database Design	Database Design
3	Teradata SQL	SQL
4	Teradata DBA	DBA
5	Teradata Appl Dev	Appl Dev

COALESCE

COALESCE finds the **first non-null value** in a **list** and returns it. If **everything in the list is NULL** then **Coalesce will return a NULL value**. You can use columns or literal values in the coalesce list.

Manager_Call_Table

Emp_no	First_name	Last_name	Work_phone	Cell_phone	Home_phone
2	Leona	Coffing	NULL	513 300-0321	513 123-1345
4	Gareth	Walter	303 834-1342	303 876-1245	303 423-1234
6	Mark	Ferguson	NULL	817 456-1435	817 342-9081
9	Sara	Wilson	NULL	NULL	NULL
10	Mike	Larkins	523 310-4392	NULL	523 434-9875

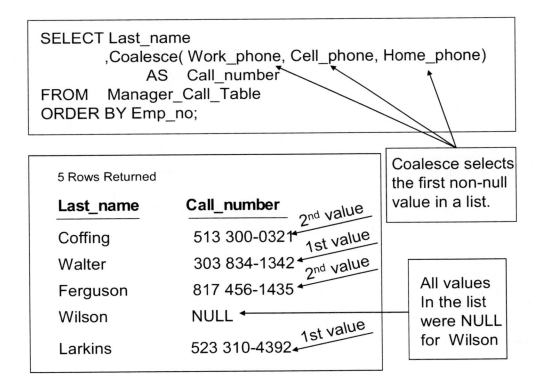

```
SELECT Last_name
        ,Coalesce( Work_phone, Cell_phone, Home_phone)
            AS   Call_number
FROM   Manager_Call_Table
ORDER BY Emp_no;
```

Coalesce selects the first non-null value in a list.

5 Rows Returned

Last_name	Call_number
Coffing	513 300-0321	2nd value
Walter	303 834-1342	1st value
Ferguson	817 456-1435	2nd value
Wilson	NULL
Larkins	523 310-4392	1st value

All values In the list were NULL for Wilson

COALESCE with Literals

COALESCE finds the first non-null value in a list and returns it. If everything in the list is NULL then Coalesce will return a NULL value. You can use columns or literal values in the coalesce list. One benefit of literals is that they will never return a NULL value. Notice our literal 'No Phone' value in our Coalesce list? We will never return NULL now.

Manager_Call_Table

Emp_no	First_name	Last_name	Work_phone	Cell_phone	Home_phone
2	Leona	Coffing	NULL	513 300-0321	513 123-1345
4	Gareth	Walter	303 834-1342	303 876-1245	303 423-1234
6	Mark	Ferguson	NULL	817 456-1435	817 342-9081
9	Sara	Wilson	NULL	NULL	NULL
10	Mike	Larkins	523 310-4392	NULL	523 434-9875

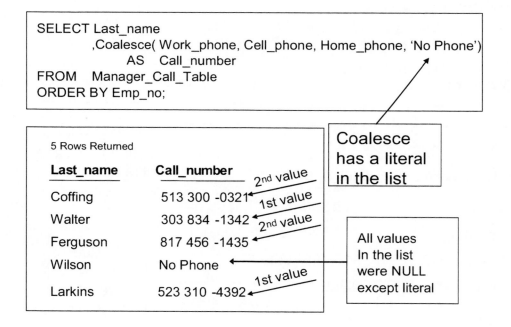

```
SELECT Last_name
        ,Coalesce( Work_phone, Cell_phone, Home_phone, 'No Phone')
            AS   Call_number
FROM   Manager_Call_Table
ORDER BY Emp_no;
```

Coalesce
has a literal
in the list

5 Rows Returned

Last_name	Call_number
Coffing	513 300 -0321
Walter	303 834 -1342
Ferguson	817 456 -1435
Wilson	No Phone
Larkins	523 310 -4392

2nd value
1st value
2nd value
1st value

All values
In the list
were NULL
except literal

ZEROIFNULL

The purpose of the **ZEROIFNULL function** is to compare the data value in a column and when it contains a **NULL**, transform it, for the life of the SQL statement, to a **zero**.

Employee_Table				
Employee_No	Dept_No	First_Name	Last_Name	Salary
1	10	Tom	Coffing	50000.00
2	10	Leona	Coffing	75000.50
3	20	Steve	Wilmes	95054.30
4	20	Gareth	Walter	94986.35
5	30	Robert	Hines	120987.45
6	30	Mark	Ferguson	97087.67
7	30	Scott	Smith	143987.94
8	40	Marsha	Lewis	98453.88
9	40	Sara	Wilson	97450.75
10	50	Mike	Larkins	245098.00
11	999	Arfy	Coffing	NULL
12	999	Spot	Coffing	NULL

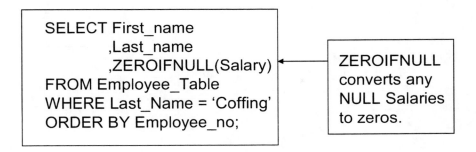

```
SELECT First_name
       ,Last_name
       ,ZEROIFNULL(Salary)
FROM Employee_Table
WHERE Last_Name = 'Coffing'
ORDER BY Employee_no;
```

ZEROIFNULL converts any NULL Salaries to zeros.

4 Rows Returned		
First_name	Last_name	Salary
Tom	Coffing	50000.00
Leona	Coffing	75000.50
Arfy	Coffing	0.00
Spot	Coffing	0.00

NULLIFZERO

The purpose of the **NULLIFZERO** function is to compare the data value in a column and when it contains a **zero**, transform it, **for the life of the SQL statement**, to a **NULL**.

Sales_Table

Store_No	Product_ID	Sale_Date	Total_Sales
1	100	01-10-2004	34000.00
2	100	01-10-2004	0.00
3	100	01-10-2004	23000.00
1	200	01-10-2004	12000.00
2	200	01-10-2004	43000.00
3	200	01-10-2004	17000.00
1	300	01-10-2004	12000.00
2	300	01-10-2004	0.00
3	300	01-10-2004	17000.00

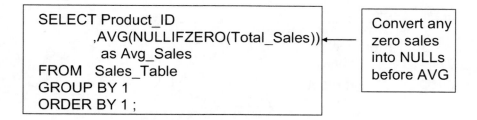

```
SELECT Product_ID
      ,AVG(NULLIFZERO(Total_Sales))
       as Avg_Sales
FROM   Sales_Table
GROUP BY 1
ORDER BY 1 ;
```

Convert any zero sales into NULLs before AVG

3 Rows Returned

Product_ID	Avg_Sales
100	28500
200	24000
300	14500

NULLIF Command

NULLIF is an ANSI standard command that works similarly to NULLIFZERO. **NULLIFZERO** only coverts a **zero to a NULL**, but **NULLIF** can **convert a zero** to a NULL, but it can also convert **anything to a NULL**. To use NULLIF all you have to do is pass the name of the column to compare and the value to compare for equal. NULLIF works with two values. If the two values are equal then the result is NULL. If the two values are not equal then the first value is returned.

Our next example will use the NULLIF command to check for credits of 4. We will replace all 4 credit classes with the word NULL. **The logic is if X = Y then NULL else X.**

Course_Table

Course_ID	Course_Name	Credits	Seats
1	Teradata Basics	3	100
2	Teradata Database Design	3	25
3	Teradata SQL	3	20
4	Teradata DBA	4	12
5	Teradata Appl Dev	3	16

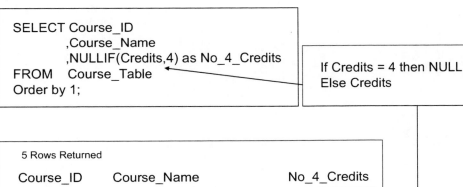

```
SELECT Course_ID
      ,Course_Name
      ,NULLIF(Credits,4) as No_4_Credits
FROM    Course_Table
Order by 1;
```

If Credits = 4 then NULL
Else Credits

5 Rows Returned

Course_ID	Course_Name	No_4_Credits
1	Teradata Basics	3
2	Teradata Database Design	3
3	Teradata SQL	3
4	Teradata DBA	NULL
5	Teradata Appl Dev	3

The CASE Command (Valued CASE)

The CASE command is excellent for interrogating data and then acting accordingly. **Each row is** evaluated by the **CASE command** only **once**. Once a comparison is met then the next row is evaluated. For each **CASE statement** you will have a corresponding **END statement**. You can even have nested CASE commands.

There are two different syntax differences for the CASE command. If you CASE a particular column then you can only **check for equality (Valued Case).** That is apparent in our example below.

Course_Table

Course_ID	Course_Name	Credits	Seats
1	Teradata Basics	3	100
2	Teradata Database Design	3	25
3	Teradata SQL	3	20
4	Teradata DBA	4	12
5	Teradata Appl Dev	3	16

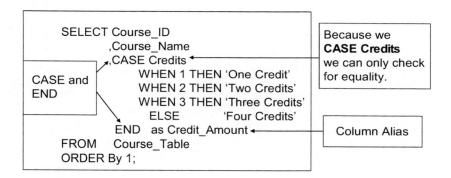

```
                 SELECT Course_ID
                        ,Course_Name
                        ,CASE Credits
                             WHEN 1 THEN 'One Credit'
                             WHEN 2 THEN 'Two Credits'
                             WHEN 3 THEN 'Three Credits'
                              ELSE           'Four Credits'
                        END   as Credit_Amount
                 FROM    Course_Table
                 ORDER By 1;
```

CASE and END

Because we **CASE Credits** we can only check for equality.

Column Alias

5 Rows Returned

Course_ID	Course_Name	Credit_Amount
1	Teradata Basics	Three Credits
2	Teradata Database Design	Three Credits
3	Teradata SQL	Three Credits
4	Teradata DBA	Four Credits
5	Teradata Appl Dev	Three Credits

The CASE Command (Searched CASE)

There are two different syntax differences for the CASE command. If you CASE a particular column then you can only **check for equality .(Valued Case)**. If you use the **CASE command without specifying the column name immediately** after the **word CASE** you can then check many different columns and you can also check for things other than equality. This is called a **Searched CASE**.

Course_Table

Course_ID	Course_Name	Credits	Seats
1	Teradata Basics	3	100
2	Teradata Database Design	3	25
3	Teradata SQL	3	20
4	Teradata DBA	4	12
5	Teradata Appl Dev	3	16

```
SELECT Course_ID
       ,Course_Name
       ,CASE  ◄
            WHEN Credits = 1 THEN 'One Credit'
            WHEN Credits < 3 THEN 'Two Credits'
            WHEN Credits < 4 THEN 'Three Credits'
            ELSE          'Four Credits'
        END   as Credit_Amount
FROM    Course_Table
ORDER By 1;
```

Because there is no column name after CASE we can check for equality or inequality using any valid statement.

5 Rows Returned

Course_ID	Course_Name	Credit_Amount
1	Teradata Basics	Three Credits
2	Teradata Database Design	Three Credits
3	Teradata SQL	Three Credits
4	Teradata DBA	Four Credits
5	Teradata Appl Dev	Three Credits

Nested CASE Statement

You can have nested CASE statements. These are CASE statements within CASE statements. For each CASE you must have a corresponding END statement.

Course_Table

Course_ID	Course_Name	Credits	Seats
1	Teradata Basics	3	100
2	Teradata Database Design	3	25
3	Teradata SQL	3	20
4	Teradata DBA	4	12
5	Teradata Appl Dev	3	16

```
SELECT Course_ID
        ,Course_Name
        ,CASE Credits
            WHEN 3
              THEN 'Three Credits – '
                || (CASE WHEN Seats > 25 THEN 'Large Class'
                         WHEN Seats BETWEEN 18 and 25 THEN 'Med Class'
                         WHEN Seats < 18 THEN 'Small Class'
                         ELSE 'Unknown Size'
                    END)
            WHEN 4
              THEN 'Four Credits – '
                || (CASE WHEN Seats > 25 THEN 'Large Class'
                         WHEN Seats BETWEEN 18 and 25 THEN 'Med Class'
                         WHEN Seats < 18 THEN 'Small Class'
                         ELSE 'Unknown Size'
                    END)
            ELSE 'Credits Unknown'
        END as Credits_and_Class_Size
FROM Course_Table
ORDER BY 1 ;
```

5 Rows Returned

Course_ID	Course_Name	Credits_And_Class_Size
1	Teradata Basics	3 Credits – Large Class
2	Teradata Database Design	3 Credits – Med Class
3	Teradata SQL	3 Credits – Med Class
4	Teradata DBA	4 Credits – Small Class
5	Teradata Appl Dev	3 Credits – Small Class

Chapter 12 – Temporary Tables

"I've got to follow them - I am their leader."

Alexandre Ledru-Rollin

Derived Tables

Derived Tables are temporary tables that are created within a user's SQL and the **derived table and all of its data are deleted when the query is done**. The **Users Spool space** is used to materialize the rows. Derived tables **do not create DDL** and so they are **not** part of the **data dictionary**. **Any user** with **spool space** can create a **derived table**.

In our next example we will CREATE a derived table to hold the average salary.

Employee_Table

Employee_No	Dept_No	First_Name	Last_Name	Salary
1	10	Tom	Coffing	50000.00
2	10	Leona	Coffing	75000.50
3	20	Steve	Wilmes	95054.30
4	20	Gareth	Walter	94986.35
5	30	Robert	Hines	120987.45
6	30	Mark	Ferguson	97087.67
7	30	Scott	Smith	143987.94
8	40	Marsha	Lewis	98453.88
9	40	Sara	Wilson	97450.75
10	50	Mike	Larkins	245098.00
11	999	Arfy	Coffing	NULL
12	999	Spot	Coffing	NULL

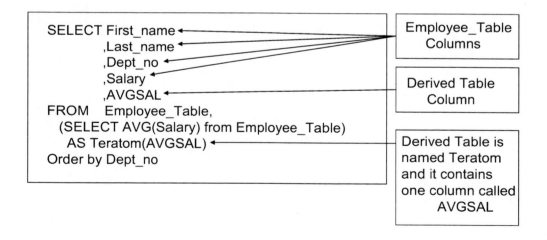

```
SELECT First_name
       ,Last_name
       ,Dept_no
       ,Salary
       ,AVGSAL
FROM   Employee_Table,
   (SELECT AVG(Salary) from Employee_Table)
    AS Teratom(AVGSAL)
Order by Dept_no
```

Employee_Table Columns

Derived Table Column

Derived Table is named Teratom and it contains one column called AVGSAL

Derived Tables Continued

Below is another way to run the previous Derived Table query with the exact same results.

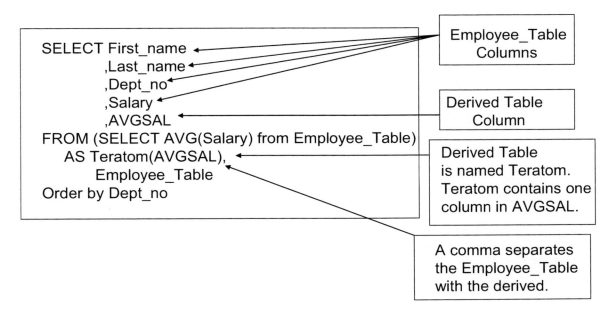

```
SELECT First_name
      ,Last_name
      ,Dept_no
      ,Salary
      ,AVGSAL
FROM (SELECT AVG(Salary) from Employee_Table)
  AS Teratom(AVGSAL),
     Employee_Table
Order by Dept_no
```

Employee_Table Columns

Derived Table Column

Derived Table is named Teratom. Teratom contains one column in AVGSAL.

A comma separates the Employee_Table with the derived.

12 Rows Returned

First_name	Last_name	Dept_no	Salary	AVGSAL
Tom	Coffing	10	50000.00	111810.68
Leona	Coffing	10	75000.50	111810.68
Steve	Wilmes	20	95054.30	111810.68
Gareth	Walter	20	94986.35	111810.68
Robert	Hines	30	120987.45	111810.68
Mark	Ferguson	30	97087.67	111810.68
Scott	Smith	30	143987.94	111810.68
Marsha	Lewis	40	98453.88	111810.68
Sara	Wilson	40	97450.75	111810.68
Mike	Larkins	50	245098.00	111810.68
Arfy	Coffing	999	NULL	111810.68
Spot	Coffing	999	NULL	111810.68

AVGSAL stored in the derived table named Teratom

Multiple Columns in a Derived Table

Our next query will build a derived table that will hold the AVGSAL for each dept_no. We will then join the derived information to the Employee_Table to deliver all employees making more than the average salary in their particular dept_no.

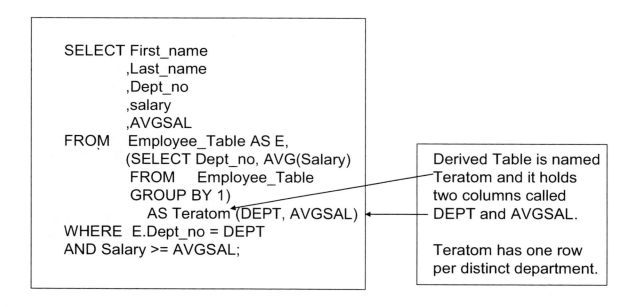

```
SELECT First_name
       ,Last_name
       ,Dept_no
       ,salary
       ,AVGSAL
FROM   Employee_Table AS E,
       (SELECT Dept_no, AVG(Salary)
        FROM     Employee_Table
        GROUP BY 1)
          AS Teratom (DEPT, AVGSAL)
WHERE  E.Dept_no = DEPT
AND Salary >= AVGSAL;
```

Derived Table is named Teratom and it holds two columns called DEPT and AVGSAL.

Teratom has one row per distinct department.

6 Rows Returned

First_name	Last_name	Dept_no	Salary	AVGSAL
Leona	Coffing	10	75000.50	62500.25
Steve	Wilmes	20	95054.30	95020.17
Robert	Hines	30	120987.45	120687.68
Scott	Smith	30	143987.94	120687.68
Marsha	Lewis	40	98453.88	97952.31
Mike	Larkins	50	245098.00	245098.00

Derived Table using with a Different Format

A derived table can utilize multiple formats. Our query below is the same query with the same answer set from the previous page, but it uses a different format. The example defines the derived column names in the SELECT of the derived table.

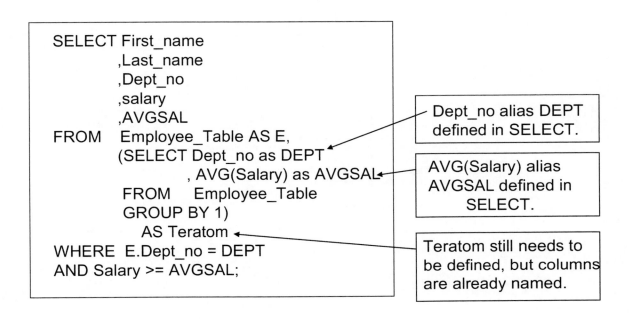

```
SELECT First_name
       ,Last_name
       ,Dept_no
       ,salary
       ,AVGSAL
FROM   Employee_Table AS E,
       (SELECT Dept_no as DEPT
              , AVG(Salary) as AVGSAL
       FROM    Employee_Table
       GROUP BY 1)
         AS Teratom
WHERE  E.Dept_no = DEPT
AND Salary >= AVGSAL;
```

Dept_no alias DEPT defined in SELECT.

AVG(Salary) alias AVGSAL defined in SELECT.

Teratom still needs to be defined, but columns are already named.

6 Rows Returned

First_name	Last_name	Dept_no	Salary	AVGSAL
Leona	Coffing	10	75000.50	62500.25
Steve	Wilmes	20	95054.30	95020.17
Robert	Hines	30	120987.45	120687.68
Scott	Smith	30	143987.94	120687.68
Marsha	Lewis	40	98453.88	97952.31
Mike	Larkins	50	245098.00	245098.00

Derived Table

Here we have created a derived table named DavesDerived. This function will allow us to create a table for the time of the query so we can join our Employee_Table to DavesDerived which in this case shows us the average salary for each department.

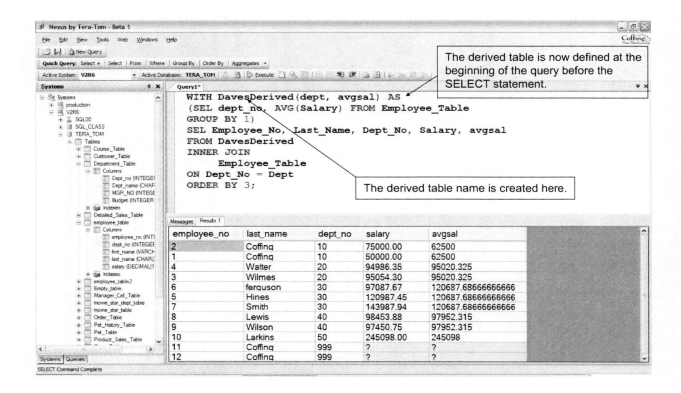

SELECT Command Complete

Derived Tables Using a WITH RECURISVE

A new variation of a Derived table in V2R6 is a Recursive Derived Table. The major difference is that normally a Set Operator is also used and one of the SELECT statements within the derived table references the derived table name. The recursive nature is that the table is joined multiple times as long as there were matching rows in the previous iteration.

With Recursive internally performs a self-join of the table(s) referenced in the first SELECT following the AS. It is for building output such as bill of material, organizational structure and any output that benefits from a hierarchical arrangement.

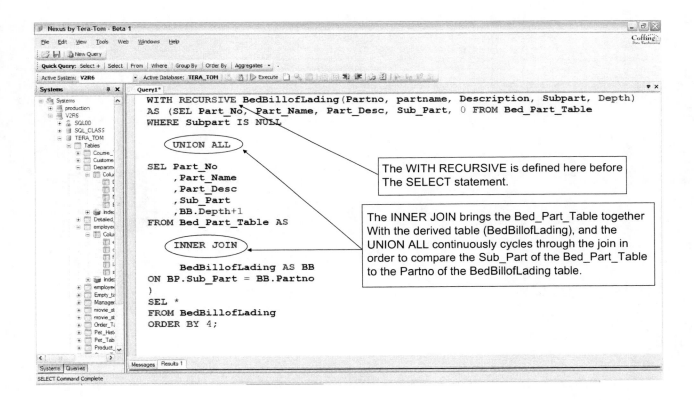

Derived Tables Using a WITH RECURISVE Cont.

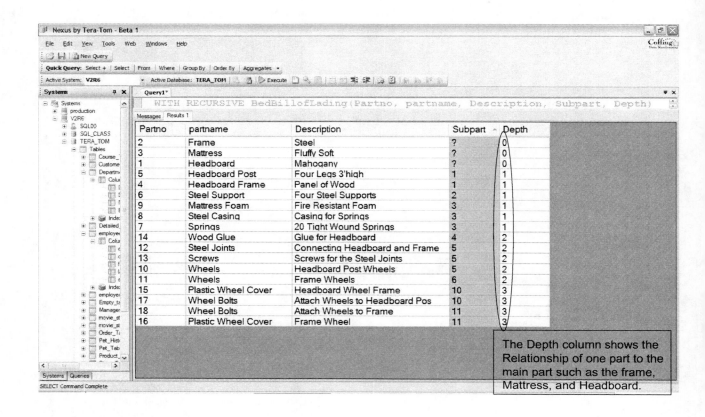

Partno	partname	Description	Subpart	Depth
2	Frame	Steel	?	0
3	Mattress	Fluffy Soft	?	0
1	Headboard	Mahogany	?	0
5	Headboard Post	Four Legs 3'high	1	1
4	Headboard Frame	Panel of Wood	1	1
6	Steel Support	Four Steel Supports	2	1
9	Mattress Foam	Fire Resistant Foam	3	1
8	Steel Casing	Casing for Springs	3	1
7	Springs	20 Tight Wound Springs	3	1
14	Wood Glue	Glue for Headboard	4	2
12	Steel Joints	Connecting Headboard and Frame	5	2
13	Screws	Screws for the Steel Joints	5	2
10	Wheels	Headboard Post Wheels	5	2
11	Wheels	Frame Wheels	6	2
15	Plastic Wheel Cover	Headboard Wheel Frame	10	3
17	Wheel Bolts	Attach Wheels to Headboard Pos	10	3
18	Wheel Bolts	Attach Wheels to Frame	11	3
16	Plastic Wheel Cover	Frame Wheel	11	3

The Depth column shows the Relationship of one part to the main part such as the frame, Mattress, and Headboard.

With Recursive showing specified values

This example shows how we can display certain relationships between two parts while limiting what is being shown at the same time.

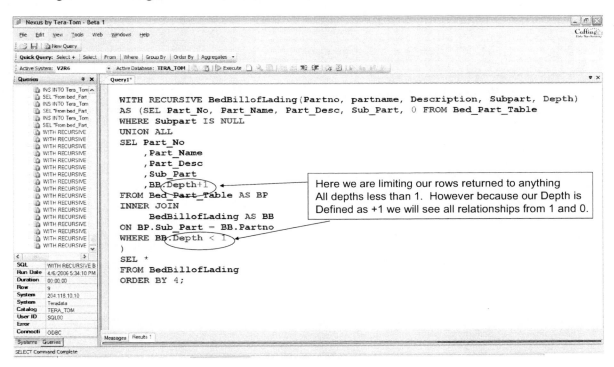

```
WITH RECURSIVE BedBillofLading(Partno, partname, Description, Subpart, Depth)
AS (SEL Part_No, Part_Name, Part_Desc, Sub_Part, 0 FROM Bed_Part_Table
WHERE Subpart IS NULL
UNION ALL
SEL Part_No
    ,Part_Name
    ,Part_Desc
    ,Sub_Part
    ,BB.Depth+1
FROM Bed_Part_Table AS BP
INNER JOIN
        BedBillofLading AS BB
ON BP.Sub_Part = BB.Partno
WHERE BB.Depth < 1
)
SEL *
FROM BedBillofLading
ORDER BY 4;
```

Here we are limiting our rows returned to anything All depths less than 1. However because our Depth is Defined as +1 we will see all relationships from 1 and 0.

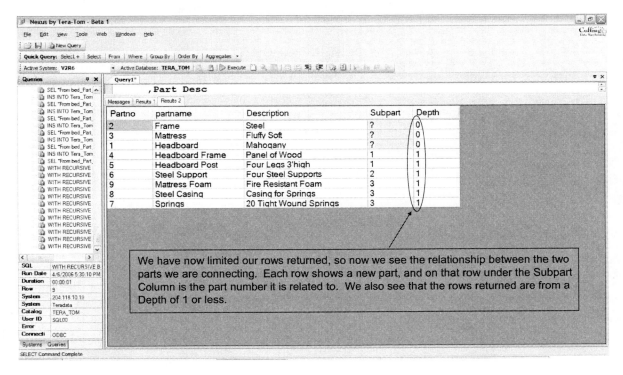

	,Part Desc			
Partno	partname	Description	Subpart	Depth
2	Frame	Steel	?	0
3	Mattress	Fluffy Soft	?	0
1	Headboard	Mahogany	?	0
4	Headboard Frame	Panel of Wood	1	1
5	Headboard Post	Four Legs 3'high	1	1
6	Steel Support	Four Steel Supports	2	1
9	Mattress Foam	Fire Resistant Foam	3	1
8	Steel Casing	Casing for Springs	3	1
7	Springs	20 Tight Wound Springs	3	1

We have now limited our rows returned, so now we see the relationship between the two parts we are connecting. Each row shows a new part, and on that row under the Subpart Column is the part number it is related to. We also see that the rows returned are from a Depth of 1 or less.

OLAP

DDL
Data Dictionary Language

Volatile Table

A Volatile table is materialized by a users spool and it **does not store DDL in the Data Dictionary.** A Volatile Table is created by a user and then populated with an INSERT/SELECT statement. A Volatile Table is automatically dropped after the session is over. You **CAN'T Collect Statistics** on a **Volatile Table**.

1 – A USER CREATES a Volatile Table

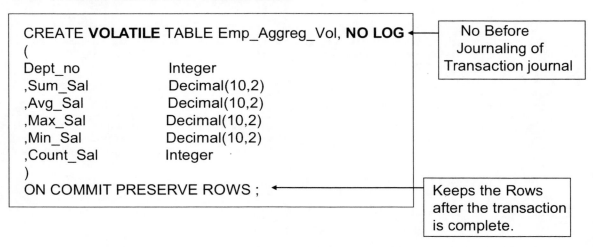

```
CREATE VOLATILE TABLE Emp_Aggreg_Vol, NO LOG
(
Dept_no                 Integer
,Sum_Sal                Decimal(10,2)
,Avg_Sal                Decimal(10,2)
,Max_Sal                Decimal(10,2)
,Min_Sal                Decimal(10,2)
,Count_Sal              Integer
)
ON COMMIT PRESERVE ROWS ;
```

No Before Journaling of Transaction journal

Keeps the Rows after the transaction is complete.

2 – The USER Populates the Volatile table with an INSERT/SELECT

```
INSERT INTO Emp_Aggreg_Vol
SELECT Dept_no
        ,Sum(Salary)
        ,AVG(Salary)
        ,MAX(Salary)
        ,MIN (Salary)
        ,Count(Salary)
FROM   Employee_Table
GROUP By 1;
```

3 – The USER can query the Volatile Table until they logoff

```
SELECT  * from Emp_Aggreg_Vol
ORDER BY 1;
```

Volatile Table Restrictions

The following CREATE TABLE options are not permitted for volatile tables:
- **Permanent journaling**
- **Referential integrity constraints**
- **Check constraints**
- **TITLE clause**
- **Named indexes**
- **PARTITION BY clause**
- **Compressed columns**
- **DEFAULT clause**

Volatile tables do **not allow Statistics to be collected.**

When Volatile Tables are CREATED certain restrictions apply. You **can't have**:

Permanent journaling
Referential integrity constraints
Check constraints
TITLE clause
Named indexes
PARTITION BY clause
Compressed columns
DEFAULT clause

Global Temporary Tables

A **Global Temporary Table** is materialized in a users **TEMP Space** and Teradata stores the **DDL in the Data Dictionary**. A Global Temporary Table is created by a user and the table definition will be placed in the Data Dictionary. Anyone with TEMP Space assigned can use an INSERT/SELECT statement to populate their own version of the table. A **Global Temporary Table drops** the **data after a user session is over**, but the **table definition is not deleted**.

1 – The USER CREATES a Global Temporary Table

```
CREATE GLOBAL TEMPORARY Table Emp_Aggreg_Global
(Dept_no          Integer
,SUM_Sal           Decimal(10,2)
,AVG_Sal           Decimal(10,2)
,MAX_Sal           Decimal(10,2)
,MIN_Sal           Decimal(10,2)
,Count_Sal         Integer
)
ON COMMIT PRESERVE ROWS ;
```

2 – Any User with TEMP Space can populate a Global Temporary Table with an INSERT/SELECT

```
INSERT INTO Emp_Aggreg_Global
SELECT        Dept_No
              ,SUM(Salary)
              ,AVG(Salary)
              ,MAX(Salary)
              ,MIN(Salary)
              ,COUNT(Salary)
FROM          Employee_Table
GROUP BY   Dept_No;
```

Since a Global Temporary Table is in the Data Dictionary and it can be altered the following operations can be used:
- **Add/Drop Columns**
- **Add/Drop Attributes**
- **CREATE/DROP Indices**
- **You can COLLECT Statistics on a Global (Not a Volatile)**

Chapter 13 — SET Operators

If you are planning for a year, sow rice; if you are planning for a decade, plant trees; if you are planning for a lifetime, educate people."

Chinese Proverb

INTERSECT

There are three SET operators and they are **UNION, INTERSECT** and **EXCEPT**. **MINUS** is also used and **works exactly like EXCEPT. The keywords MINUS and EXCEPT are interchangeable.** Below is an example of two tables. They are Table_A and Table_B. When a SET Operator query is run both queries are run simultaneously and then the answer sets are merged together after duplicates are eliminated. Because duplicates are eliminated **SET Operators demand** that the **same number of columns** be **used in both queries.** They matching columns must be in the same order and the columns need to be from the same domain.

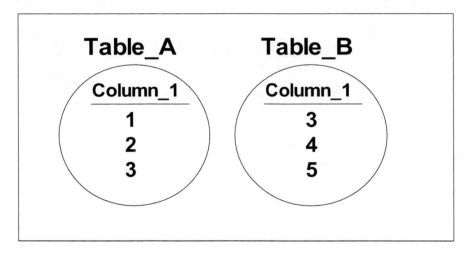

Here is an example of a SET Operator query.

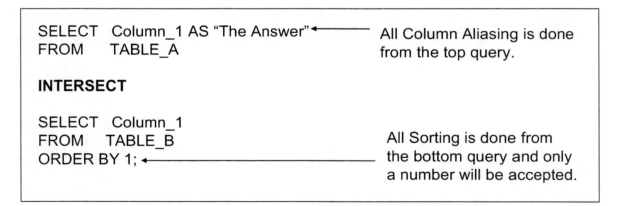

```
SELECT   Column_1 AS "The Answer"          All Column Aliasing is done
FROM     TABLE_A                           from the top query.

INTERSECT

SELECT   Column_1
FROM     TABLE_B                           All Sorting is done from
ORDER BY 1;                                the bottom query and only
                                           a number will be accepted.
```

```
1 row returned

The Answer
_____
    3
```

INTERSECT Example

Using the keyword INTERSECT provide the employee_no for all valid managers in both the Employee_Table and the Department_Table.

Employee_Table

Employee_No	Dept_No	First_Name	Last_Name	Salary
1	10	Tom	Coffing	50000.00
2	10	Leona	Coffing	75000.50
3	20	Steve	Wilmes	95054.30
4	20	Gareth	Walter	94986.35
5	30	Robert	Hines	120987.45
6	30	Mark	Ferguson	97087.67
7	30	Scott	Smith	143987.94
8	40	Marsha	Lewis	98453.88
9	40	Sara	Wilson	97450.75
10	50	Mike	Larkins	245098.00
11	999	Arfy	Coffing	NULL
12	999	Spot	Coffing	NULL

Department_Table

Dept_No	Dept_name	MGR_No	Budget
10	Sales	2	266000
20	Marketing	4	356000
30	HR	6	200000
40	Development	9	2000 00
50	IT	10	25000000

Equal number of **columns** from the same **domain** (both integers with the same range of values).

Select **employee_no** as Manager
FROM Employee_Table
INTERSECT
Select **Mgr_No**
FROM Department_Table
Order by 1;

Aliasing done in the top query.

ORDER BY done in bottom Query with a number only!

5 rows returned

Manager

2

4

6

9

10

UNION

The UNION command will run two queries simultaneously placing both answer sets in spool. The two spools are combined after duplicates are eliminated. If you don't want the duplicates eliminated you utilize the UNION ALL command. **UNION** is performed just like an **OUTER JOIN**.

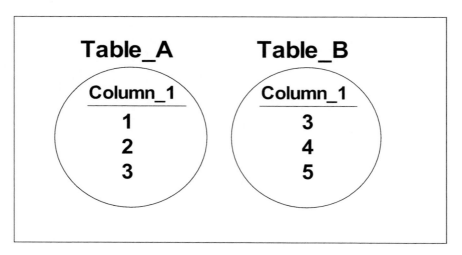

```
SELECT   Column_1 AS "The Answer"          All Column Aliasing is done
FROM     TABLE_A                            from the top query.

UNION

SELECT   Column_1
FROM     TABLE_B                            All Sorting is done from
ORDER BY 1;                                 the bottom query and only
                                            a number will be accepted.
```

```
5 rows returned

The Answer
_____
    1
    2
    3
    4
    5
```

UNION with INSERT SELECT to Eliminate Transient Journal

UNION works brilliantly with an INSERT/SELECT to eliminate the Transient Journal. The Transient Journal is an automatic protection feature in Teradata that is on 100% of the time. Transient Journal takes a before picture of all rows being updated and uses those pictures for ROLLBACK purposes.

A Transient Journal is on each AMP and if 100 rows are being updated in a single transaction then each AMP keeps track of its changes and 100 pictures are taken by varying AMPs. If the query runs successfully a COMMIT will take place and the Transient Journals will be discarded. If there is a problem and the query has to ROLLBACK then the AMPs can use the Transient Journal.

The only time the Transient Journal is not used is when a table starts completely empty. Knowing this can save you an enormous amount of time. Let's imagine you had two tables representing the East and West Regions. If you want to consolidate them you could do an INSERT/SELECT from one table to another. The Transient Journal would be snapping an enormous amount of before pictures and this can slow down the system.

We suggest you use a UNION or a UNION ALL and INSERT/SELECT them both into one table that starts empty. No Transient Journal before pictures will be taken because if a ROLLBACK is needed the table was already empty. Normally a **UNION runs** two queries and then combines the results **together eliminating duplicates**. A **UNION ALL** does **NOT eliminate duplicates**. That also makes the query even faster.

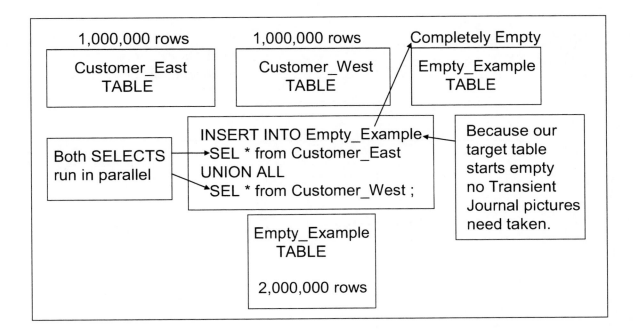

EXCEPT or MINUS

The EXCEPT or MINUS command will run two queries. The order of the queries is extremely important. The top query and the bottom query run simultaneously placing their answer sets in spool. The top query will bring every row in spool back, EXCEPT if it finds a match for a row in the bottom query. If a match is found the row is eliminated.

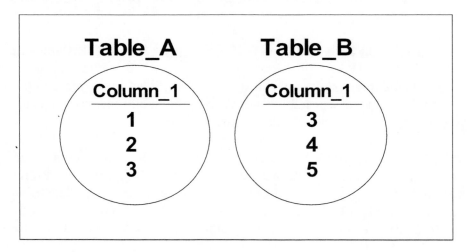

Table_A	Table_B
Column_1	Column_1
1	3
2	4
3	5

```
SELECT   Column_1 AS "The Answer"          All Column Aliasing is done
FROM     TABLE_A                           from the top query.

EXCEPT

SELECT   Column_1
FROM     TABLE_B                           All Sorting is done from
ORDER BY 1;                                the bottom query and only
                                           a number will be accepted.
```

2 rows returned

The Answer
_____

1

2

Group by Grouping Sets through Unions

Group by Grouping Sets are a great way to break down the data to make it easier to analyze what is going on in multiple scenarios. This Group by Grouping query shows a break down of total sales for each product, a total of all sales for the year of 2004, a break down of the total sales in each month listed in the table and finally a total of all sales made since the table was created.

This example shows only a total for the year 2004, however if there was three years worth of information, this would be broken down by year with a total of all three years sales at the end of the result set.

```
/* Group by Grouping Sets through Unions*/

SEL product_id
        ,Null AS Yr
        ,Null AS Mth
        ,sum(total_sales)
FROM product_sales_Table
GROUP BY 1, 2, 3
UNION
SEL Null
        ,extract(year from sale_date)
        ,Null
        ,sum(total_sales)
FROM product_sales_Table
GROUP BY 1, 2, 3
UNION
SEL Null
        ,Null
        ,extract(month from sale_date)
        ,sum(total_sales)
FROM product_sales_Table
GROUP BY 1, 2, 3
ORDER BY 1 desc, 2 desc, 3 desc
```

Group by Grouping Sets through Unions Cont.

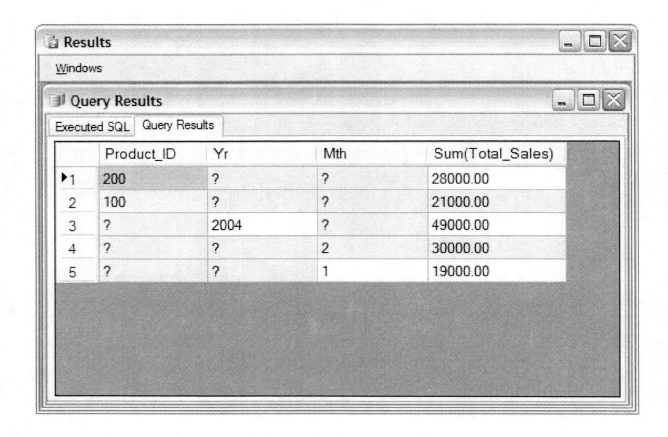

Group by Rollup

Group by Rollup will allow me to see a complete breakdown of total sales per product with every possible scenario, ending with an overall total.

```
/* Group by Rollup */
SEL product_id
        ,extract(year from sale_date) AS Yr
        ,extract(month from sale_date) AS Mth
        ,sum(total_sales)
FROM product_sales_Table
GROUP BY 1, 2, 3
UNION
SEL product_id
        ,extract(year from sale_date)
        ,Null
        ,sum(total_sales)
FROM product_sales_Table
GROUP BY 1, 2, 3
UNION
SEL product_id
        ,Null
        ,Null
        ,sum(total_sales)
FROM product_sales_Table
GROUP BY 1, 2, 3
UNION
SEL Null
        ,Null
        ,Null
        ,sum(total_sales)
FROM product_sales_Table
GROUP BY 1, 2, 3
ORDER BY 1 desc, 2 desc, 3 desc
```

Group by Rollup Cont.

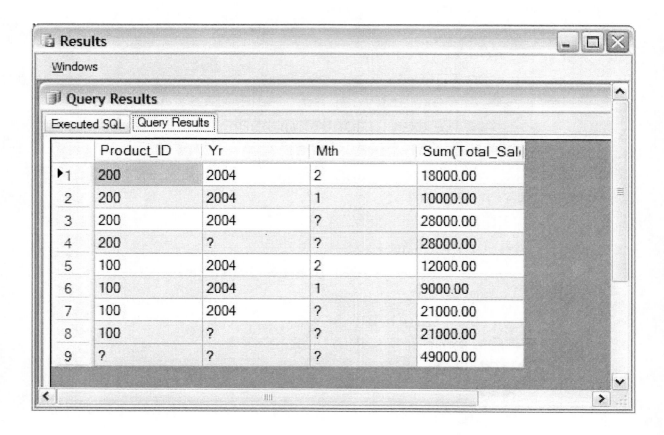

Group by Cube

Group by Cube is the king of all group by statements. This will literally show you every possible scenario and give a total for each one. This is showing you what both the Group by Grouping sets would show as well as the Group by Rollup in one query!

```
/* Group by Cube */
SEL product_id
        ,extract(year from sale_date) AS Yr
        ,extract(month from sale_date) AS Mth
        ,sum(total_sales)
FROM product_sales_Table
GROUP BY 1, 2, 3
UNION
SEL product_id
        ,Null
        ,extract(month from sale_date)
        ,sum(total_sales)
FROM product_sales_Table
GROUP BY 1, 2, 3
UNION
SEL product_id
        ,Null
        ,Null
        ,sum(total_sales)
FROM product_sales_Table
GROUP BY 1, 2, 3
UNION
SEL Null
        ,extract(year from sale_date)
        ,extract(month from sale_date)
        ,sum(total_sales)
FROM product_sales_Table
GROUP BY 1, 2, 3
UNION
SEL Null
        ,extract(year from sale_date)
        ,Null
        ,sum(total_sales)
FROM product_sales_Table
GROUP BY 1, 2, 3
UNION
SEL Null
        ,Null
        ,extract(month from sale_date)
        ,sum(total_sales)
FROM product_sales_Table
GROUP BY 1, 2, 3
UNION
SEL Null
        ,Null
        ,Null
        ,sum(total_sales)
FROM product_sales_Table
GROUP BY 1, 2, 3
ORDER BY 1 desc, 2 desc, 3 desc
```

Group by Cube Cont.

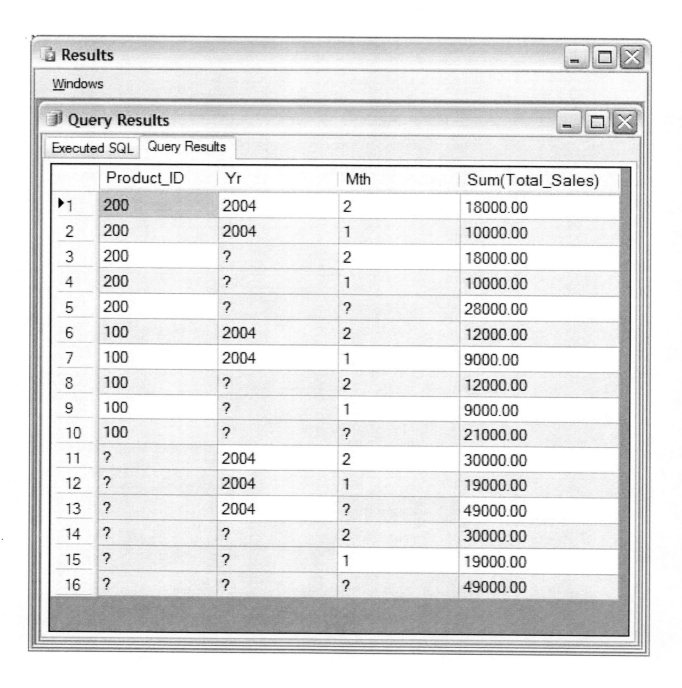

Chapter 14 — Views

"You can make more friends in two months by becoming interested in other people, than you will in two years by trying to get other people interested in you."

Dale Carnegie

View Basics

A **View** is a SELECT statement that is **stored in the Data Dictionary (DD)**. It is sometimes referred to as a virtual table because a view is used exactly like a table with columns and rows.

Restricting access to columns from one or more data tables is normally done for reasons of security. If the view does not select a column, it is not available to the user. By creating a view to explicitly request the desired column names from the data table(s) and omitting the restricted columns, it looks as though the columns do not exist. Therefore, they are secure from the users' restricted access to columns through the view.

To restrict rows from user access, the view can be written to disallow access to rows by using a WHERE clause in the stored SELECT. The WHERE clause limits the rows returned to the user by rejecting all rows that do not meet the stated criteria.

When creating a view, there are certain considerations that must be taken into account. In Teradata, a view may **NOT** contain:
- An **ORDER BY** – rows are not ordered in a table, nor in a view
- **Indices** – however, any index on underlying tables may be used
- Column names must use valid characters
    - **Aggregates must be assigned an alias**
    - **Derived data** with **mathematics symbols** must have **an alias**

There are a few restrictions that disallow maintenance activity on a view with an **INSERT**, **UPDATE** or **DELETE request**. A view cannot be used for maintenance if it:
- **Performs a join operation** – more than one table
- Selects the **same column twice** – wouldn't know which one to use
- **Derives data** – does not undo the math or calculation
- **Performs aggregation** – eliminates detail data
- Uses **OLAP functions** – data does not exist in a column
- Uses a **DISTINCT** or GROUP BY – eliminate duplicate rows

How to CREATE a View

Views are an excellent way to protect sensitive data from being seen. Views limit the columns or rows a user can access. Our example below will create a view.

Employee_Table

Employee_No	Dept_No	First_Name	Last_Name	Salary
1	10	Tom	Coffing	50000.00
2	10	Leona	Coffing	75000.50
3	20	Steve	Wilmes	95054.30
4	20	Gareth	Walter	94986.35
5	30	Robert	Hines	120987.45
6	30	Mark	Ferguson	97087.67
7	30	Scott	Smith	143987.94
8	40	Marsha	Lewis	98453.88
9	40	Sara	Wilson	97450.75
10	50	Mike	Larkins	245098.00
11	999	Arfy	Coffing	NULL
12	999	Spot	Coffing	NULL

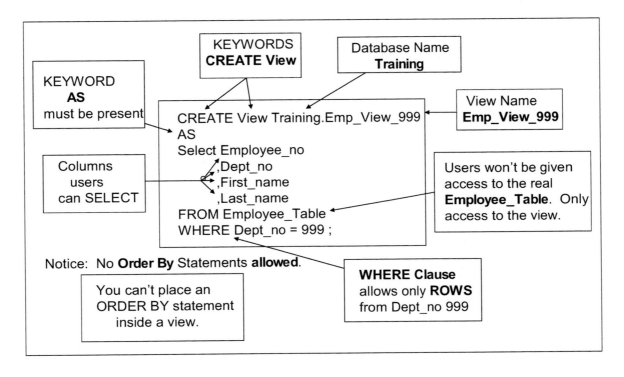

You SELECT from a View

You can now SELECT from your view as is seen in the example below. Notice that you are now allowed to use the ORDER BY statement.

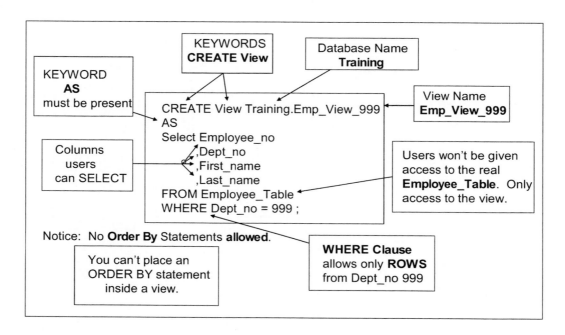

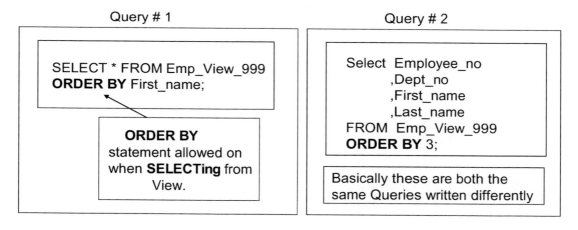

Change a View with the Keyword REPLACE

You CHANGE a view with the keyword REPLACE instead of CREATE. The best way to do this is to first perform a SHOW View *Viewname*. This will give you the DDL (Old CREATE or REPLACE statement for the view). You can then copy this into your query window and make sure you use the word REPLACE instead of CREATE. Then make the changes you desire.

> SHOW View Emp_View_999 ;

	1 Row Processed **Request Text**
1	Create view Emp_view_999 as
2	Sel employee_no, Dept_no, First_name, Last_name
3	From Employee_table where
4	Where Dept_no = 999 ;

Copy in the DDL, use the word REPLACE and make your changes.

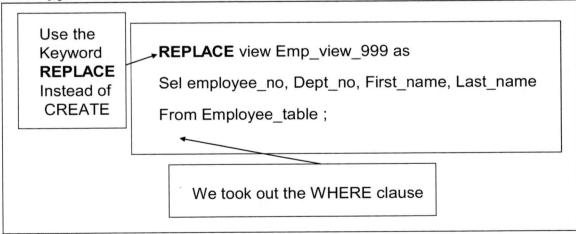

Use the Keyword **REPLACE** Instead of CREATE

REPLACE view Emp_view_999 as

Sel employee_no, Dept_no, First_name, Last_name

From Employee_table ;

We took out the WHERE clause

Drop View

The DROP VIEW statement has only one function. It deletes a view out of the DD. Therefore, it is a very powerful and easy command to use. Additionally, there is no question that asks if you are sure you want to DROP THE VIEW and there is no undo functionality. If a user has the privilege to DROP a view and executes a DROP VIEW command, the view is gone.

```
Drop view emp_view_999 ;
```

Placing Aggregates inside a View

Anytime you utilize an **Aggregate in a view or a macro** you must give the aggregate an **ALIAS name**. If you don't you will receive an error during the CREATE VIEW or CREATE MACRO statement so don't forget to ALIAS.

Here is an example of creating a view using aggregates and aliasing the aggregates.

```
CREATE VIEW Employee_Salary_View
AS
SELECT Dept_no
         ,SUM(Salary) as SUMMY
         ,Max (Salary) as "MAX"
FROM    Employee_Table
GROUP BY Dept_no ;
```

Now that the view has been created and the aggregates have been aliased you can SELECT any columns you need in your query from the view.

```
SELECT Dept_no
         ,"MAX"
 FROM   Employee_salary_View
Order By 1 ;
```

6 rows returned

Dept_no	"MAX"
10	75000.50
20	95054.30
30	143987.94
40	98453.88
50	245098.00
999	?

Using "Locking for Access" in Views

Views are an excellent place for **Access Locks**. You can specify them in the **CREATE View Statement**. Whenever our view below is utilized an ACCESS lock will be placed on the Employee_Table. This will allow a user access even if the table is being updated. An access lock is also called a dirty read or a read without integrity because results may be off. This is because access locks allow access to rows being updated. When a row is being updated you can't be sure if you are calculating the old value or the new value. It all depends on where the update was at when you were accessing the record.

The rule of thumb is that **Access Locks** are great for queries that read millions of records and whose **results don't have to be perfect**.

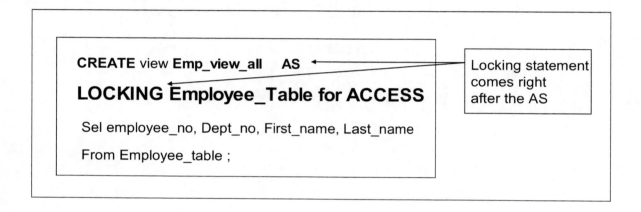

CREATE view **Emp_view_all**   **AS**

LOCKING Employee_Table for ACCESS

Sel employee_no, Dept_no, First_name, Last_name

From Employee_table ;

Locking statement comes right after the AS

You can UPDATE Tables through Views

If you have the ACCESS RIGHTS you can **UPDATE table rows** through a **view**. You can even update table rows that are restricted by the view WHERE Clause. You can prevent ignoring of the WHERE Clause on an update with a **WITH CHECK OPTION** statement.

Remember our Emp_View_999 view?

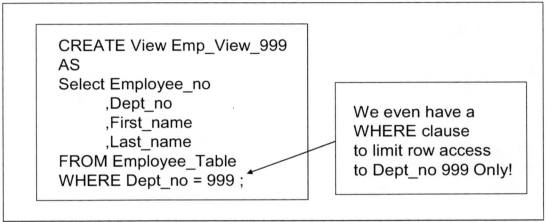

```
CREATE View Emp_View_999
AS
Select Employee_no
        ,Dept_no
        ,First_name
        ,Last_name
FROM Employee_Table
WHERE Dept_no = 999 ;
```

We even have a WHERE clause to limit row access to Dept_no 999 Only!

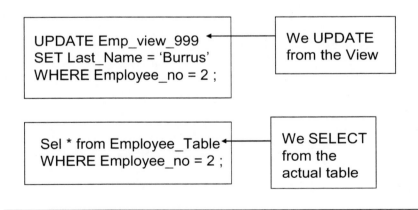

```
UPDATE Emp_view_999
SET Last_Name = 'Burrus'
WHERE Employee_no = 2 ;
```

We UPDATE from the View

```
Sel * from Employee_Table
WHERE Employee_no = 2 ;
```

We SELECT from the actual table

1 Row Returned

Employee_no	Dept_no	First_name	Last_name	Salary
2	10	Leona	**Burrus**	75000.50

Restricting UPDATE rows WITH CHECK OPTION

If you have the ACCESS RIGHTS you can UPDATE table rows through a view. You can even update table rows that are restricted by the view WHERE Clause. You can prevent ignoring of the WHERE Clause on an update with a WITH CHECK OPTION statement.

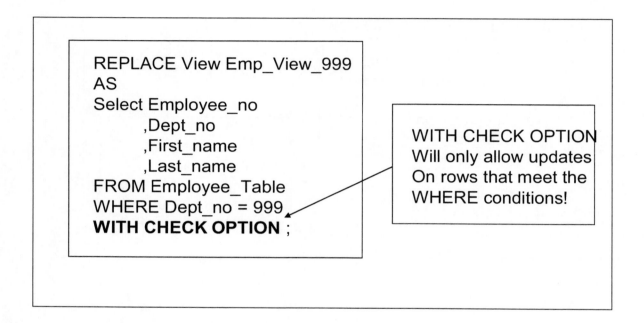

Chapter 15 — Macros

"We're fools whether we dance or not, so we might as well dance."

Japanese Proverb

Macro Basics

Macros are SQL statements stored as an object **in the Data Dictionary (DD)**. Unlike a view, a macro can store one or multiple SQL statements. Once you create a MACRO you EXEC the Macro. Where you **SELECT from a view** you **EXECute a macro**.

Additionally, the SQL is not restricted to only SELECT operations. INSERT, UPDATE, and DELETE commands are valid within a macro. When using BTEQ, conditional logic and BTEQ commands may also be incorporated into the macro.

Macros are stored in DBC's Data Dictionary, can be shared by multiple users and greatly reduce the network since they are not sent across the network or channel. They provide excellent security to tables.

All updates within a macro are considered one transaction. They either all work or they all rollback. Parameters can be passed to a macro dynamically.

Data Definition Language (DDL) is used to create, delete or modify a macro. The main restriction is that all objects in a database must have unique names. Additionally, since Teradata is case blind, names like Mymacro and mymacro are identical.

Although a macro can have multiple SQL statements within it, if a macro contains **DDL**, it must be the last statement in the macro. The reason for this is based on the transactional nature of a macro. Since DDL locks one or more rows within the DD and this could prevent user access to the DD, it is desirable to release these locks as soon as possible. Therefore, a macro's DDL transaction needs to finish quickly. Hence, you can **only have one DDL statement within a macro**.

The **fully expanded maximum text size of a macro** is **2MB**.

You can reference both global temporary tables and volatile tables from a macro.

The following data attributes are NOT valid as macro parameters.
- CHECK Constraint
- COMPRESS

How to CREATE a Macro

The CREATE MACRO statement initially builds a new macro. It names the macro and optionally the database where it is to be created. Additionally, it must specify the SQL statement(s) that comprise the execution of the macro.

Each SQL statement within a macro must have its own semi-colon to help the optimizer delineate one SQL statement from another. All the SQL statements must be enclosed in parentheses to be created and treated as a single transaction.

You must have CREATE Macro privilege on the database or user where the macro will be created. The creator of the macro is also give DROP MACRO and EXEC privileges with GRANT OPTION on the macro. You must have the DROP Macro privilege to REPLACE a macro.

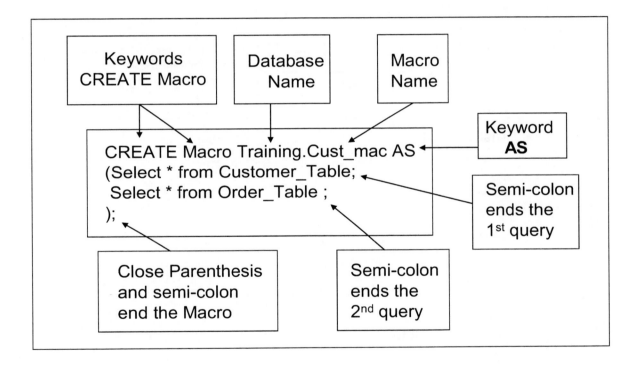

How to EXECute a Macro

To execute a Macro you utilize the EXEC statement.

Here is our original CREATE Statement

```
CREATE Macro Training.Cust_mac AS
(Select * from Customer_Table;
 Select * from Order_Table ;
);
```

Never use the word **MACRO** to EXECUTE a MACRO. Only the keyword EXEC and the MACRO NAME are needed.

EXEC cust_mac ;

This is because the only Object that uses the keyword **EXEC is a MACRO**.

Answer Set 1

Cust_Name	Phone	Cust_Num
CPUDoctor	816 140-3423	3
ABC Consulting	937 855-4838	1
TempHelpers	513 300-0346	2
Fergie's	456 334-1543	4

Answer Set 2

Cust_Num	Order_No	Order_Date	Order_Total
1	100	2004-06-06	5000.00
2	200	2004-06-07	4000.00
3	300	2004-06-08	2000.00
5	400	2004-06-09	1000000.00

Completed: 8 rows processed

How to CREATE a Macro with Input Parameters

Macros can be **passed input parameters** that work inside the macro. The parameters are passed in the **EXEC statement**. Below we are going to update the Employee_table by changing the Last_name of 'Burrus' back to 'Coffing'. What is excellent about parameters is that each time you execute the macro you can change the input. The example below shows a parameterized macro. Each time it is executed it will expect and demand two input parameters.

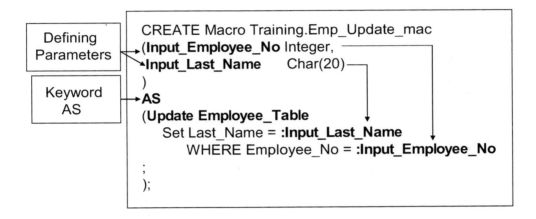

The first example below **must have** the **input parameters** in the **proper order**. The **second example does not** have to have **an order** because the input parameters are specifically **named** in the EXEC statement.

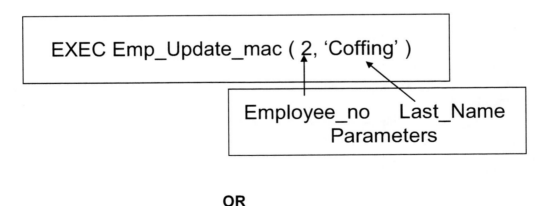

OR

EXEC Emp_Update_mac (Input_Last_Name = 'Coffing', Input_Employee_no = 2) ;

219

How to change a Macro

To change a Macro you merely copy the DDL and change the word CREATE with REPLACE. Then make your changes. Follow the examples below.

SHOW Macro Emp_Update_Mac ;

Answer Set 1

Create macro emp_update_mac
(input_employee_no integer
,input_last_name char(20)**)**
AS
(update employee_table
Set last_name = :input_last_name
    where employee_no = :input_Employee_No
;);

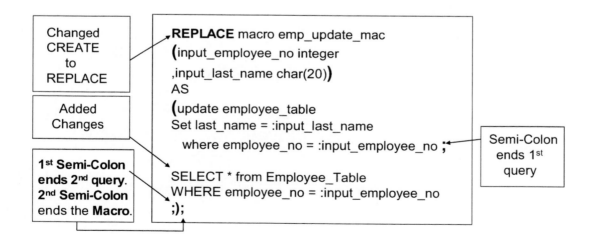

Changed CREATE to REPLACE	**REPLACE** macro emp_update_mac **(**input_employee_no integer ,input_last_name char(20)**)** AS **(**update employee_table Set last_name = :input_last_name where employee_no = :input_employee_no **;**
Added Changes	SELECT * from Employee_Table WHERE employee_no = :input_employee_no **;);**
1st Semi-Colon ends 2nd query. 2nd Semi-Colon ends the **Macro**.	Semi-Colon ends 1st query

Drop Macro

The DROP MACRO statement has only one function. It deletes a macro out of the DD. Therefore, it is a very powerful and easy command to use. Additionally, there is no question that asks if you are sure you want to DROP THE MACRO and there is no undo functionality. If a user has the privilege to DROP a macro and executes a DROP MACRO command, the macro is gone.

```
Drop macro emp_update_mac ;
```

Macros that will not work

The macros below will not work. Can you figure out why? Macros are considered implicit transactions. This means that everything inside a macro is considered part of the same transaction. Implicit transactions **can't have DDL unless it is the only statement**. **Multiple queries inside a macro can't contain any DDL**.

```
CREATE Macro update_Mac
AS
(SELECT * FROM Employee_Table;
CREATE TABLE Test2
(employee integer
,dept_no    integer
) primary index (dept_no););
```

FAILURE:

You can't have DDL
In a macro unless
it is the only
STATEMENT!

```
CREATE Macro Create_Tab
(input_tablename CHAR(20))
AS
(CREATE TABLE :input_tablenam
(employee integer
,dept_no    integer
) primary index (dept_no););
```

FAILURE:

You **can't have DDL** that **passes parameters** as the **table name**

Chapter 16 – Dates and Times

"Choose your friends carefully. Your enemies will choose you."

Yassir Arafat

RESERVED Words such as DATE and TIME

Below is a BTEQ example using RESERVED words. You can select these keywords in SQL Assistant, Queryman or BTEQ.

RESERVED Words you can SELECT

BTEQ – Enter your DBC/SQL request or BTEQ Command:

```
.SET FOLDLINE ON ALL
.SET SIDETITLES ON

SELECT      DATE                    as Teradata_Date
            ,CURRENT_DATE           as ANSI_Date
            ,TIME                   as Teradata_Time
            ,CURRENT_TIME           as ANSI_Time
            ,CURRENT_TIMESTAMP      as ANSI_Timestamp
            ,DATABASE               as I_Am_In_Database
            ,USER                   as I_Logged_In_As
            ,ACCOUNT                as My_Account
            ,SESSION                as My_Session_#_Is
            ,ROLE                   as My_Role
            ,PROFILE                as My_Profile
```

```
*** Query Completed.  One row found.  11 columns returned.

*** Total elapsed time was 1 second.

        Teradata_Date    04/05/26
          ANSI_Date      04/05/26
        Teradata_Time    22:52:22
          ANSI_Time      22:52:22+00:00
       ANSI_Timestamp    2004-05-26 22:52:22.470000+00:00
      I_Am_In_Database   Training
       I_Logged_In_As    TeraTom
         My_Account      $M
      My_Session_#_Is    1000
           My_Role       ?
          My_Profile     ?
```

How Dates are Stored on Disk

All dates in Teradata are stored in a **YYYMMDD** fashion. Notice that **internally** the year is stored in **3 digits**.

> **DATES** are always **stored internally** on Teradata as **INTEGERS** with a **format** of **YYYMMDD**

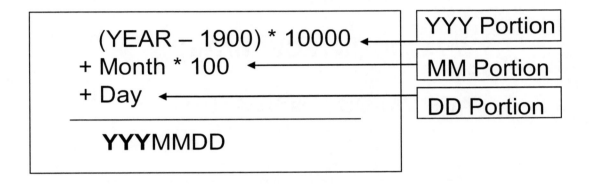

(YEAR − 1900) * 10000 ← YYY Portion
+ Month * 100 ← MM Portion
+ Day ← DD Portion
─────────────
YYYMMDD

Some Sample Dates

January 10, 19**59** stored as: **59**0110

October 15, 19**98** stored as: **98**1015

December 1, 19**99** stored as: **99**1201

February 25, **2000** stored as: **100**0225

August 23 , 20**05** stored as: **105**0823
────────────
YYYMMDD

How Teradata Displays the Date

Teradata will display the date as either **YY/MM/DD** or **YYYY-MM-DD**. The YY/MM/DD is the traditional Teradata format, which is referred to as **INTEGERDATE**. The **YYYY-MM-DD is ANSI** compliant and referred to as **ANSIDATE**. You normally can choose the DATEFORM you want, but SQL Assistant is the exception to the rule because it uses ODBC and that defaults to ANSIDATE.

Teradata displays the **DATE Two Ways**.
The choice is called **DATEFORM**
and you can pick:

YY/MM/DD (**INTEGERDATE**)

YYYY-MM-DD (**ANSIDATE**)

When Teradata is first installed:

System defaults to **YY/MM/DD** (INTEGERDATE)

DBA can change the default to **ANSIDATE** by **Modifying** the **DBSCONTROL record**.

USERS can choose their **DATEFORM** at either **USER CREATE** time or at the **Session Level**.

How to change the DATEFORM

Teradata will display the date as either YY/MM/DD or YYYY-MM-DD. **YY/MM/DD** represents a form called **INTEGERDATE**. **YYYY-MM-DD** represents **ANSIDATE**. You have a system default choice for your DATEFORM and that is either INTEGERDATE or ANSIDATE.

The DATEFORM can be changed at **3 levels.**

SYSTEM LEVEL

System Level Modification by updating the DBSControl Record # 14
   DBSControl
      MODIFY GENERAL 14= 0 /*   (YY/MM/DD) INTEGERDATE */
      or
      MODIFY GENERAL 14 = 1 /* (YYYY-MM-DD) ANSIDATE   */

USER CREATE LEVEL

CREATE USER username ....

        ■
        ■
        ■
     DATEFORM={INTEGERDATE | ANSIDATE}

Session LEVEL

SET SESSION DATEFORM = {ANSIDATE | INTEGERDATE}

Session level settings do not work with QueryMan or SQL Assistant (ODBC Driven clients).

Teradata Dates stored as Integers for a Reason

Teradata stores dates internally as an integer in the form of YYYMMDD. The year 1999 is represented as 99 and the year 2000 is represented as 100. This is done because dates can be added to or subtracted from. Dates can be compared to other dates and intervals, extracts, and calculations can be performed.

Order_Table

Cust_Num	Order_No	Order_Date	Order_Total
1	100	2004-06-06	5000.00
2	200	2004-06-07	4000.00
3	300	2004-06-08	2000.00
5	400	2004-06-09	1000000.00

```
SELECT Cust_Num
      ,Order_No
      ,Order_Date
      ,Order_Total
      ,Order_Date + 20 as Payment_Due_Date
      ,Order_Date + 30 as Shipment_Date
FROM   Order_Table
ORDER BY 1 ;
```

4 Rows Returned

Cust_Num	Order_No	Order_Date	Order_Total	Payment_Due_Date	Shipment_Date
1	100	2004-06-06	5000.00	2004-06-26	2004-07-06
2	200	2004-06-07	4000.00	2004-06-27	2004-07-07
3	300	2004-06-08	2000.00	2004-06-28	2004-07-08
5	400	2004-06-09	1000000.00	2004-06-29	2004-07-09

ADD_MONTHS Command

The **ADD_MONTHS function** will add months to a date using **calendar intelligence** that **handles leap year calculations** and **number of day processing**.

```
SELECT Cust_Num
       ,Order_No
       ,Order_Date
       ,Order_Total
       ,ADD_MONTHS (Order_Date, 12) as One_Year_Later
       ,ADD_MONTHS (Order_Date, 12 * 5) as Five_Years_Later
FROM Order_Table
ORDER BY 1;
```

4 Rows Returned

Cust_Num	Order_No	Order_Date	Order_Total	One_Year_Later	Five_Years_Later
1	100	**2004-06-06**	5000.00	**2005-06-06**	**2009-06-06**
2	200	**2004-06-07**	4000.00	**2005-06-07**	**2009-06-07**
3	300	**2004-06-08**	2000.00	**2005-06-08**	**2009-06-08**
5	400	**2004-06-09**	1000000.00	**2005-06-09**	**2009-06-09**

EXTRACT Command with Dates

The EXTRACT command will **extract the day, month, or year from a date**. It can also extract the **hours, minutes, or seconds from a time**.

```
SELECT Cust_Num
       ,Order_No
       ,Order_Date
       ,EXTRACT (Year from Order_Date) as "Year"
       ,EXTRACT (Month from Order_Date) as "Month"
       ,EXTRACT (Day from Order_Date) as "Day"
FROM Order_Table
ORDER BY 1;
```

4 Rows Returned

Cust_Num	Order_No	Order_Date	Year	Month	Day
1	100	**2004-06-06**	2004	6	6
2	200	**2004-06-07**	2004	6	7
3	300	**2004-06-08**	2004	6	8
5	400	**2004-06-09**	2004	6	9

EXTRACT Command with TIME

The EXTRACT command will extract the day, month, or year from a date. It can also extract the hours, minutes, or seconds from a time. Below is an example of extracting portions of the time.

```
SELECT EXTRACT (HOUR FROM '11:02:45') as The_Hour
      ,EXTRACT (MINUTE FROM '11:02:45') as The_Minute
      ,EXTRACT (SECOND FROM '11:02:45') as The_Second
```

```
1 Row Returned

The_Hour      The_Minute      The_Second
_____     _____      _____
      11               2              45
```

The System Calendar

Teradata has a system calendar that is detailed and makes dealing with dates much easier. The purpose is to provide an easy way to compare dates. Teradata's **calendar** uses a base table named **caldates** with a **single column** named **CDATES**. There is one row for every day since **January 1, 1900** through **December 31, 2100.** The base table is never referenced by the user. A view called CALENDAR is used instead. CALENDAR resides in the database called Sys_Calendar. To access the System Calendar you use the full name of **Sys_Calendar.calendar.**

USING BTEQWIN

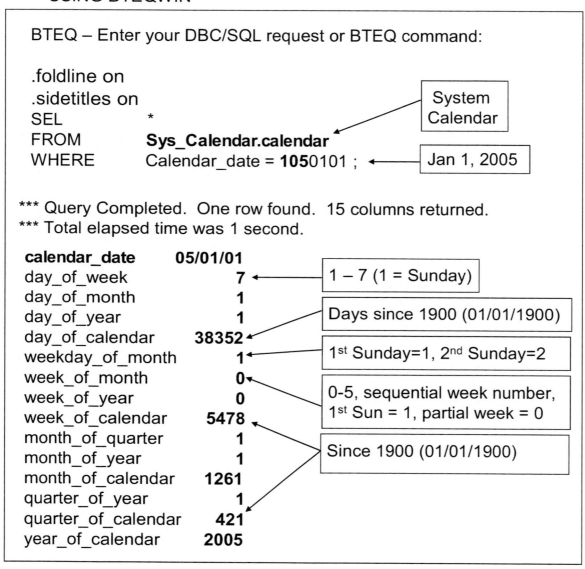

IN SQL Assistant merely type: **SEL   * FROM Sys_Calendar.calendar**
WHERE   calendar_date = 1050101;

232

Using the System Calendar for Date Comparison

You can best **utilize the System Calendar** by **joining it with another table**. You can then **compare for dates such as days, months, quarters, days of weeks** etc.,

Order_Table

Cust_Num	Order_No	Order_Date	Order_Total
1	100	2004-06-06	5000.00
2	200	2004-06-07	4000.00
3	300	2004-06-08	2000.00
5	400	2004-06-09	1000000.00

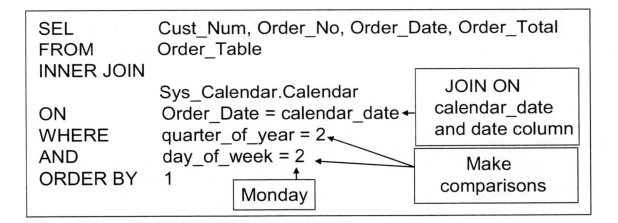

```
SEL             Cust_Num, Order_No, Order_Date, Order_Total
FROM            Order_Table
INNER JOIN
                Sys_Calendar.Calendar
ON              Order_Date = calendar_date
WHERE           quarter_of_year = 2
AND             day_of_week = 2
ORDER BY        1
                        Monday
```

JOIN ON calendar_date and date column

Make comparisons

1 Row Returned

Cust_Num	Order_No	Order_Date	Order_Total
2	200	2004-06-07	4000.00

INTERVAL Processing for Arithmetic and Conversion

Intervals are used to perform **DATE, TIME** and **TIMESTAMP arithmetic** and **conversion**.

Simple INTERVALS	Complex INTERVALS
DAY	DAY TO SECOND
MONTH	DAY TO MINUTE
YEAR	DAY TO SECOND
HOUR	HOUR TO SECOND
MINUTE	HOUR TO MINUTE
SECOND	MINUTE TO SECOND

```
SELECT date '2004-01-01' as Our_Date
        ,date '2004-01-01' + INTERVAL '1' DAY as Plus_1_Day
        ,date '2004-01-01' + INTERVAL '3' MONTH as Plus_3_Months
        ,date '2004-01-01' + INTERVAL '5' YEAR as Plus_5_YEARS ;
```

```
1 Row Returned

Our_Date     Plus_1_Day    Plus_3_Months    Plus_5_Years

2004-01-01   2004-01-02    2004-04-01       2009-01-01
```

INTERVAL Processing that Fails

Intervals are used to perform DATE, TIME and TIMESTAMP arithmetic and conversion. Intervals have intelligence built in so the query will fail if an invalid date is a result. Here are some examples below.

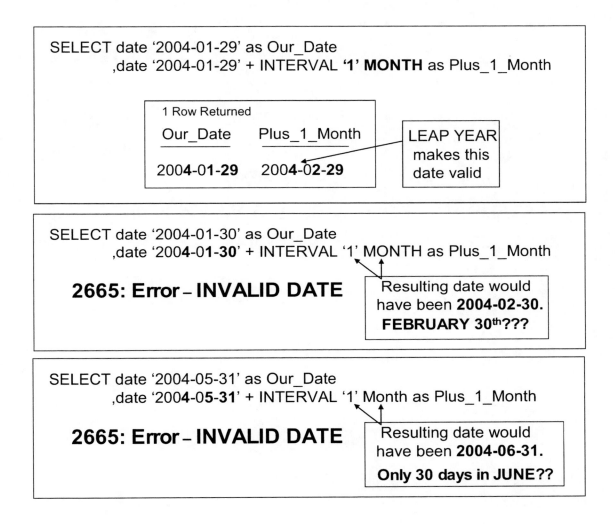

INTERVAL Arithmetic with Date and Time

Date and Time operations will produce varying results based on either ANSI mode or Teradata mode (BTET). Let the chart below be your guide. It is important to memorize the options below.

Date and Time explicit arithmetic results

DATE	-	Date	=	**INTERVAL**
DATE	+ or -	INTERVAL	=	**DATE**
INTERVAL	+ or -	INTERVAL	=	**INTERVAL**
TIME	-	TIME	=	**INTERVAL**
TIME	+ or	INTERVAL	=	**TIME**
TIMESTAMP	-	TIMESTAMP	=	**INTERVAL**
TIMESTAMP	+ or -	INTERVAL	=	**TIMESTAMP**

TIMESTAMP

A TIMESTAMP combines together into a single column the DATE and TIME. TIMESTAMP is a reserved word. TIMESTAMP is also a display format and a new data type. The fields in CURRENT_TIMESTAMP are:

- **YEAR**
- **MONTH**
- **DAY**
- **HOUR**
- **MINUTE**
- **SECOND**
- **TIMEZONE_HOUR**
- **TIMEZONE_MINUTE**

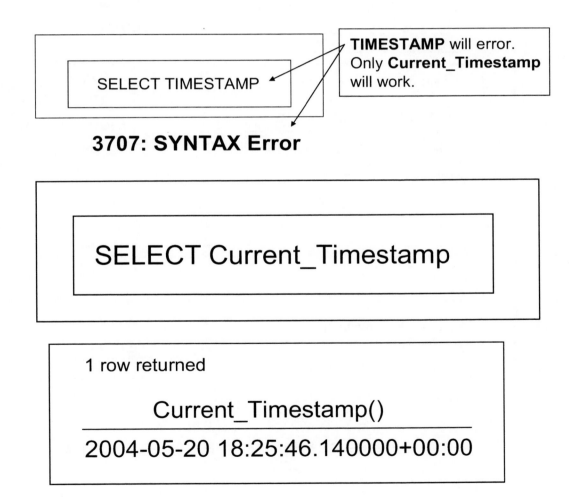

SELECT TIMESTAMP

TIMESTAMP will error. Only **Current_Timestamp** will work.

3707: SYNTAX Error

SELECT Current_Timestamp

1 row returned

Current_Timestamp()
_____
2004-05-20 18:25:46.140000+00:00

CURRENT_TIMESTAMP

A **TIMESTAMP** combines together into a single column the **DATE** and **TIME**. TIMESTAMP is a reserved word. TIMESTAMP is also a display format and a new data type.

TIMESTAMP is TIMESTAMP WITH TIMEZONE(12) length internally, but will either be represented as CHARACTER length CHAR(19) or CHAR(26) depending on the display of seconds (6).

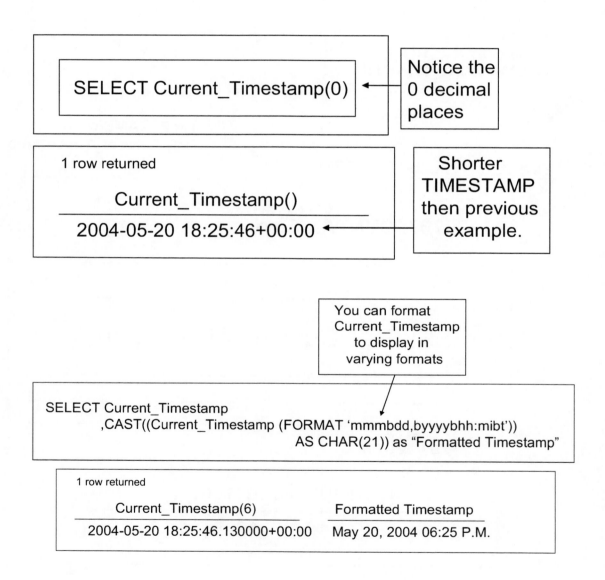

| SELECT Current_Timestamp(0) | Notice the 0 decimal places |

1 row returned

Current_Timestamp()
2004-05-20 18:25:46+00:00

Shorter TIMESTAMP then previous example.

You can format Current_Timestamp to display in varying formats

```
SELECT Current_Timestamp
      ,CAST((Current_Timestamp (FORMAT 'mmmbdd,byyyybhh:mibt'))
                         AS CHAR(21)) as "Formatted Timestamp"
```

1 row returned

Current_Timestamp(6)	Formatted Timestamp
2004-05-20 18:25:46.130000+00:00	May 20, 2004 06:25 P.M.

Time Table Create Insert

"Wisdom doesn't automatically come with old age. Nothing does – except wrinkles. It's true, some wines improve with age. But only if the grapes were good in the first place."

— **Abigail Van Buren**

It's true that data doesn't come with old age. However as we store more data, we are able to analyze our past to better predict our future. The diagram below shows five ways of recording time; Time(0), Time(6), Time with Time Zone, TIMESTAMP(6), and TIMESTAMP(6) WITH TIME ZONE. Each one of these commands records time in a different fashion.

```
CREATE SET TABLE TERA_TOM.time_table
     (
     Standard_time CHAR(3),
     Time_Normal time(0),
     Time_Normal6 time(6),
     Time_Time_Zone Time with Time Zone,
     Time_stamp_Normal TIMESTAMP(6),
     Time_Stamp_Time_Zone TIMESTAMP(6) WITH TIME ZONE)
PRIMARY INDEX ( Standard_time);


INSERT INTO Time_Table
     ('EST'
     ,Time '11:00:00'
     ,Time '11:00:00.123456'
     ,Time '11:00:00'
     ,timestamp '2007-01-01 11:00:00'
     ,timestamp '2007-01-01 11:00:00');
```

Time Zone CST Time

Considering that most Teradata systems are incorporated into international corporations, we realize that these corporations need to keep track of a multitude of different time zones. But have no fear because Teradata is here! With the TIME ZONE INTERVAL we are able to differentiate between time zones.

Taking the illustration below into consideration, we see that we are switching our time zone from EST to CST. All we need to do is let Teradata know what the time zone differential is and our system takes care of the rest for us.

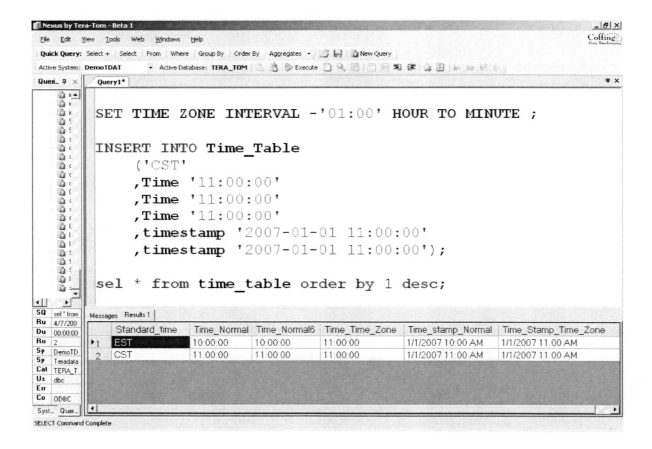

Time Table Results with Cast CST

Now that we have a basic understanding of our time commands, lets look a little deeper to find out what is really going on. Looking at the table below we see two rows; EST and CST. Within the Time_Normal column we see that the EST result shows a value of 10:00:00 and the CST shows a value of 11:00:00 even though they were both entered at the 11:00:00 in their respective time zones. Our time is now local at CST so Teradata knows that anything being recorded in EST at 11:00:00 will be 10:00:00 local time. The Time_Time_Zone column shows the time in which the transaction was made at the respective location.

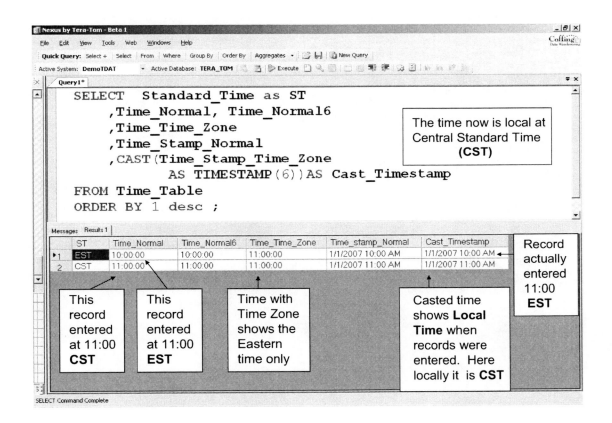

Time Table Results with Cast EST

We have now changed our local time from CST to EST. If you look at the result set in the diagram below you will see that in both EST as well as CST their transactions have both been made at 11:00 locally. However, now that the local time has been set to EST the second row of the Time_Normal column shows a time of 12:00 because even though in CST the transaction was made at 11:00, in EST the time was 12:00, and that is what is being shown; the time of the transaction locally (in this case that time is EST).

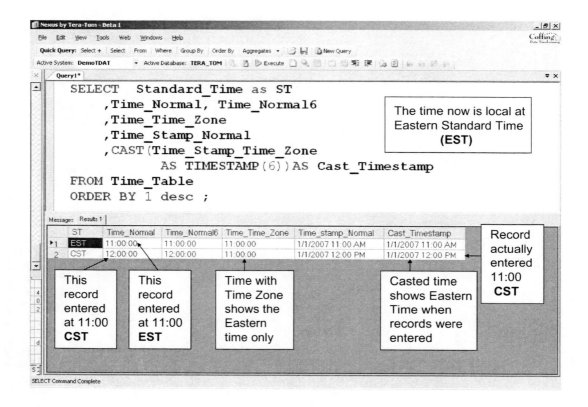

Time Zone CST with Results

Now that we are able to understand the different ways of recording time and how they can work together to keep our world wide data warehouses correlated, we are able to take several different regions and allow them to work together as one. We can see that in the first result set it is 11:00:00 across the board. However not until it is being compared to the second result set are we able to see at what time a specific transaction was made in their time zone displayed in our local time.

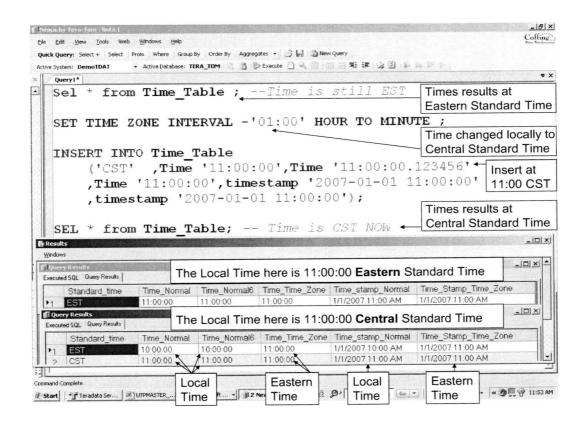

Chapter 17 – Creating Tables

"Copy from one, it's plagiarism; copy from two, it's research."

Wilson Mizner

A Simple CREATE Statement

Teradata is fantastic at creating tables easily. All you need is a CREATE TABLE statement and the table is created. Here is a simple example.

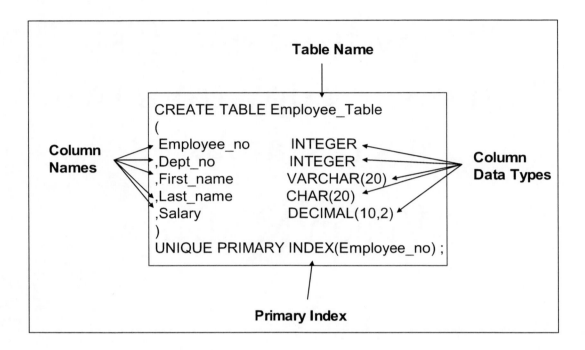

The basic information needed to create a table is the table name, column names and their respective data types, and you must define one and only one Primary Index for the table. If you don't define a Primary Index Teradata will do so for you.

A Simple INSERT Statement

Below is an example of an INSERT statement to populate our employee_table.

```
INSERT INTO Employee_Table
Values (1, 999, 'Arfy', 'Coffing', NULL) ;
```

CREATING SET TABLES

Below is an example of a CREATE SET Table statement. **SET Tables** are tables that will **NOT ALLOW DUPLICATE ROWS!** If you INSERT data into a Teradata SET Table the Teradata database will do a duplicate row check and deny the INSERT if a duplicate row already exists. The duplicate row check can take time so it is recommended that when creating a set table that you define at least one column as unique or create a UNIQUE PRIMARY INDEX. If you have a UNIQUE constraint or a UNIQUE INDEX the system will not have to do a duplicate row check.

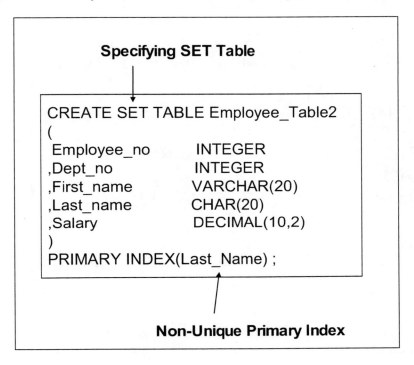

Specifying SET Table

```
CREATE SET TABLE Employee_Table2
(
 Employee_no        INTEGER
,Dept_no            INTEGER
,First_name         VARCHAR(20)
,Last_name          CHAR(20)
,Salary             DECIMAL(10,2)
)
PRIMARY INDEX(Last_Name) ;
```

Non-Unique Primary Index

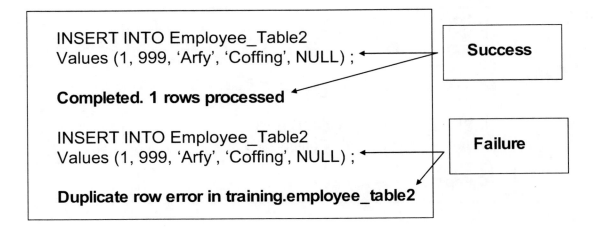

```
INSERT INTO Employee_Table2
Values (1, 999, 'Arfy', 'Coffing', NULL) ;
```

Success

Completed. 1 rows processed

```
INSERT INTO Employee_Table2
Values (1, 999, 'Arfy', 'Coffing', NULL) ;
```

Failure

Duplicate row error in training.employee_table2

CREATING MULTISET TABLES

Below is an example of a CREATE MULTISET Table statement. **MULTISET Tables** are tables that **ALLOW DUPLICATE ROWS!** In our example please notice that we have a Non-Unique Primary Index on the Last_name column.

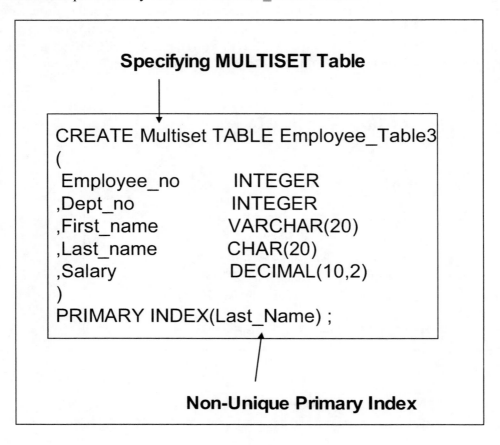

Specifying MULTISET Table

```
CREATE Multiset TABLE Employee_Table3
(
 Employee_no        INTEGER
,Dept_no            INTEGER
,First_name         VARCHAR(20)
,Last_name          CHAR(20)
,Salary             DECIMAL(10,2)
)
PRIMARY INDEX(Last_Name) ;
```

Non-Unique Primary Index

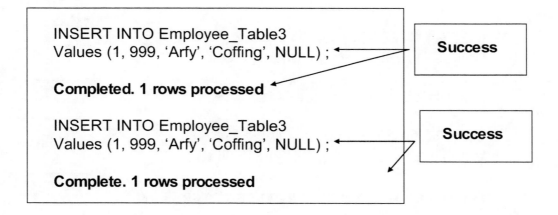

```
INSERT INTO Employee_Table3
Values (1, 999, 'Arfy', 'Coffing', NULL) ;
```
Success

Completed. 1 rows processed

```
INSERT INTO Employee_Table3
Values (1, 999, 'Arfy', 'Coffing', NULL) ;
```
Success

Complete. 1 rows processed

UNIQUE PRIMARY INDEX

Whether or not a table is SET or MULTISET is mute when you have a UNIQUE PRIMARY INDEX (UPI). A Unique Primary Index means that no duplicate values can exist for the column or columns that make up the primary index.

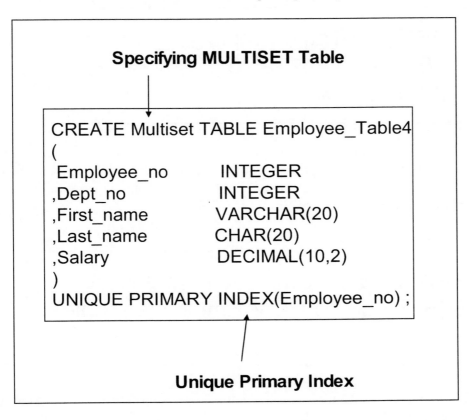

Specifying MULTISET Table

```
CREATE Multiset TABLE Employee_Table4
(
 Employee_no        INTEGER
,Dept_no            INTEGER
,First_name         VARCHAR(20)
,Last_name          CHAR(20)
,Salary             DECIMAL(10,2)
)
UNIQUE PRIMARY INDEX(Employee_no) ;
```

Unique Primary Index

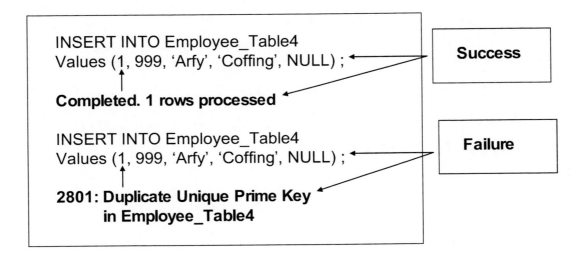

```
INSERT INTO Employee_Table4
Values (1, 999, 'Arfy', 'Coffing', NULL) ;
```
Success

Completed. 1 rows processed

```
INSERT INTO Employee_Table4
Values (1, 999, 'Arfy', 'Coffing', NULL) ;
```
Failure

**2801: Duplicate Unique Prime Key
        in Employee_Table4**

A Quick Way to Copy Tables

Teradata allows you to create a new table exactly like another table including its data. Here are two syntax examples that will do exactly this.

```
CREATE Table Employee_Table5
AS Employee_Table
WITH DATA ;
```

The above example has created Employee_Table5. Employee_Table5 has the exact Data Definition Language (DDL) as Employee_Table. Employee_Table5 also contains the exact data rows contained in Employee_Table. We have essentially copied Employee_Table in another table called Employee_Table5.

```
CREATE Table Employee_Table6
AS (SELECT * FROM Employee_Table)
WITH DATA ;
```

The above example has created Employee_Table6. Employee_Table6 has the exact Data Definition Language (DDL) as Employee_Table. Employee_Table6 also contains the exact data rows contained in Employee_Table. We have essentially copied Employee_Table in another table called Employee_Table6.

```
CREATE Table Employee_Table7
AS (SELECT * FROM Employee_Table)
WITH NO DATA ;
```

The Table Definition is copied, but NOT the Data.

Copying a table with a different Primary Index

Has there ever been an instance where you want to take a table that already exists and create a duplicate table with all the same information but with a different Primary Index? Well you're in luck! This example shows how to copy a table. After the table is copied we have the option of creating the table With Data, or With No Data. In this case we wanted to have all of the same information, and at the end of the command we define our new Primary Index.

In order to duplicate an existing table while changing the Primary Index we copy the existing table we want to duplicate and change the Primary Index

```
Create Table   <Table Name> AS
(SEL *  FROM <Table2 Name>)
With Data
Primary Index (<New Primary Index>)
```

Copying a table with a different Primary Index Cont.

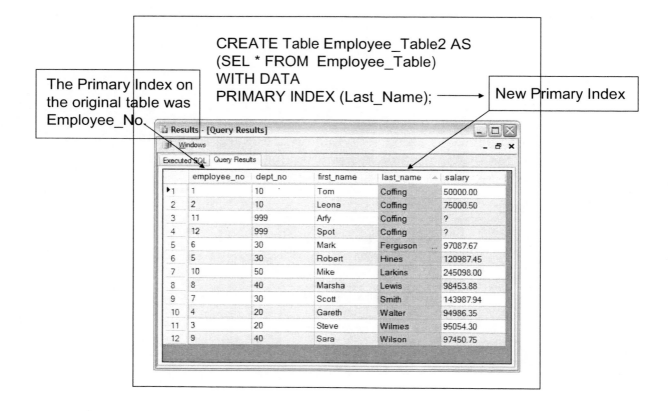

The Primary Index on the original table was Employee_No.

CREATE Table Employee_Table2 AS
(SEL * FROM Employee_Table)
WITH DATA
PRIMARY INDEX (Last_Name);

New Primary Index

Results - [Query Results]

Windows

Executed SQL   Query Results

	employee_no	dept_no	first_name	last_name	salary
1	1	10	Tom	Coffing	50000.00
2	2	10	Leona	Coffing	75000.50
3	11	999	Arfy	Coffing	?
4	12	999	Spot	Coffing	?
5	6	30	Mark	Ferguson	97087.67
6	5	30	Robert	Hines	120987.45
7	10	50	Mike	Larkins	245098.00
8	8	40	Marsha	Lewis	98453.88
9	7	30	Scott	Smith	143987.94
10	4	20	Gareth	Walter	94986.35
11	3	20	Steve	Wilmes	95054.30
12	9	40	Sara	Wilson	97450.75

CREATE Table Options

FALLBACK requests that a second copy of each row inserted into a table be stored on another AMP in the same cluster. This is done in case the AMP fails. If an AMP fails and FALLBACK is on the table the system will keep running. When rows from the failed AMP are needed they are obtained from the FALLBACK copy residing on another AMP.

PERMANENT JOUNALING keeps an audit trail of any new updates, inserts, or deletions. You can specify BEFORE JOURNALS or AFTER JOURNALS. A BEFORE JOURNAL will allow you to roll backward in time. This might be needed if a programmer makes a mistake and it is necessary to go back to the way the data used to look. An AFTER JOURNAL is the most popular journal. It works in conjunction with Full System Backups to make sure the system is backed up. An After Journal will take a picture of any change AFTER the change has occurred.

The **FREESPACE PERCENTAGE** tells Teradata at what percentage Teradata should keep a cylinder free of rows on data loads when using Fastload and Multiload utilities to load the table. A FREESPACE 10 PERCENT keeps 10% of a cylinder's sector space free when loading the data. Valid values for the percentage of free space range from 0-75. If you only load a table with the load utilities Fastload or Multiload then you can set the number to 0. If you load with Fastload and Multiload, but also utilize straight SQL to load additional data you might want to set the value to 10% or 20% depending on how often you INSERT data with straight SQL.

The **DATABLOCKSIZE** determines a maximum block size for multiple row storage on disk. Larger block sizes enhance full table scan operations and smaller block sizes are best of on-line transaction-orientated tables.

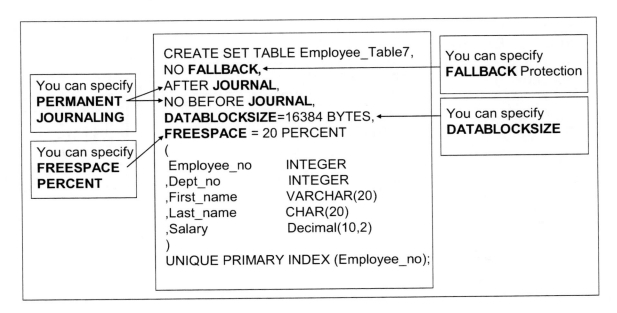

Defining Constraints at the Column Level

You can establish constraints at the column or table level. Establishing constraints at the column level directly on the column definition is easy, but it does spread the constraints throughout the DDL Statement. Below is an example.

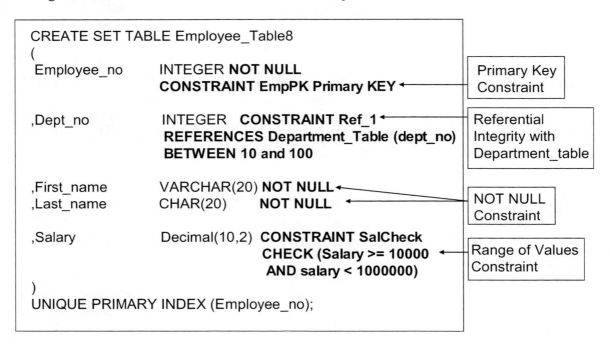

The Employee_Table8 and the Department_Table have referential integrity between them. You can't insert or update a new employee if their dept_no does not exist in the Department_Table.

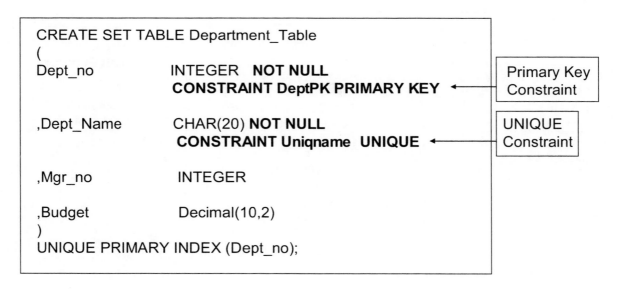

Defining Constraints at the Table Level

You can establish constraints at the column or table level. Establishing constraints at the column level directly on the column definition is easy, but it does spread the constraints throughout the DDL Statement. Below is an example.

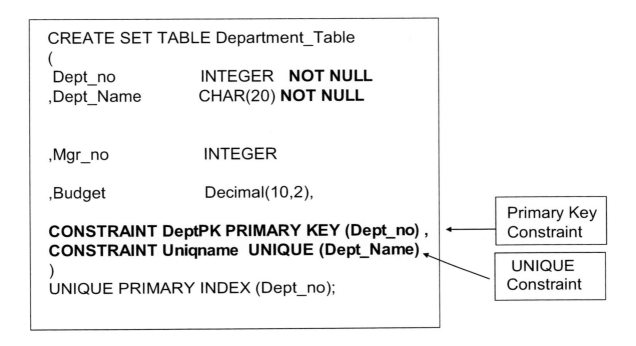

```
CREATE SET TABLE Department_Table
(
 Dept_no              INTEGER   NOT NULL
,Dept_Name            CHAR(20) NOT NULL


,Mgr_no               INTEGER

,Budget               Decimal(10,2),

CONSTRAINT DeptPK PRIMARY KEY (Dept_no) ,
CONSTRAINT Uniqname  UNIQUE (Dept_Name)
)
UNIQUE PRIMARY INDEX (Dept_no);
```

Primary Key Constraint

UNIQUE Constraint

Defining constraints at the table level makes the definition easier to read and understand than looking for constraints throughout the DDL.

Partitioned Primary Index Tables

Teradata allows you to partition tables by column(s) that are different then the tables Primary Index. Remember, data in a table is always distributed by the Primary Index to the proper AMP. The table can be partitioned by any column(s). You can also have the same column

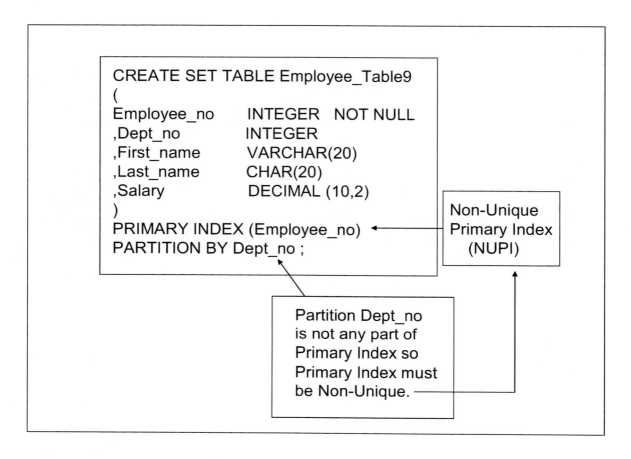

```
CREATE SET TABLE Employee_Table9
(
Employee_no      INTEGER   NOT NULL
,Dept_no          INTEGER
,First_name       VARCHAR(20)
,Last_name        CHAR(20)
,Salary           DECIMAL (10,2)
)
PRIMARY INDEX (Employee_no)
PARTITION BY Dept_no ;
```

Non-Unique Primary Index (NUPI)

Partition Dept_no is not any part of Primary Index so Primary Index must be Non-Unique.

You can NOT have a UNIQUE PRIMARY INDEX on a table that is partitioned by something not included in the Primary Index.

Remember, data is never distributed based on the partition. **Data is only distributed** based on the **Primary Index** of a table (even if it is a **PPI Table**).

Partitions can eliminate full table scans

AMP 1			AMP 2		
Employee_Table			**Employee_Table**		
Employee	**Dept**	**First_Name**	**Employee**	**Dept**	**First_Name**

Part 1

Employee	Dept	First_Name	Employee	Dept	First_Name
99	10	Tom	13	10	Ray
75	10	Mike	12	10	Jeff
56	10	Sandy	21	10	Randy

Part 2

Employee	Dept	First_Name	Employee	Dept	First_Name
30	20	Leona	16	20	Janie
54	20	Robert	55	20	Chris
40	20	Morgan	70	20	Gareth

Partition Primary Index is Dept

How many partitions on each AMP will need to be read for the following query?

SELECT *
FROM Employee_Table
WHERE Dept = 20;

Answer: 1

Partition Primary Indexes reduce the **number of rows** that are processed by using **partition elimination**.

Partitioning with CASE_N

Teradata now allows you to crack the CASE statement as a partitioning option. Here are the fundamentals:

Use of CASE_N results in:

- Just like the CASE statement it evaluates a list of conditions picking only the first condition met.

- The data row will be placed into a partition associated with that condition.

```
CREATE TABLE Order_Table
(
Order_Number       Integer   NOT NULL
,Customer_Number Integer   NOT NULL
,Order_Date       Date
,Order_Total       Decimal (10,2)
)
PRIMARY INDEX(Customer_Number)
PARTITION BY CASE_N
   (Order_Total < 1000
    ,Order_Total < 5000
    ,Order_Total < 10000
    ,Order_Total < 50000, NO Case, Unknown
);
```

We can't have a Unique Primary Index (UPI) here because we are partitioning by ORDER_TOTAL and ORDER_TOTAL is not part of the Primary Index. Data Distribution of a Partitioned Primary Index table is based only on the Primary Index.

Partitioning with RANGE_N

Teradata also has a western theme because they allow your partitions to go "Home on the Range" by using the RANGE_N function. Here are the fundamentals. Use of RANGE_N results in:

- The expression is evaluated and associated to one of a list of ranges.

- Ranges are always listed in increasing order and can't overlap

- The data row is placed into the partition that falls within the associated range.

- The test value in RANGE_N function must be an INTEGER or DATE. (This includes BYTEINT or SMALLINT)

In the example below please notice the arrows. They are designed to illustrate that you can use a UNIQUE PRIMARY INDEX on a Partitioned table when the Partition is part of the PRIMARY INDEX.

```
CREATE TABLE Order_Table
(
Order_Number            Integer  NOT NULL
,Customer_Number        Integer  NOT NULL
,Order_Date             Date
,Order_Total            Decimal(10,2)
)UNIQUE PRIMARY INDEX
(Customer_Number, Order_Date)
PARTITION BY Range_N
   (Order_Date
      BETWEEN DATE '2003-01-01'
         AND DATE '2003-06-30'
EACH INTERVAL '1' DAY
);
```

NO CASE, NO RANGE, or UNKNOWN

If you specify NO Case, NO Range, or Unknown with partitioning their will be no fighting amongst the partitions. These keywords tell Teradata which partition to place bad data.

You can specify a NO CASE or NO RANGE Partition as well as a partition for UNKNOWN.

A NO CASE or NO RANGE partition is for any value, which isn't true for any previous CASE_N or RANGE_N expression.

If UNKNOWN is included as part of the NO CASE or NO RANGE option with an OR condition, then any values that are not true for any previous CASE_N or RANGE_N expression and any unknown (e.g., NULL) will be put in the same partition. This example has a total of 5 partitions.

        Partition by CASE_N
                (Salary < 30000,
                  Salary < 50000,
                  Salary < 100000
                  Salary < 1000000,
                  NO CASE OR UNKNOWN)

If you don't see the OR operand associated with UNKNOWN then NULLs will be placed in the UNKNOWN Partition and all other rows that don't meet the CASE criteria will be placed in the NO CASE partition. This example has a total of 6 partitions.

Partition by CASE_N
        (Salary < 30000,
          Salary < 50000,
          Salary < 100000
          Salary < 1000000,
          NO CASE, UNKNOWN)

PPI Advantages and Disadvantages

You partition a table to avoid Full Table Scans on Range Queries (BETWEEN Statements). Below are listed some of the advantages and disadvantages of PPI tables.

Advantages:

- Range queries don't have to utilize a Full Table Scan.

- Deletions of entire partitions are lightning fast.

- PPI provides an excellent solution instead of using secondary indexes

- Tables that hold yearly information don't have to be split into 12 smaller tables to avoid Full Table Scans (FTS). This can make modeling and querying easier.

- Fastload and Multiload work with PPI tables, but not with all Secondary Indexes.

Disadvantages:

- A two-byte Partition number is added to the ROW-ID and it is now called a ROW KEY. The two-bytes per row will add more Perm Space to a table.

- Joins to Non-Partitioned Tables can take longer and become more complicated for Teradata to perform.

- Basic select queries utilizing the Primary Index can take longer if the Partition number is not also mentioned in the WHERE clause of the query.

- You can't have a Unique Primary Index (UPI) if the Partition Number is not at least part of the Primary Index. You must therefore create a Unique Secondary Index to maintain uniqueness.

ROW KEY = 10 Bytes Partition, Row Hash, Uniqueness Value	Data is sorted on each AMP by Row Key PI ↓ PPI ↓				
20,10010011001110010110011011010001, 1	99	20	Dave	Jones	75000.50
20,11110011001110010110011011010001, 1	88	20	Mary	Dawn	82000.50
30,10110011001110010110011011010001, 1	77	30	Will	Bear	78000.50
30,11110011001110010110011011010001, 1	66	30	Ken	Lasen	86000.50

PPI Date Range in Months

The table below shows an outstanding example of Partitioning a table with a RANGE_N based on Month. The example shows that the partitions will start with January 1, 2004 and end with partition December 31, 2005. It is two years worth of Order data. Each month will hold its own partition. This will allow users to run queries that analyze a particular month with each AMP only having to read one partition to satisfy a monthly query. This table can also be used to analyze weeks and years, but it is intended for the majority of the queries to be based on single or multiple months.

```
CREATE TABLE Order_Table
(
Order_Number            Integer NOT NULL
,Customer_Number        Integer NOT NULL
,Order_Date             Date
,Order_Total            Decimal(10,2)
)
PRIMARY INDEX (Order_Number)
PARTITION BY RANGE_N
(
Order_Date
   BETWEEN DATE '2004-01-01'
        AND DATE '2005-12-31'
      EACH INTERVAL '1' MONTH
);
```

PPI Date Range in Weeks

The table below shows an outstanding example of Partitioning a table with a RANGE_N based on weeks. The example shows that the partitions will start with January 1, 2004 and end with partition December 31, 2005. It is two years worth of Order data. Each week will hold its own partition. This will allow users to run queries that analyze a particular week with each AMP only having to read one partition to satisfy a weekly query. This table can also be used to analyze months and years, but it is intended for the majority of the queries to be based on single or multiple weeks.

```
CREATE TABLE Order_Table
(
Order_Number          Integer NOT NULL
,Customer_Number      Integer NOT NULL
,Order_Date           Date
,Order_Total          Decimal(10,2)
)
PRIMARY INDEX (Order_Number)
PARTITION BY RANGE_N
(
Order_Date
  BETWEEN DATE '2004-01-01'  AND DATE '2004-12-31'
                EACH INTERVAL '7' DAY
            ,DATE '2005-01-01' AND DATE '2005-12-31'
                EACH INTERVAL '7' DAY
);
```

PPI Date Range in Days

The table below shows an outstanding example of partitioning a table with a RANGE_N based on each partition representing 1 day. The example shows that the table holds Orders for two years. Each Day will be its own partition. This will allow users to run queries that analyze a particular Day with each AMP only having to read one partition to satisfy a Daily query. This table can also be used to analyze weeks, months and years, but it is intended for the majority of the queries to be based on single or multiple Days. This table will hold at least 730 partitions. (365 days per year for a two-year period).

```
CREATE TABLE Order_Table
(
Order_Number          Integer NOT NULL
,Customer_Number      Integer NOT NULL
,Order_Date           Date
,Order_Total          Decimal(10,2)
)
PRIMARY INDEX (Order_Number)
PARTITION BY RANGE_N
(
Order_Date
   BETWEEN DATE '2004-01-01'
        AND DATE '2005-12-31'
            EACH INTERVAL '1' DAY
);
```

Finding the Rows in each Partition

The word PARTITION is a keyword in Teradata and therefore can be used in SQL Queries. The picture below shows an excellent example of SQL that will show the partition number and the number of rows in the partition.

```
Select Partition as Partition_Number
        COUNT(*) AS Rows_In_Partition
FROM Order_Table
GROUP BY 1
ORDER BY 1;
```

Altering a Table to Add or Delete Partitions

You can ALTER a Table to Add or Delete Partitions, but you can only Add or Delete Partitions that are on the ends. This does NOT mean you can only Add or Delete Partitions that are the first and last partition. You can Add or Delete many partitions as long as they are at the beginning or end. In the picture below you can see we are deleting an entire year (12 months) at the beginning of the Order_Table and adding another year (12 months) to the end of the table's partition.

You will use the WITH DELETE option if the table is populated with data and you don't want to save the data being removed.

If a table is populated then there are restrictions to the ALTER Table command with PPI Tables:

- You can't ALTER the primary index columns.

- You can ALTER the table to change to a UNIQUE PRIMARY INDEX only if the NUPI had a Unique Secondary Index already.

- You can't Add or Drop the NO RANGE or UNKNOWN Partitions

- You can only ADD RANGE or DROP RANGE at the ends.

ALTER TABLE Order_table
  MODIFY PRIMARY INDEX
    DROP RANGE BETWEEN DATE
      '2004-01-01 AND DATE '2004-12-31'
      EACH INTERVAL '1' MONTH
    ADD RANGE BETWEEN DATE
      '2006-01-01 AND DATE '2006-12-31'
      EACH INTERVAL '1' MONTH
    WITH DELETE ;

Altering a Table's Partitions but saving the Data

You can ALTER a Table to Add or Delete Partitions, but you can only Add or Delete Partitions that are on the ends. This does NOT mean you can only Add or Delete Partitions that are the first and last partition. You can Add or Delete many partitions as long as they are at the beginning or end. In the picture below you can see we are deleting an entire year (12 months) at the beginning of the Order_Table and adding another year (12 months) to the end of the table's partition.

You will use the WITH INSERT option if the table is populated with data and you want to move the data to another table for safe keeping. The table you want to move the partition data to before removing the partition and data must already exist. If the table does exist and it is empty it will be fast because Teradata will not have to use the Transient Journal. If a table is populated then there are restrictions to the ALTER Table command with PPI Tables:

- You can't ALTER the primary index columns.

- You can ALTER the table to change to a UNIQUE PRIMARY INDEX only if the NUPI had a Unique Secondary Index already.

- You can't Add or Drop the NO RANGE or UNKNOWN Partitions

- You can only ADD RANGE or DROP RANGE at the ends.

```
ALTER TABLE Order_table
  MODIFY PRIMARY INDEX
    DROP RANGE BETWEEN DATE
      '2004-01-01 AND DATE '2004-12-31'
      EACH INTERVAL '1' MONTH
    ADD RANGE BETWEEN DATE
      '2006-01-01 AND DATE '2006-12-31'
      EACH INTERVAL '1' MONTH
    WITH INSERT INTO
      Order_Table_Backup ;
```

Altering a Table's Partitions on Empty Tables

If a table is empty there are fewer restrictions on the ALTER command for PPI tables. In our example below we don't need the WITH DELETE or WITH INSERT INTO command to drop partitions. This is because the table is empty. We can also change the NO RANGE or UNKNOWN partitions. This is again only because the table is empty.

```
ALTER TABLE Order_table
  MODIFY PRIMARY INDEX
    DROP RANGE BETWEEN DATE
      '2004-01-01 AND DATE '2004-12-31'
      EACH INTERVAL '1' MONTH
    ADD RANGE BETWEEN DATE
      '2006-01-01 AND DATE '2006-12-31'
      EACH INTERVAL '1' MONTH ;
```

```
ALTER TABLE Order_table
  MODIFY PRIMARY INDEX
    ADD RANGE
      NO RANGE
      OR UNKNOWN:
```

Chapter 18 – WITH and WITH BY for Totals and Subtotals

"If you're falling off a cliff, you may as well try to fly."

Captain John Sheridan, Babylon 5

The WITH Statement

The WITH statement will bring a grand total to the end of a report, but it does not work with SQL Assistant or Queryman. The before mentioned products use ODBC and the WITH and WITH BY statements don't work. They do work however in BTEQ. The WITH statement will work with aggregation to produce a grand total.

Course_Table

Course_ID	Course_Name	Credits	Seats
1	Teradata Basics	3	100
2	Teradata Database Design	3	25
3	Teradata SQL	3	20
4	Teradata DBA	4	12
5	Teradata Appl Dev	3	16

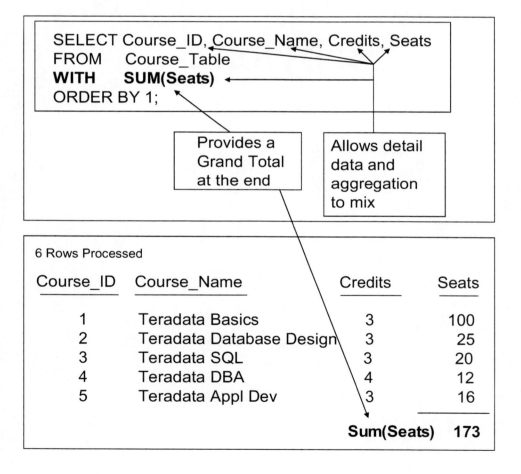

```
SELECT Course_ID, Course_Name, Credits, Seats
FROM    Course_Table
WITH    SUM(Seats)
ORDER BY 1;
```

Provides a Grand Total at the end

Allows detail data and aggregation to mix

6 Rows Processed

Course_ID	Course_Name	Credits	Seats
1	Teradata Basics	3	100
2	Teradata Database Design	3	25
3	Teradata SQL	3	20
4	Teradata DBA	4	12
5	Teradata Appl Dev	3	16
		Sum(Seats)	173

The WITH BY Statement

The WITH BY statement allows detail data to mix with aggregation. The WITH BY statement will not work with SQL Assistant or Queryman. The before mentioned products use ODBC and the WITH and WITH BY statements don't work with ODBC products. They do work however in BTEQ.

Employee_Table				
Employee_No	**Dept_No**	**First_Name**	**Last_Name**	**Salary**
1	10	Tom	Coffing	50000.00
2	10	Leona	Coffing	75000.50
3	20	Steve	Wilmes	95054.30
4	20	Gareth	Walter	94986.35
5	30	Robert	Hines	120987.45
6	30	Mark	Ferguson	97087.67
7	30	Scott	Smith	143987.94
8	40	Marsha	Lewis	98453.88
9	40	Sara	Wilson	97450.75
10	50	Mike	Larkins	245098.00
11	999	Arfy	Coffing	NULL
12	999	Spot	Coffing	NULL

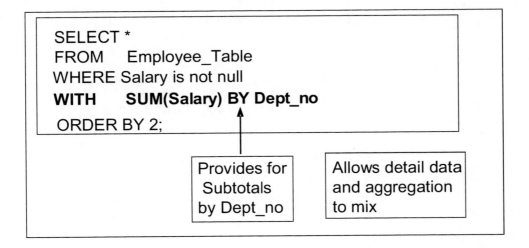

```
SELECT *
FROM    Employee_Table
WHERE Salary is not null
WITH      SUM(Salary) BY Dept_no
ORDER BY 2;
```

Provides for Subtotals by Dept_no

Allows detail data and aggregation to mix

The WITH BY Statement Cont.

18 Rows Processed

Employee_No	Dept_no	First_name	Last_name	Salary
1	10	Tom	Coffing	50000.00
2	10	Leona	Coffing	75000.50
			Sum(Salary)	125000.50
3	20	Steve	Wilmes	95054.30
2	20	Gareth	Walter	94986.35
			Sum(Salary)	190040.65
5	30	Robert	Hines	120987.45
6	30	Mark	Ferguson	97087.67
7	30	Scott	Smith	143987.94
			Sum(Salary)	362062.91
8	40	Marsha	Lewis	98453.88
9	40	Sara	Wilson	97450.75
			Sum(Salary)	195904.63
10	50	Mike	Larkins	245098.00
			Sum(Salary)	245098.00

Combining WITH BY and WITH

The WITH BY statement provides subtotals and the WITH provides a grand total. They can both be used together.

Employee_Table				
Employee_No	**Dept_No**	**First_Name**	**Last_Name**	**Salary**
1	10	Tom	Coffing	50000.00
2	10	Leona	Coffing	75000.50
3	20	Steve	Wilmes	95054.30
4	20	Gareth	Walter	94986.35
5	30	Robert	Hines	120987.45
6	30	Mark	Ferguson	97087.67
7	30	Scott	Smith	143987.94
8	40	Marsha	Lewis	98453.88
9	40	Sara	Wilson	97450.75
10	50	Mike	Larkins	245098.00
11	999	Arfy	Coffing	NULL
12	999	Spot	Coffing	NULL

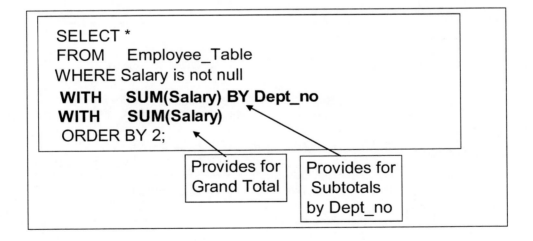

```
SELECT *
FROM    Employee_Table
WHERE Salary is not null
  WITH    SUM(Salary) BY Dept_no
  WITH    SUM(Salary)
ORDER BY 2;
```

Provides for Grand Total

Provides for Subtotals by Dept_no

Combining Multiple WITH BY statements and WITH

The WITH BY statement provides subtotals and the WITH provides a grand total. You can have multiple WITH BY statements.

Product_Sales_Table

Product_ID	Sale_Date	Total_Sales
100	01-28-2004	4000.00
100	01-29-2004	5000.00
100	02-01-2004	5000.00
100	02-10-2004	7000.00
200	01-28-2004	4000.00
200	01-29-2004	6000.00
200	02-01-2004	5000.00
200	02-02-2004	4000.00
200	02-10-2004	9000.00

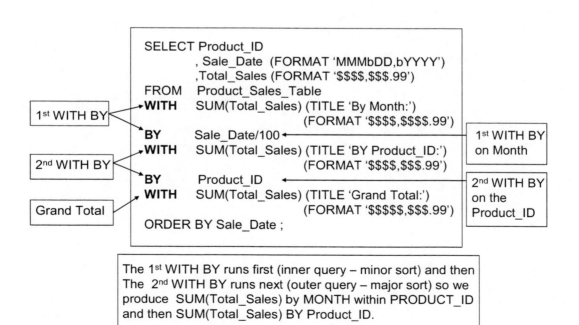

```
SELECT Product_ID
       , Sale_Date  (FORMAT 'MMMbDD,bYYYY')
       ,Total_Sales (FORMAT '$$$$,$$$.99')
FROM   Product_Sales_Table
WITH   SUM(Total_Sales) (TITLE 'By Month:')
                        (FORMAT '$$$$,$$$$.99')
BY     Sale_Date/100
WITH   SUM(Total_Sales) (TITLE 'BY Product_ID:')
                        (FORMAT '$$$$,$$$.99')
BY       Product_ID
WITH   SUM(Total_Sales) (TITLE 'Grand Total:')
                        (FORMAT '$$$$$,$$$.99')
ORDER BY Sale_Date ;
```

1st WITH BY
2nd WITH BY
Grand Total

1st WITH BY on Month
2nd WITH BY on the Product_ID

The 1st WITH BY runs first (inner query – minor sort) and then The 2nd WITH BY runs next (outer query – major sort) so we produce SUM(Total_Sales) by MONTH within PRODUCT_ID and then SUM(Total_Sales) BY Product_ID.

Combining Multiple WITH BY statements and WITH (Continued)

```
16 Rows Returned
```

Product_ID	Sale_Date	Total_Sales
100	Jan 28, 2004	$4,000.00
100	Jan 29, 2004	$5,000.00
	By Month:	**$9,000.00**
100	Feb 01, 2004	$5,000.00
100	Feb 10, 2004	$7,000.00
	By Month:	**$12,000.00**
	By Product_ID:	**$21,000.00**
200	Jan 28, 2004	$4,000.00
200	Jan 29, 2004	$6,000.00
	By Month:	**$10,000.00**
200	Feb 01, 2004	$5,000.00
200	Feb 02, 2004	$4,000.00
200	Feb 10, 2004	$9,000.00
	By Month:	**$18,000.00**
	By Product_ID:	**$28,000.00**
	Grand Total:	**$49,000.00**

Chapter 19 – Sampling

"Be kind, for everyone you meet is fighting a hard battle."

John Watson

Random Sampling – Number of Rows Sample

Teradata gives you the ability to SAMPLE a table. The Sampling function (SAMPLE) permits a SELECT to return rows randomly. There are many different options. Two options to be aware of is that you can request a sample number of rows or a sample percentage of rows. Our first example will bring back exactly 5 rows.

Employee_Table

Employee_No	Dept_No	First_Name	Last_Name	Salary
1	10	Tom	Coffing	50000.00
2	10	Leona	Coffing	75000.50
3	20	Steve	Wilmes	95054.30
4	20	Gareth	Walter	94986.35
5	30	Robert	Hines	120987.45
6	30	Mark	Ferguson	97087.67
7	30	Scott	Smith	143987.94
8	40	Marsha	Lewis	98453.88
9	40	Sara	Wilson	97450.75
10	50	Mike	Larkins	245098.00
11	999	Arfy	Coffing	NULL
12	999	Spot	Coffing	NULL

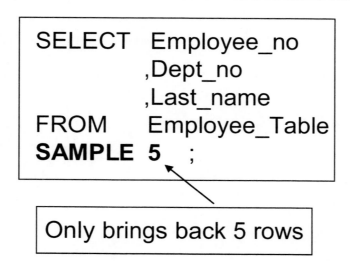

```
SELECT   Employee_no
         ,Dept_no
         ,Last_name
FROM     Employee_Table
SAMPLE 5   ;
```

Only brings back 5 rows

Random Sampling – Number of Rows Sample Cont.

5 Rows Returned

Employee_no	Dept_no	Last_name
3	20	Wilmes
11	999	Coffing
6	30	Ferguson
8	40	Lewis
10	50	Larkins

The above result set came back the first time our SAMPLE query was run. If you ran the same query over and over again you would get different result sets each time. Teradata is actually attempting to take an equal number of rows per AMP in its sampling function.

Random Sampling – Percentage of the Table Sample

You can request a SAMPLE by percentage. The example below will bring 50% of the rows back.

```
SELECT   Employee_no
         ,Dept_no
         ,Last_name
FROM     Employee_Table
SAMPLE  .5   ;
```

Brings back 50% of the rows

6 Rows Returned

Employee_no	Dept_no	Last_name
3	20	Wilmes
5	30	Hines
6	30	Ferguson
9	40	Wilson
12	999	Coffing
4	20	Walter

Multiple Samples

Sometimes it is better to get multiple samples and Teradata allows you to do so by listing either the number or rows or the percentage of the rows to be returned. The numbers of different samples are each separated by a comma. Also notice that we have captured a keyword named SAMPLEID. **SAMPLEID** can only be used in the **SELECT** list or on the **ORDER BY** statement. SAMPLEID is never used in the WHERE clause.

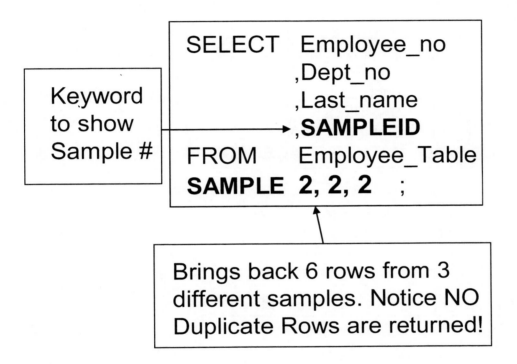

Keyword to show Sample #

```
SELECT  Employee_no
        ,Dept_no
        ,Last_name
       ,SAMPLEID
FROM    Employee_Table
SAMPLE  2, 2, 2   ;
```

Brings back 6 rows from 3 different samples. Notice NO Duplicate Rows are returned!

6 Rows Returned

Employee_no	Dept_no	Last_name	SampleID
9	40	Wilson	2
4	20	Walter	3
6	30	Ferguson	1
3	20	Wilmes	2
12	999	Coffing	3
5	30	Hines	1

SAMPLE WITH REPLACEMENT

In all of our previous SAMPLE examples you should have noticed that no duplicate rows are ever returned. For example, if a table has only 12 rows and you request a SAMPLE 15 or a SAMPLE 5, 5, 5 you will only get back 12 rows. This again is because no duplicate rows are placed in the sample.

SAMPLE WITH REPLACEMENT will allow duplicate rows in a SAMPLE function. If you use the SAMPLE WITH REPLACEMENT 15 on a table with only 12 rows you will get 15 rows back.

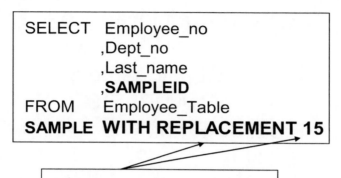

```
SELECT   Employee_no
         ,Dept_no
         ,Last_name
         ,SAMPLEID
FROM     Employee_Table
SAMPLE  WITH REPLACEMENT 15  ;
```

Brings back 15 rows. There can be duplicate rows.

15 Rows Returned

Employee_no	Dept_no	Last_name	SampleID
9	40	Wilson	1
4	20	Walter	1
6	30	Ferguson	1
3	20	Wilmes	1
12	999	Coffing	1
5	30	Hines	1
7	**30**	**Smith**	**1**
7	**30**	**Smith**	**1**
7	**30**	**Smith**	**1**
5	30	Hines	1
2	**10**	**Coffing**	**1**
2	**10**	**Coffing**	**1**
6	30	Ferguson	1
4	20	Walter	1
8	40	Lewis	1

Duplicate rows are returned

SAMPLE with RANDOMIZED ALLOCATION

The SAMPLE function does a proportional sampling across all AMPs in the system. This is not a simple random sample across the entire population of a table's rows. If you truly want a random sample across the entire population of a table's rows then use the Randomized Allocation keywords.

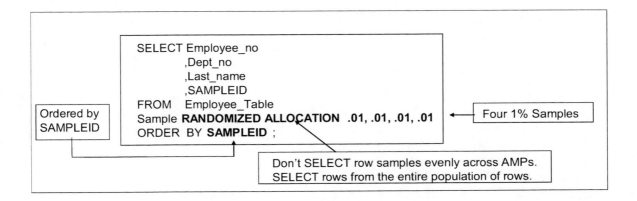

4 Rows Returned

Employee_no	Dept_no	Last_name	SampleID
1	10	Coffing	1
9	40	Wilson	2
8	40	Lewis	3
7	30	Smith	4

SAMPLE WITH REPLACEMENT and RANDOMIZED ALLOCATION together

You can utilize the SAMPLE WITH REPLACEMENT and the RANDOMIZED ALLOCATION in the same query. Notice the syntax below that takes four 1% samples. The SAMPLE WITH REPLACEMENT allows duplicate rows to be in the same sample or return set. The RANDOMIZED ALLOCATION takes a sample of the rows from the entire population of the table and does not take an even amount of rows from each AMP.

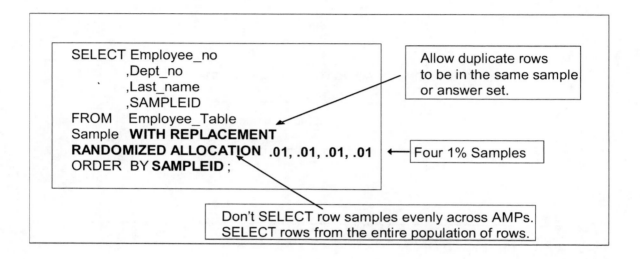

```
SELECT Employee_no
       ,Dept_no
       ,Last_name
       ,SAMPLEID
FROM    Employee_Table
Sample  WITH REPLACEMENT
RANDOMIZED ALLOCATION  .01, .01, .01, .01
ORDER  BY SAMPLEID ;
```

Allow duplicate rows to be in the same sample or answer set.

Four 1% Samples

Don't SELECT row samples evenly across AMPs. SELECT rows from the entire population of rows.

4 Rows Returned

Employee_no	Dept_no	Last_name	SampleID
7	30	Smith	1
7	30	Smith	2
9	40	Wilson	3
5	30	Hines	4

SAMPLE with Conditional Test using WHEN

A truly great function of the SAMPLE function is conditional testing using the keyword WHEN.

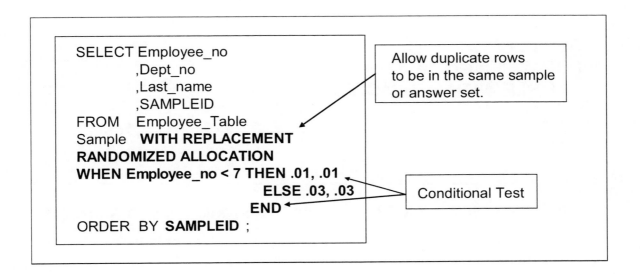

```
SELECT Employee_no
        ,Dept_no
        ,Last_name
        ,SAMPLEID
FROM    Employee_Table
Sample  WITH REPLACEMENT
RANDOMIZED ALLOCATION
WHEN Employee_no < 7 THEN .01, .01
                    ELSE .03, .03
                    END
ORDER  BY  SAMPLEID ;
```

Allow duplicate rows to be in the same sample or answer set.

Conditional Test

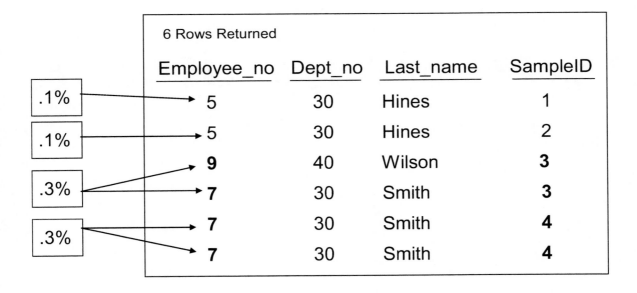

6 Rows Returned

Employee_no	Dept_no	Last_name	SampleID
5	30	Hines	1
5	30	Hines	2
9	40	Wilson	3
7	30	Smith	3
7	30	Smith	4
7	30	Smith	4

.1%

.1%

.3%

.3%

SAMPLE example that Errors

You can't have a percentage sample that is greater then 1. The system will give you an error saying "5473: SAMPLE clause has invalid set of arguments".

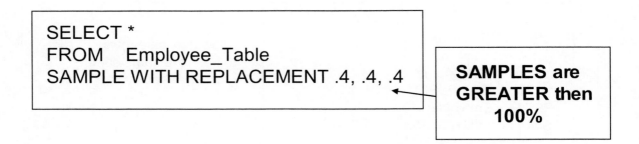

SELECT *
FROM   Employee_Table
SAMPLE WITH REPLACEMENT .4, .4, .4

SAMPLES are GREATER then 100%

ERROR – 5473: SAMPLE clause has **invalid set of arguments**

TOP Rows Option

With V2R6, Teradata provides the ANSI capability of using TOP to limit the output rows to a specific number or the percentage for the total number of rows in an ordered answer set. The keyword here is ordered answer set. The bottom line is that TOP will sort the data based on the ORDER BY statement and then bring back the number of rows requested from the TOP of the sorted list.

The syntax for using TOP:

```
SELECT TOP      }<integer-value> | <decimal-value>} [PERCENT] [WITH TIES]
        <column-list>
FROM    <table-name>;
```

Because of the location of TOP within the SELECT and the elimination of some of the rows, it is not compatible with the following SQL constructs:
DISTINCT
QUALIFY
SAMPLE
WITH and WITH BY

TOP Rows Option

Top is used to limit the output rows to a specific number of the percentage for the total number of rows in an ordered answer set. In the SELECT statement we put the TOP request then a number to indicate how many rows returned the user desires.

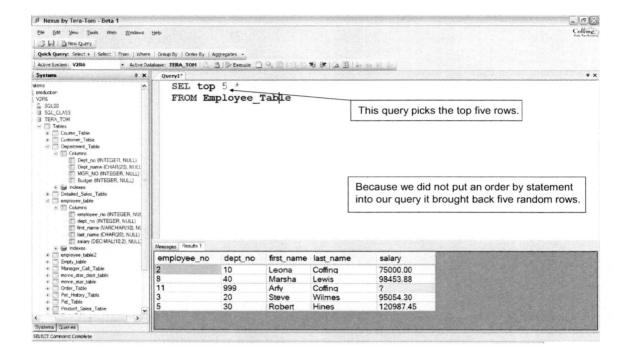

TOP Rows Option Using Percent

This example shows how a specific percent of the table can be requested and returned. Following the TOP request is the percent desired and then the word percent. However, since Teradata cannot return a portion of a row; it must return only whole numbers so if there is an undividable percent requested then Teradata is smart enough to round up to the next whole row for you!

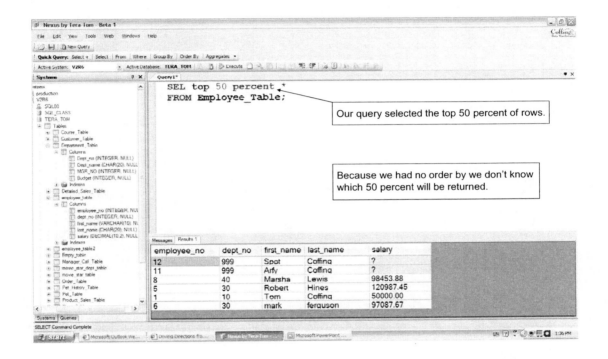

TOP Rows Option Using Order By

When using the TOP request with an ORDER BY, the system will sort the table bringing back the first three rows.

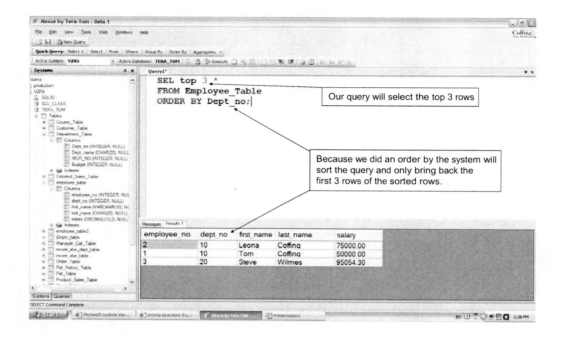

TOP Rows Option Using With Ties

When using the TOP request with the "With Ties" option, we are asking for the top 3 rows, but if the third row returned (in this case having a Dept_No of 20) has a duplicate value or a tie, the top 3 rows will be returned along with all ties from the third row.

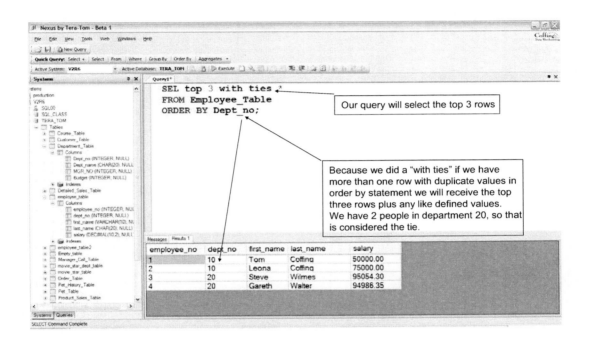

TOP Rows Option Using ORDER BY with Multiple Values

This slide shows the user requesting the top row from the Employee_Table, but 2 were returned. There were two columns listed in the ORDER BY clause asking for both Dept_No and Last_Name. We have a result set of two rows because we had a tie in both the Dept_No as well as the Last_Name.

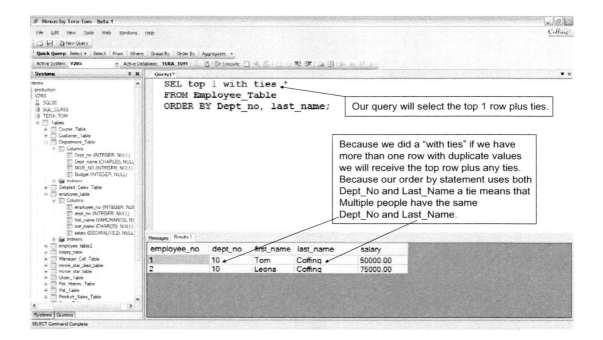

TOP Rows Option with Ties

Here we asked for the top three rows from the Employee_Table and received all three. The reason we do not see 4 rows returned is because even though we saw three rows returned when we ran a similar query earlier on, we only see three here because we have two columns listed in the ORDER BY clause rather than the one column the last time, we have more restrictions. So even though we have more than one Dept_No of 20, we see no ties with this row because we have only one Dept_No of 20 with the last name of Walter.

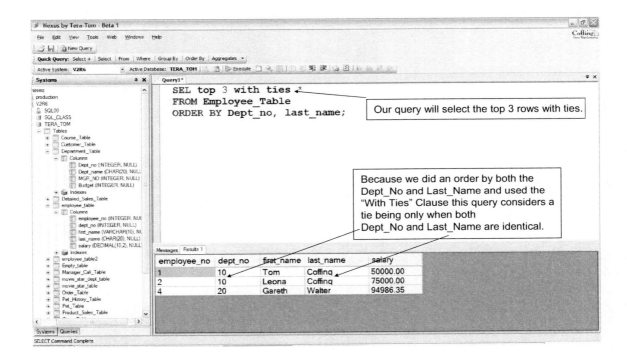

Chapter 20 – Rank and Quantile

"The man on top of the mountain did not fall there."

Longfellow

RANK

The Ranking function (RANK) permits a column to be ranked against all other rows. This means a column can be evaluated and compared, either based on high or low order, resulting in a descending (default) ranking.

The output of the RANK function is the highest or the lowest data values in a column, depending on the sort request. You always sort inside the RANK function and you never use an ORDER BY statement with an OLAP function.

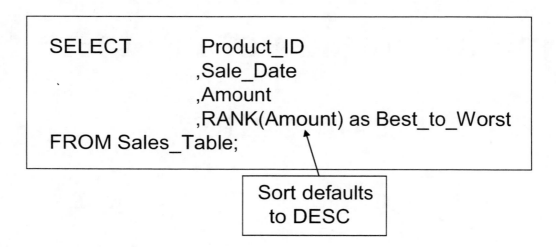

```
SELECT          Product_ID
                ,Sale_Date
                ,Amount
                ,RANK(Amount) as Best_to_Worst
FROM Sales_Table;
```

Sort defaults
to DESC

10 Rows Returned

Product_ID	Sale_Date	Amount	Best_To_Worst
20	2004-01-04	20000.00	1
20	2004-01-03	15000.00	2
20	2004-01-02	13000.00	3
20	2004-01-01	12000.00	4
10	2004-01-04	6000.00	5
10	2004-01-01	5000.00	6
10	2004-01-05	5000.00	6
20	2004-01-05	4000.00	8
10	2004-01-02	3000.00	9
10	2004-01-03	2000.00	10

RANK in ASC Order

The RANK function normally defaults to a DESC order, but you can RANK in ASC order also. You do so by placing the keyword ASC inside the RANK function.

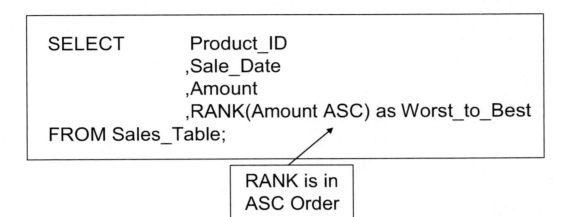

```
SELECT          Product_ID
                ,Sale_Date
                ,Amount
                ,RANK(Amount ASC) as Worst_to_Best
FROM Sales_Table;
```

RANK is in
ASC Order

10 Rows Returned

Product_ID	Sale_Date	Amount	Worst_to_Best
10	2004-01-03	2000.00	1
10	2004-01-02	3000.00	2
20	2004-01-05	4000.00	3
10	2004-01-05	5000.00	4
10	2004-01-01	5000.00	4
10	2004-01-04	6000.00	6
20	2004-01-01	12000.00	7
20	2004-01-02	13000.00	8
20	2004-01-03	15000.00	9
20	2004-01-04	20000.00	10

QUALIFY RANK is like a HAVING Statement

Like the aggregate functions, OLAP functions must read all required rows before performing their operation. Therefore, the **WHERE clause cannot be used**. Where the **aggregates use HAVING**, the **OLAP functions uses QUALIFY**. HAVING and QUALIFY are **considered equivalent**. The QUALIFY evaluates the result to determine which rows to return for OLAP and HAVING does the same for aggregates.

Our example below will only bring back the worst 5 product sales.

```
SELECT          Product_ID
                ,Sale_Date
                ,Amount
                ,RANK(Amount) as Best_Five
FROM Sales_Table
QUALIFY RANK(Amount) < 7;
```

Only the
RANKS of
the best 6

298

QUALIFY RANK with a GROUP BY

The QUALIFY RANK command allows only the best or worst number of rows to come back. Think of the QUALIFY RANK as a way of limiting the output rows just like a WHERE clause on a SELECT. The QUALIFY RANK can be used with the GROUP BY to reset the qualifying within the group.

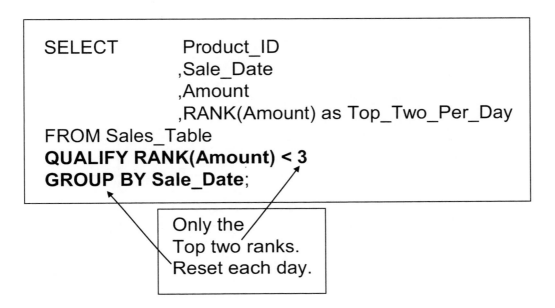

```
SELECT          Product_ID
                ,Sale_Date
                ,Amount
                ,RANK(Amount) as Top_Two_Per_Day
FROM Sales_Table
QUALIFY RANK(Amount) < 3
GROUP BY Sale_Date;
```

Only the
Top two ranks.
Reset each day.

10 Rows Returned

Product_ID	Sale_Date	Amount	Top_Two_Per_Day
20	2004-01-01	12000.00	1
10	2004-01-01	5000.00	2
20	**2004-01-02**	13000.00	1
10	**2004-01-02**	3000.00	2
20	2004-01-03	15000.00	1
10	2004-01-03	2000.00	2
20	2004-01-04	20000.00	1
10	2004-01-04	6000.00	2
10	2004-01-05	5000.00	1
20	2004-01-05	4000.00	2

New Day

QUANTILE Function

A Quantile is used to divide rows into a number of evenly distributed partitions. A percentile is actually a Quantile of 100. You can also have many other Quantiles such as quartiles (based on 4 partitions), tertiles (based on 3 partitions) and deciles (based on 10).

Here is an example of ranking our products in the Sales_Table from 1 to 10.

```
SELECT        Product_ID
              ,Sale_Date
              ,Amount
              ,QUANTILE(10, Amount) as Top_Ten_Partitions
FROM Sales_Table   ;
```

Divide all rows evenly
(by Amount) into Partitions of 10

10 Rows Returned

Product_ID	Sale_Date	Amount	Top_Ten_Partitions
10	2004-01-03	2000.00	0
10	2004-01-02	3000.00	1
20	2004-01-05	4000.00	2
10	2004-01-05	**5000.00**	**3**
10	2004-01-01	**5000.00**	**3**
10	2004-01-04	6000.00	**5**
20	2004-01-01	12000.00	6
20	2004-01-02	13000.00	7
20	2004-01-03	15000.00	8
20	2004-01-04	20000.00	9

QUANTILE Function Example using 5

Our next Quantile will break down our 10 row table into partitions of 5. It would appear that there would be two rows per partition, but that is not the case.

```
SELECT        Product_ID
              ,Sale_Date
              ,Amount
              ,QUANTILE(5, Amount) as Top_Five_Partitions
FROM Sales_Table   ;
```

Divide all rows evenly
(by Amount) into Partitions of 5

10 Rows Returned

Product_ID	Sale_Date	Amount	Top_Five_Partitions
10	2004-01-03	2000.00	0
10	2004-01-02	3000.00	0
20	2004-01-05	4000.00	1
10	2004-01-05	5000.00	1
10	2004-01-01	5000.00	1
10	2004-01-04	6000.00	2
20	2004-01-01	12000.00	3
20	2004-01-02	13000.00	3
20	2004-01-03	15000.00	4
20	2004-01-04	20000.00	4

QUANTILE Function using 100 (Percentile)

Our next Quantile will break down our 10 row table into partitions of 100.

```
SELECT        Product_ID
              ,Sale_Date
              ,Amount
              ,QUANTILE(100, Amount) as Top_100_Partitions
FROM Sales_Table   ;
```

Divide all rows evenly
(**by Amount**) into Partitions of 100

10 Rows Returned

Product_ID	Sale_Date	Amount	Top_100_Partitions
10	2004-01-03	2000.00	0
10	2004-01-02	3000.00	10
20	2004-01-05	4000.00	20
10	2004-01-05	5000.00	30
10	2004-01-01	5000.00	30
10	2004-01-04	6000.00	50
20	2004-01-01	12000.00	60
20	2004-01-02	13000.00	70
20	2004-01-03	15000.00	80
20	2004-01-04	20000.00	90

QUANTILE Function sorted ASC

Our next Quantile will break down our 10 row table into partitions of 10 and sort in ASCENDING order.

```
SELECT        Product_ID
              ,Sale_Date
              ,Amount
              ,QUANTILE(10, Amount asc) as Sorted_Ascending
FROM Sales_Table   ;
```

Bring back top amounts first

10 Rows Returned

Product_ID	Sale_Date	Amount	Sorted_Ascending
20	2004-01-04	20000.00	0
20	2004-01-03	15000.00	1
20	2004-01-02	13000.00	2
20	2004-01-01	12000.00	3
10	2004-01-04	6000.00	4
10	2004-01-01	5000.00	5
10	2004-01-05	5000.00	5
20	2004-01-05	4000.00	7
10	2004-01-02	3000.00	8
10	2004-01-03	2000.00	9

QUANTILE Function with Percentile (100)

Our next Quantile will break down our 10 row table into partitions of 100.

```
SELECT        Product_ID
              ,Sale_Date
              ,Amount
              ,QUANTILE(100, Amount) as Partitions_of_100
FROM Sales_Table   ;
```

The most common QUANTILE is the Percentile (100)

10 Rows Returned

Product_ID	Sale_Date	Amount	Partitions_of_100
10	2004-01-03	2000.00	0
10	2004-01-02	3000.00	10
20	2004-01-05	4000.00	20
10	2004-01-01	5000.00	30
10	2004-01-05	5000.00	30
10	2004-01-04	6000.00	50
20	2004-01-01	12000.00	60
20	2004-01-02	13000.00	70
20	2004-01-03	15000.00	80
20	2004-01-04	20000.00	90

Chapter 21 – OLAP

"Time is the coin of your life. It is the only coin you have, and only you can determine how it will be spent. Be careful lest you let other people spend it for you."

Carl Sandburg

Cumulative Sum (CSUM)

The Cumulative Sum (CSUM) function is an OLAP (On-Line Analytical Processing) function that provides a cumulative total for a column's numeric value. This running total provides users insight into a columns continued progression.

You can mix and match normal columns with OLAP functions. The key to understanding OLAP is in understanding that the first step is to sort the rows and then to perform the calculations. You never sort an OLAP with an ORDER BY statement. You always sort inside the OLAP function.

We will use the Sales_Table to provide us an example for calculations.

Sales_Table

Product_ID	Sale_Date	Amount
10	2004-01-01	5000.00
20	2004-01-01	12000.00
10	2004-01-02	3000.00
20	2004-01-02	13000.00
10	2004-01-03	2000.00
20	2004-01-03	15000.00
10	2004-01-04	6000.00
20	2004-01-04	20000.00
10	2004-01-05	5000.00
20	2004-01-05	4000.00

Cumulative Sum (CSUM)

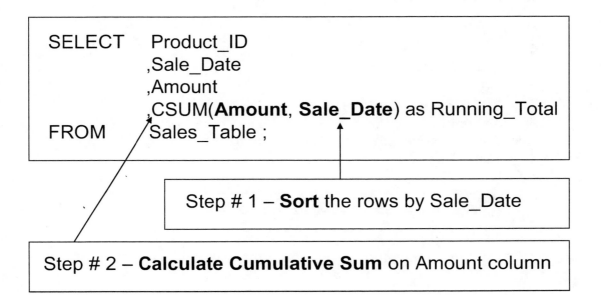

```
SELECT     Product_ID
           ,Sale_Date
           ,Amount
           ,CSUM(Amount, Sale_Date) as Running_Total
FROM       Sales_Table ;
```

Step # 1 – **Sort** the rows by Sale_Date

Step # 2 – **Calculate Cumulative Sum** on Amount column

10 Rows Returned

Product_ID	Sale_Date	Amount	Running_total
20	2004-01-01	**12000.00**	**12000.00**
10	2004-01-01	**5000.00**	**17000.00**
20	2004-01-02	13000.00	30000.00
10	2004-01-02	3000.00	33000.00
10	2004-01-03	2000.00	35000.00
20	2004-01-03	15000.00	50000.00
20	2004-01-04	20000.00	70000.00
10	2004-01-04	6000.00	76000.00
10	2004-01-05	5000.00	81000.00
20	2004-01-05	4000.00	85000.00

Step # 1
Sort by Sale_Date

Step # 2
Calculate CSUM

Cumulative Sum (CSUM) with Multiple Sort Keys

Our next example shows sorting by Sale_Date and then Product_ID.

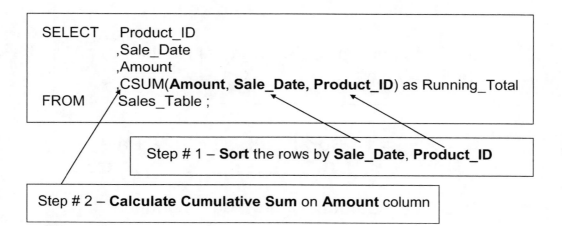

```
SELECT      Product_ID
            ,Sale_Date
            ,Amount
            ,CSUM(Amount, Sale_Date, Product_ID) as Running_Total
FROM        Sales_Table ;
```

Step # 1 – **Sort** the rows by **Sale_Date**, **Product_ID**

Step # 2 – **Calculate Cumulative Sum** on **Amount** column

10 Rows Returned

Product_ID	Sale_Date	Amount	Running_total
10	2004-01-01	5000.00	5000.00
20	2004-01-01	12000.00	17000.00
10	2004-01-02	3000.00	20000.00
20	2004-01-02	13000.00	33000.00
10	2004-01-03	2000.00	35000.00
20	2004-01-03	15000.00	50000.00
10	2004-01-04	6000.00	56000.00
20	2004-01-04	20000.00	76000.00
10	2004-01-05	5000.00	81000.00
20	2004-01-05	4000.00	85000.00

Cumulative Sum (CSUM) with GROUP BY

Our next example shows how to restart the CSUM calculation over with GROUP BY.

```
SELECT    Product_ID
          ,Sale_Date
          ,Amount
          ,CSUM(Amount, Sale_Date, Product_ID) as Running_Total
FROM      Sales_Table
GROUP BY Sale_Date;
```

Step # 1 – **Sort** the rows by **Sale_Date**, **Product_ID**

Step # 2 – **Calculate Cumulative Sum** on **Amount** column, but **start CSUM calculation over with each new sale date.**

10 Rows Returned

Product_ID	Sale_Date	Amount	Running_total
10	**2004-01-01**	**5000.00**	**5000.00**
20	**2004-01-01**	**12000.00**	**17000.00**
10	2004-01-**02**	**3000.00**	**3000.00**
20	2004-01-**02**	13000.00	16000.00
10	2004-01-03	2000.00	2000.00
20	2004-01-03	15000.00	17000.00
10	2004-01-04	6000.00	6000.00
20	2004-01-04	20000.00	26000.00
10	**2004-01-05**	**5000.00**	**5000.00**
20	**2004-01-05**	**4000.00**	**9000.00**

CSUM Resets on new date

Step # 1 - Sort by Sale_Date, Product_ID

Step # 2 - Calculate CSUM. Reset on each Sale_Date.

CSUM to Generate Sequential Numbers

CSUM can be used to generate sequential numbers starting with 1. Look at the example below.

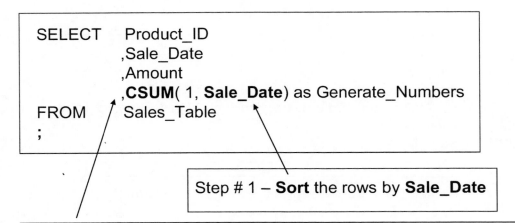

```
SELECT    Product_ID
          ,Sale_Date
          ,Amount
          ,CSUM( 1, Sale_Date) as Generate_Numbers
FROM      Sales_Table
;
```

Step # 1 – **Sort** the rows by **Sale_Date**

Step # 2 – **Starts with the number 1 and continues to add 1 thus resulting in sequential numbers.**

10 Rows Returned

Product_ID	Sale_Date	Amount	Generate_Numbers
10	2004-01-01	5000.00	1
20	2004-01-01	12000.00	2
20	2004-01-02	13000.00	3
10	2004-01-02	3000.00	4
20	2004-01-03	15000.00	5
10	2004-01-03	2000.00	6
10	2004-01-04	6000.00	7
20	2004-01-04	20000.00	8
10	2004-01-05	5000.00	9
20	2004-01-05	4000.00	10

CSUM using ANSI SUM OVER

Below is the **ANSI version** of a **CSUM**. **Unbound Preceding** can translate to **ALL Rows participate**. **Start at the beginning** and include the **first and last row**. The **OVER ()** can be translated to an **ORDER BY**.

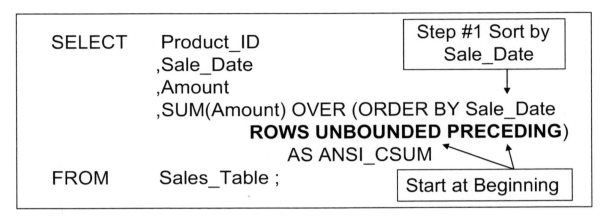

Product_ID	Sale_Date	Amount	ANSI_CSUM
10	2004-01-01	5000.00	5000.00
20	2004-01-01	12000.00	17000,00
20	2004-01-02	13000.00	30000.00
10	2004-01-02	3000.00	33000.00
20	2004-01-03	15000.00	48000.00
10	2004-01-03	2000.00	50000.00
10	2004-01-04	6000.00	56000.00
20	2004-01-04	20000.00	76000.00
10	2004-01-05	5000.00	81000.00
20	2004-01-05	4000.00	85000.00

10 Rows Returned

ANSI SUM OVER with PARTITION BY for Grouping

The ANSI SUM OVER syntax does not use the GROUP BY statement, but instead uses the term PARTITION BY to designate a grouping. One of the major advantages to the PARTITION is that each column that is a SUM ban be based on a different value. Whereas, there can only be a single GROUP BY in a SELECT.

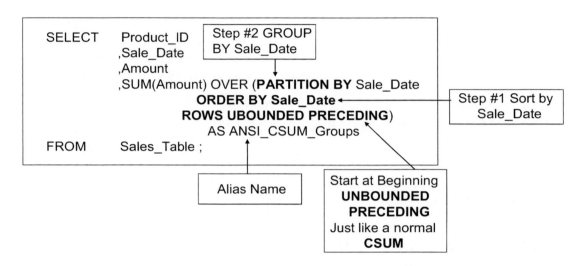

10 Rows Returned			
Product_ID	Sale_Date	Amount	ANSI_CSUM_Groups
10	2004-01-01	5000.00	5000.00
20	2004-01-01	12000.00	17000.00
10	2004-01-02	3000.00	3000.00
20	2004-01-02	13000.00	16000.00
20	2004-01-03	15000.00	15000.00
10	2004-01-03	2000.00	17000.00
20	2004-01-04	20000.00	20000.00
10	2004-01-04	6000.00	26000.00
20	2004-01-05	4000.00	4000.00
10	2004-01-05	5000.00	9000.00

Moving Sum (MSUM)

The Moving Sum (CSUM) function is an OLAP (On-Line Analytical Processing) function that provides a Moving total based on a window (number of rows) for a column's numeric value. This moving total provides user's insight into a columns continued progression in hopes that spikes and abnormalities will appear.

You can mix and match normal columns with OLAP functions. The key to understanding OLAP is in understanding that the first step is to sort the rows and then to perform the calculations. You never sort an OLAP with an ORDER BY statement. You always sort inside the OLAP function.

We will use the Sales_Table to provide us an example for calculations.

Sales_Table

Product_ID	Sale_Date	Amount
10	2004-01-01	5000.00
20	2004-01-01	12000.00
10	2004-01-02	3000.00
20	2004-01-02	13000.00
10	2004-01-03	2000.00
20	2004-01-03	15000.00
10	2004-01-04	6000.00
20	2004-01-04	20000.00
10	2004-01-05	5000.00
20	2004-01-05	4000.00

Moving Sum (MSUM)

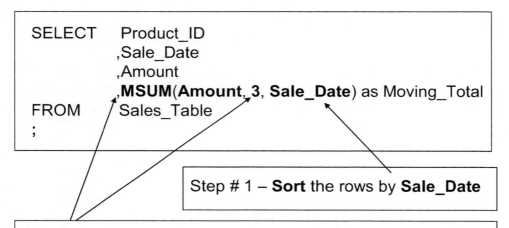

```
SELECT    Product_ID
          ,Sale_Date
          ,Amount
          ,MSUM(Amount, 3, Sale_Date) as Moving_Total
FROM      Sales_Table
;
```

Step # 1 – **Sort** the rows by **Sale_Date**

Step # 2 – **Calculate Moving Sum** on **Amount** column every **3 rows**. Calculation = Current Row plus two previous rows.

10 Rows Returned

Product_ID	Sale_Date	Amount	Moving_total
10	2004-01-01	5000.00	5000.00
20	2004-01-01	12000.00	17000.00
20	2004-01-02	13000.00	30000.00
10	2004-01-02	3000.00	28000.00
20	2004-01-03	15000.00	31000.00
10	2004-01-03	2000.00	20000.00
10	2004-01-04	6000.00	23000.00
20	2004-01-04	20000.00	28000.00
10	2004-01-05	5000.00	31000.00
20	2004-01-05	4000.00	29000.00

Moving Sum (MSUM) with Multiple Sort Keys

Our next example shows sorting by Sale_Date and then Product_ID.

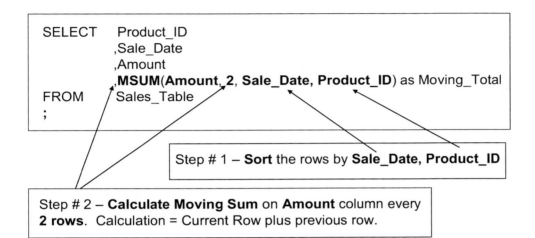

```
SELECT    Product_ID
          ,Sale_Date
          ,Amount
          ,MSUM(Amount, 2, Sale_Date, Product_ID) as Moving_Total
FROM      Sales_Table
;
```

Step # 1 – **Sort** the rows by **Sale_Date, Product_ID**

Step # 2 – **Calculate Moving Sum** on **Amount** column every **2 rows**. Calculation = Current Row plus previous row.

10 Rows Returned

Product_ID	Sale_Date	Amount	Moving_Total
10	2004-01-01	5000.00	5000.00
20	2004-01-01	12000.00	17000.00
10	2004-01-02	3000.00	15000.00
20	2004-01-02	13000.00	16000.00
10	2004-01-03	2000.00	15000.00
20	2004-01-03	15000.00	17000.00
10	2004-01-04	6000.00	21000.00
20	2004-01-04	20000.00	26000.00
10	2004-01-05	5000.00	25000.00
20	2004-01-05	4000.00	9000.00

Moving Sum (MSUM) with GROUP BY

Our next example shows how to restart the MCSUM calculation over with GROUP BY.

```
SELECT    Product_ID
          ,Sale_Date
          ,Amount
          ,MSUM(Amount, 2, Sale_Date, Product_ID) as Moving_Total
FROM      Sales_Table
GROUP BY Sale_Date;
```

Step # 1 – **Sort** the rows by **Sale_Date, Product_ID**

Step # 2 – **Calculate Moving Sum** on **Amount** column every **2 rows, but GROUP BY resets calculation**.

10 Rows Returned

Product_ID	Sale_Date	Amount	Moving_Total
10	2004-01-01	5000.00	5000.00
20	2004-01-01	12000.00	17000.00
10	**2004-01-02**	3000.00	3000.00
20	2004-01-02	13000.00	16000.00
10	2004-01-03	2000.00	2000.00
20	2004-01-03	15000.00	17000.00
10	2004-01-04	6000.00	6000.00
20	2004-01-04	20000.00	26000.00
10	2004-01-05	5000.00	5000.00
20	2004-01-05	4000.00	9000.00

Group By Resets

Moving Sum (MSUM) with ANSI SUM OVER

Our next example shows how to perform an MSUM with the ANSI SUM OVER syntax.

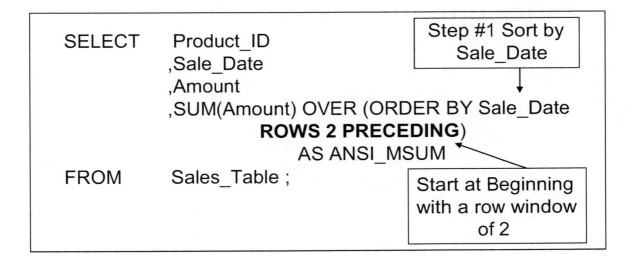

SELECT	Product_ID		Step #1 Sort by Sale_Date
	,Sale_Date		
	,Amount		
	,SUM(Amount) OVER (ORDER BY Sale_Date		
	ROWS 2 PRECEDING)		
	AS ANSI_MSUM		
FROM	Sales_Table ;		Start at Beginning with a row window of 2

10 Rows Returned

Product_ID	Sale_Date	Amount	ANSI_MSUM
10	2004-01-01	5000.00	5000.00
20	2004-01-01	12000.00	17000,00
20	2004-01-02	13000.00	30000.00
10	2004-01-02	3000.00	28000.00
20	2004-01-03	15000.00	31000.00
10	2004-01-03	2000.00	20000.00
10	2004-01-04	6000.00	23000.00
20	2004-01-04	20000.00	28000.00
10	2004-01-05	5000.00	31000.00
20	2004-01-05	4000.00	29000.00

MSUM with ANSI SUM OVER and PARTITION BY for Grouping

Our next example shows how to perform an MSUM with the ANSI SUM OVER syntax with the PARTITION BY statement for grouping. The **ANSI syntax does not use GROUP BY**, but instead uses **PARTITION BY**.

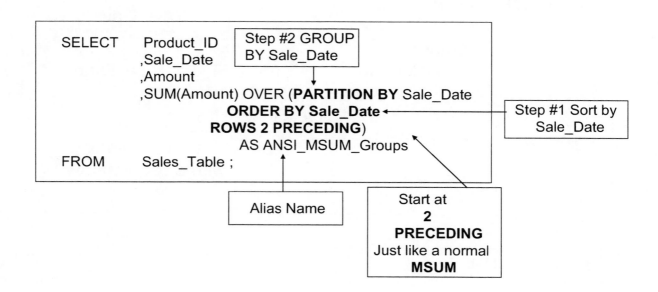

Product_ID	Sale_Date	Amount	ANSI_MSUM_Groups
10	2004-01-01	5000.00	5000.00
20	2004-01-01	12000.00	17000.00
10	2004-01-02	3000.00	3000.00
20	2004-01-02	13000.00	16000.00
20	2004-01-03	15000.00	15000.00
10	2004-01-03	2000.00	17000.00
20	2004-01-04	20000.00	20000.00
10	2004-01-04	6000.00	26000.00
20	2004-01-05	4000.00	4000.00
10	2004-01-05	5000.00	9000.00

10 Rows Returned

Moving Average (MAVG)

The Moving Average (MAVG) function is an OLAP (On-Line Analytical Processing) function that provides a Moving Average based on a window (number of rows) for a column's numeric value. This moving total provides user's insight into a columns continued progression in hopes that spikes and abnormalities will appear.

You can mix and match normal columns with OLAP functions. The key to understanding OLAP is in understanding that the first step is to sort the rows and then to perform the calculations. You never sort an OLAP with an ORDER BY statement. You always sort inside the OLAP function.

We will use the Sales_Table to provide us an example for calculations.

Sales_Table

Product_ID	Sale_Date	Amount
10	2004-01-01	5000.00
20	2004-01-01	12000.00
10	2004-01-02	3000.00
20	2004-01-02	13000.00
10	2004-01-03	2000.00
20	2004-01-03	15000.00
10	2004-01-04	6000.00
20	2004-01-04	20000.00
10	2004-01-05	5000.00
20	2004-01-05	4000.00

Moving Average (MAVG) Cont.

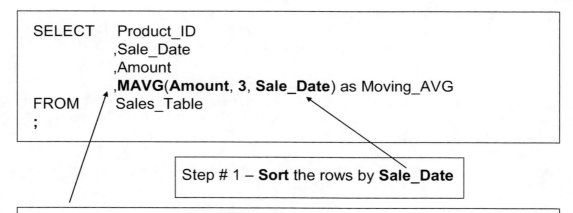

```
SELECT    Product_ID
          ,Sale_Date
          ,Amount
          ,MAVG(Amount, 3, Sale_Date) as Moving_AVG
FROM      Sales_Table
;
```

Step # 1 – **Sort** the rows by **Sale_Date**

Step # 2 – **Calculate Moving AVG** on **Amount** column every **3 rows**.
Calculation = Current Row + 2 previous rows.

10 Rows Returned

Product_ID	Sale_Date	Amount	Moving_AVG
10	2004-01-01	5000.00	5000.00
20	2004-01-01	12000.00	8500.00
20	2004-01-02	13000.00	10000.00
10	2004-01-02	3000.00	9333.00
20	2004-01-03	15000.00	10333.00
10	2004-01-03	2000.00	6667.00
10	2004-01-04	6000.00	7667.00
20	2004-01-04	20000.00	93330.00
10	2004-01-05	5000.00	10333.00
20	2004-01-05	4000.00	9667.00

Moving Average (MAVG) with Multiple Sort Keys

Our next example shows sorting by Sale_Date and then Product_ID.

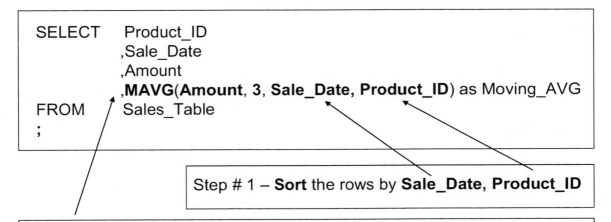

```
SELECT    Product_ID
          ,Sale_Date
          ,Amount
          ,MAVG(Amount, 3, Sale_Date, Product_ID) as Moving_AVG
FROM      Sales_Table
;
```

Step # 1 – **Sort** the rows by **Sale_Date, Product_ID**

Step # 2 – **Calculate Moving AVG** on **Amount** column every **3 rows**.
Calculation = Current Row + 2 previous rows.

10 Rows Returned

Product_ID	Sale_Date	Amount	Moving_AVG
10	2004-01-01	5000.00	5000.00
20	2004-01-01	12000.00	8500.00
10	2004-01-02	3000.00	7500.00
20	2004-01-02	13000.00	8000.00
10	2004-01-03	2000.00	7500.00
20	2004-01-03	15000.00	8500.00
10	2004-01-04	6000.00	10500.00
20	2004-01-04	20000.00	13000.00
10	2004-01-05	5000.00	12500.00
20	2004-01-05	4000.00	4500.00

Moving Average (MAVG) with GROUP BY

Our next example shows how to restart the MAVG calculation over with GROUP BY.

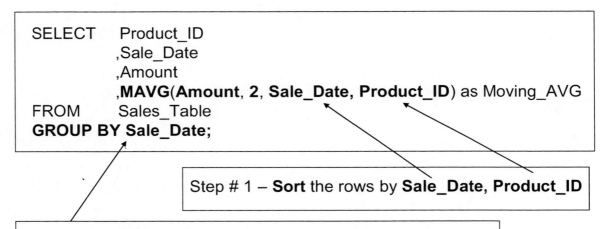

```
SELECT    Product_ID
          ,Sale_Date
          ,Amount
          ,MAVG(Amount, 2, Sale_Date, Product_ID) as Moving_AVG
FROM      Sales_Table
GROUP BY Sale_Date;
```

Step # 1 – **Sort** the rows by **Sale_Date, Product_ID**

Step # 2 – **Calculate Moving AVG** on **Amount** column every **2 rows, but GROUP BY resets calculation.**

10 Rows Returned

Product_ID	Sale_Date	Amount	Moving_AVG
10	2004-01-01	5000.00	5000.00
20	2004-01-01	12000.00	8500.00
10	**2004-01-02**	3000.00	3000.00
20	2004-01-02	13000.00	8000.00
10	2004-01-03	2000.00	2000.00
20	2004-01-03	15000.00	8500.00
10	2004-01-04	6000.00	6000.00
20	2004-01-04	20000.00	13000.00
10	2004-01-05	5000.00	5000.00
20	2004-01-05	4000.00	4500.00

Group By Resets

MAVG with ANSI AVG OVER

Our next example shows how to get a Moving Average using the ANSI syntax AVG OVER. Our example is the same thing as doing a MAVG.

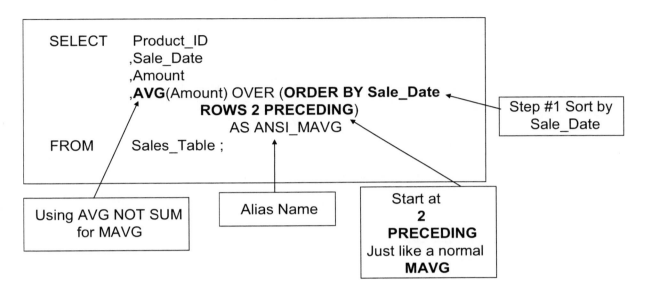

Product_ID	Sale_Date	Amount	ANSI_MAVG
10	2004-01-01	5000.00	5000.00
20	2004-01-01	12000.00	8500.00
20	2004-01-02	13000.00	10000.00
10	2004-01-02	3000.00	9333.00
20	2004-01-03	15000.00	10333.00
10	2004-01-03	2000.00	6667.00
10	2004-01-04	6000.00	7667.00
20	2004-01-04	20000.00	9333.00
10	2004-01-05	5000.00	10333.00
20	2004-01-05	4000.00	9667.00

10 Rows Returned

MAVG with ANSI AVG OVER and PARTITION BY for Grouping

Our next example shows how to get a Moving Average using the ANSI syntax AVG OVER and to PARTITION BY which is the ANSI way for grouping. Our example is the same thing as doing a MAVG with a GROUP BY on Product_ID.

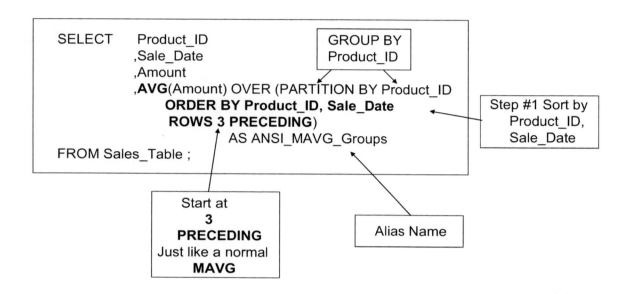

```
SELECT    Product_ID
         ,Sale_Date
         ,Amount
         ,AVG(Amount) OVER (PARTITION BY Product_ID
            ORDER BY Product_ID, Sale_Date
            ROWS 3 PRECEDING)
                AS ANSI_MAVG_Groups
FROM Sales_Table ;
```

GROUP BY Product_ID

Step #1 Sort by Product_ID, Sale_Date

Start at **3 PRECEDING** Just like a normal **MAVG**

Alias Name

10 Rows Returned

Product_ID	Sale_Date	Amount	ANSI_MAVG_Groups
10	2004-01-01	5000.00	5000.00
10	2004-01-02	3000.00	4000.00
10	2004-01-03	2000.00	3333.00
10	2004-01-04	6000.00	4000.00
10	2004-01-05	5000.00	4000.00
20	2004-01-01	12000.00	12000.00
20	2004-01-02	13000.00	12500.00
20	2004-01-03	15000.00	13333.00
20	2004-01-04	20000.00	15000.00
20	2004-01-05	4000.00	13000.00

Rows 3 Preceding

RESETS

Moving Difference (MDIFF)

The Moving Difference (MDIFF) function is an OLAP (On-Line Analytical Processing) function that provides a Moving Difference between two rows, based on a window (number of rows) for a column's numeric value. This moving difference provides user's insight into a columns continued differences in hopes that spikes and abnormalities will appear.

You can mix and match normal columns with OLAP functions. The key to understanding OLAP is in understanding that the first step is to sort the rows and then to perform the calculations. You never sort an OLAP with an ORDER BY statement. You always sort inside the OLAP function.

We will use the Sales_Table to provide us an example for calculations.

Sales_Table

Product_ID	Sale_Date	Amount
10	2004-01-01	5000.00
20	2004-01-01	12000.00
10	2004-01-02	3000.00
20	2004-01-02	13000.00
10	2004-01-03	2000.00
20	2004-01-03	15000.00
10	2004-01-04	6000.00
20	2004-01-04	20000.00
10	2004-01-05	5000.00
20	2004-01-05	4000.00

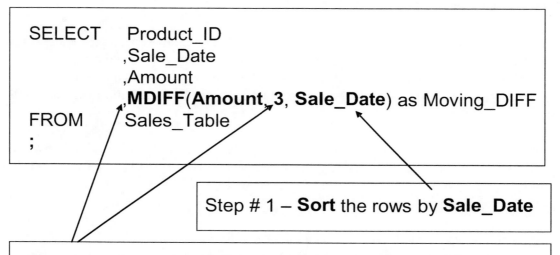

```
SELECT     Product_ID
           ,Sale_Date
           ,Amount
           ,MDIFF(Amount, 3, Sale_Date) as Moving_DIFF
FROM       Sales_Table
;
```

Step # 1 – **Sort** the rows by **Sale_Date**

Step # 2 – **Calculate Moving DIFF** on **Amount** column every **3 rows**. Calculation = Current Row and 3 rows back.

10 Rows Returned

Product_ID	Sale_Date	Amount	Moving_Diff
10	2004-01-01	5000.00	?
20	2004-01-01	12000.00	?
20	2004-01-02	13000.00	?
10	2004-01-02	3000.00	-2000.00
20	2004-01-03	15000.00	3000.00
10	2004-01-03	2000.00	-11000.00
10	2004-01-04	6000.00	3000.00
20	2004-01-04	20000.00	5000.00
10	2004-01-05	5000.00	3000.00
20	2004-01-05	4000.00	-2000.00

Moving Difference (MDIFF) with Multiple Sort Keys

Our next example shows sorting by Sale_Date and then Product_ID.

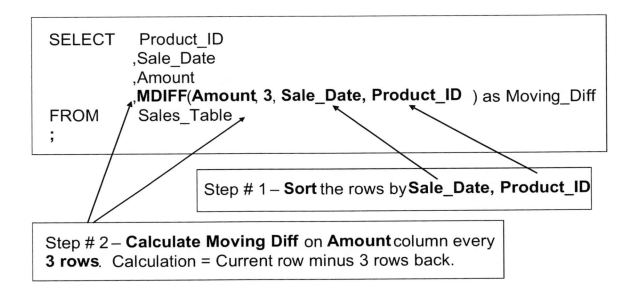

```
SELECT    Product_ID
         ,Sale_Date
         ,Amount
         ,MDIFF(Amount, 3, Sale_Date, Product_ID  ) as Moving_Diff
FROM      Sales_Table
;
```

Step # 1 – **Sort** the rows by **Sale_Date, Product_ID**

Step # 2 – **Calculate Moving Diff** on **Amount** column every
3 rows. Calculation = Current row minus 3 rows back.

10 Rows Returned

Product_ID	Sale_Date	Amount	Moving_Diff
10	2004-01-01	5000.00	?
20	2004-01-01	12000.00	?
10	2004-01-02	3000.00	?
20	2004-01-02	13000.00	8000.00
10	2004-01-03	2000.00	-10000.00
20	2004-01-03	15000.00	12000.00
10	2004-01-04	6000.00	-7000.00
20	2004-01-04	20000.00	18000.00
10	2004-01-05	5000.00	-10000.00
20	2004-01-05	4000.00	-2000.00

Moving Difference (MDIFF) with GROUP BY

Our next example shows how to restart the MDIFF calculation over with GROUP BY.

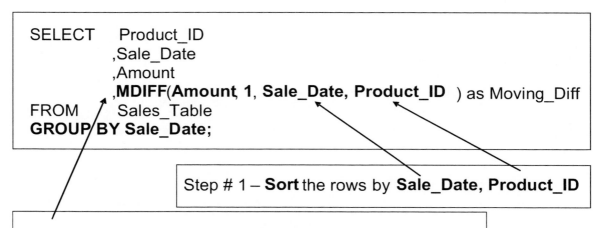

```
SELECT    Product_ID
          ,Sale_Date
          ,Amount
          ,MDIFF(Amount, 1, Sale_Date, Product_ID ) as Moving_Diff
FROM      Sales_Table
GROUP BY Sale_Date;
```

Step # 1 – **Sort** the rows by **Sale_Date, Product_ID**

Step # 2 – **Calculate Moving Diff** on **Amount** column every **1 row** . Calculation = Current row minus 1 row back.
GROUP BY Sale_Date

10 Rows Returned

Product_ID	Sale_Date	Amount	Moving_Diff
10	2004-01-01	5000.00	?
20	2004-01-01	12000.00	7000.00
10	2004-01-02	3000.00	?
20	2004-01-02	13000.00	10000.00
10	2004-01-03	2000.00	?
20	2004-01-03	15000.00	13000.00
10	2004-01-04	6000.00	?
20	2004-01-04	20000.00	14000.00
10	2004-01-05	5000.00	?
20	2004-01-05	4000.00	-1000.00

Chapter 22 – New V2R5.1 and V2R6 Features

"We owe almost all our knowledge not to those who have agreed, but to those who have differed."

G.C. Colton

New GROUP BY specifications

Teradata has some new and exciting OLAP features with V2R5.1. They are explained in the following pages with syntax and examples. We will use our Store_Table in the examples.

GROUP BY <ordinary-grouping-sets>
      | {GROUPING SETS <grouping-sets-specification> | <empty-grouping-set>}
      | CUBE <cube-list>
      | ROLLUP <rollup-list>

Extended GROUP BY operations:
GROUPING SETS
Empty Set
CUBE
ROLLUP

The following data is used to demonstrate the functionality of these new grouping operators:

Store_Table

Store_ID	Region_Num	District_Num	Product_ID	Sale_Date	Sales_Amt
Dayton-1	100	1	1000	10-01-2004	1200.00
Dayton-1	100	1	1000	10-02-2004	800.00
Dayton-1	100	1	2000	10-01-2004	1000.00
Dayton-1	100	1	1000	10-02-2004	900.00
Dayton-2	100	1	1000	10-01-2004	400.00
Dayton-2	100	1	1000	10-02-2004	300.00
Dayton-2	100	1	2000	10-01-2004	200.00
Dayton-2	100	1	2000	10-02-2004	600.00
Lansing-1	200	1	1000	10-01-2004	1000.00
Lansing-1	200	1	1000	10-01-2004	950.00
Lansing-1	200	1	1000	10-01-2004	560.00
Lansing-1	200	1	1000	10-01-2004	425.00

Original GROUP BY Example

Store_Table

Store_ID	Region_Num	District_Num	Product_ID	Sale_Date	Sales_Amt
Dayton-1	100	1	1000	10-01-2004	1200.00
Dayton-1	100	1	1000	10-02-2004	800.00
Dayton-1	100	1	2000	10-01-2004	1000.00
Dayton-1	100	1	1000	10-02-2004	900.00
Dayton-2	100	1	1000	10-01-2004	400.00
Dayton-2	100	1	1000	10-02-2004	300.00
Dayton-2	100	1	2000	10-01-2004	200.00
Dayton-2	100	1	2000	10-02-2004	600.00
Lansing-1	200	1	1000	10-01-2004	1000.00
Lansing-1	200	1	1000	10-01-2004	950.00
Lansing-1	200	1	1000	10-01-2004	560.00
Lansing-1	200	1	1000	10-01-2004	425.00

```
SELECT   Region_Num
        ,District_Num
        ,Store_ID
        ,SUM(sales_amt) AS Sales_Amount
From Store_Table
GROUP BY Store_ID, Region_Num, District_Num
ORDER 1,2,3;
```

```
3 rows returned

Region_Num      District_Num      Store_ID    Sales_Amount
_____      _____      _____    _____

       100                 1      Dayton-1         3900.00
       100                 1      Dayton-2         1500.00
       200                 1      Lansing-1        2925.00
```

GROUPING SETS

Syntax:

GROUP BY GROUPING SETS (<columnname> [, <columnname> …] [( )])

GROUP BY GROUPING SETS ((<columnname>, <columnname> [, ( )])
                 [, (<columnname>, <columnname>) …)

GROUP BY GROUPING SETS (<columnname> [, <columnname> …])
    ,GROUPING SETS ((<columnname>, <columnname>)
                [, (<columnname>, <columnname>) …)

```
SELECT   Store_ID
        ,Region_Num
        ,District_Num
        ,SUM(sales_amt) AS Sales_Amount
From Store_Table
GROUP BY GROUPING SETS (Region_Num, District_Num, Store_ID)
        ,GROUPING SETS (Region_Num ())
        ,GROUPING SETS (Region_Num, District_Num, ());
```

8 rows returned

Region_Num	District_Num	Store_ID	Sales_Amount
200	1	Lansing-1	2925.00
200	1	?	2925.00
200	?	?	2925.00
100	1	Dayton-2	1500.00
100	1	Dayton-1	3900.00
100	1	?	5400.00
100	?	?	5400.00
?	?	?	8325.00

CUBE

Syntax:

GROUP BY **CUBE (** <columnname> [, <columnname> …] [( )] **)**

GROUP BY **CUBE ((** <columnname>, <columnname> [, ( )] **)**
                [, (<columnname>, <columnname>) … **)**

GROUP BY **CUBE (** <columnname> [, <columnname> …] **)**
      ,CUBE ((<columnname>, <columnname>)
                [, (<columnname>, <columnname>) … **)**

```
SELECT   Region_Num
         ,District_Num
         ,Store_ID
         ,SUM(sales_amt) AS Sales_Amount
From Store_Table
GROUP BY CUBE (Region_Num, District_Num, Store_ID)
         ,CUBE (Region_Num) ;
```

8 rows returned

Region_Num	District_Num	Store_ID	Sales_Amount
200	1	Lansing-1	2925.00
200	1	?	2925.00
200	?	?	2925.00
100	1	Dayton-2	1500.00
100	1	Dayton-1	3900.00
100	1	?	5400.00
100	?	?	5400.00
?	?	?	8325.00

ROLLUP

Syntax:

GROUP BY **ROLLUP (** <columnname> [, <columnname> …] **)**

GROUP BY **ROLLUP (** (<columnname>, <columnname>])

```
SELECT   Store_ID
         ,Region_Num
         ,District_Num
         ,SUM(sales_amt) AS Sales_Amount
From Store_Table
GROUP BY ROLLUP (Store_ID, Region_Num, District_Num) ;
```

8 rows returned

Region_Num	District_Num	Store_ID	Sales_Amount
200	1	Lansing-1	2925.00
200	1	?	2925.00
200	?	?	2925.00
100	1	Dayton-2	1500.00
100	1	Dayton-1	3900.00
100	1	?	5400.00
100	?	?	5400.00
?	?	?	8325.00

QUEUE Tables

Beginning in release V2R6 Teradata offers the ability to use a QUEUE table as a table level option. It is defined like a normal table, however a queue table is a table that works on a First In First Out (FIFO) principle. The biggest difference is that the rows are stored and retrieved as a time stamp arrangement. The reason that the first column must be defined as a Queue Insertion Time Stamp is so Teradata can process each row only once. It does so by deleting rows after they are retrieved. Another important factor to notice is that a Queue Table can not have the Queue Insertion Time Stamp (QTIS) column as a unique column. This means the QTIS column can't be defined as an UPI, Primary Key, Unique Secondary Index (USI) or an Identity column.

The first column of a queue table must be a Queue Insertion Time Stamp (QTIS) defined as:

<QTIS-columnname> TIMESTAMP(6) NOT NULL DEFAULT CURRENT_TIMESTAMP

A QITS column *cannot* be defined as any of the following:
• UNIQUE (can be a NUPI but not advised)
• PRIMARY KEY
• Unique secondary index
• Identity column

The most significance of a QUEUE table is that as rows are retrieved, they are automatically deleted to guarantee each row will only be processed once. It is an event driven data storage area. The use of SELECT and CONSUME TOP 1 will guarantee the delivery of only the first row only.

FROM TABLE UDF Tables

The FROM TABLE UDF Table is also introduced in release V2R6 of Teradata. It facilitates the use of a User Defined Function (UDF) to create and return a row to a FROM in an SQL request.

The table and column definition is created in a user defined function. The TABLE option can only appear once in a FROM and cannot be part of a join operation.

Syntax for using FROM TABLE:

FROM TABLE (<UDF-function-name> (<parameter-list>))

The expression list is set up to match with the RETURNS TABLE clause of the CREATE FUNCTION statement. Therefore the number of expressions must match those in the UDF, they are assigned on a positional basis from first to last and they override the names used in the UDF. If the expression list is omitted, the names come from the UDF.

Since this book does not address C or C++ programming there is not an example of this capability. It is here to serve as an introduction only.

Chapter 23 – Miscellaneous

"Violence is a tool of the ignorant."

Flip Wilson

Single Row MERGE INTO Command

The MERGE-INTO feature is similar to the ANSI MERGE statement limited to a single-row source table. This is similar to the UPSERT in an UPDATE statement, but more flexible in its syntax presentation and it has considerable subquery capabilities.

You will have a source and a target table. If the two have a matching row found in the WHERE clause then an UPDATE will occur. If the two do not find a match from the WHERE clause then an INSERT is performed.

Department_Table

Dept_no	Dept_name	Mgr_no	Budget
10	**Sales**	**2**	**266000**
20	**Marketing**	**4**	**356000**
30	HR	6	200000
40	Development	9	20000
50	IT	10	25000000

Department_Table1

Dept_no	Dept_name	Mgr_no	Budget
10	**Sales**	**2**	**266000**

Only One Row In Table

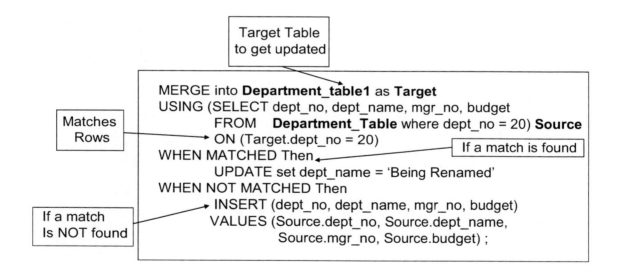

Target Table to get updated

Matches Rows

If a match is found

If a match Is NOT found

```
MERGE into Department_table1 as Target
USING (SELECT dept_no, dept_name, mgr_no, budget
       FROM   Department_Table where dept_no = 20) Source
   ON (Target.dept_no = 20)
WHEN MATCHED Then
       UPDATE set dept_name = 'Being Renamed'
WHEN NOT MATCHED Then
       INSERT (dept_no, dept_name, mgr_no, budget)
       VALUES (Source.dept_no, Source.dept_name,
               Source.mgr_no, Source.budget) ;
```

Department_Table

Dept_no	Dept_name	Mgr_no	Budget
10	**Sales**	**2**	**266000**
20	**Marketing**	**4**	**356000**
30	HR	6	200000
40	Development	9	20000
50	IT	10	25000000

Department_Table1

Dept_no	Dept_name	Mgr_no	Budget
10	**Sales**	**2**	**266000**
20	**Marketing**	**4**	**356000**

Now there are two rows

Compression

Compression is fantastic! Did you know that you could now compress up to **255 distinct values (plus NULLs)** per fixed **width column**? You can. This can significantly enhance system costs and performance. The **compressed columns** can **only be done** on **Character data types**.

. You can save quite a bit of space.

- Up to 255 columns (plus NULL) can be compressed per column.

- Only fixed-width columns can be compressed. No VarChar capabilities yet.

- Primary Index columns can't be compressed.

- Alter table does not support compression on existing columns at this time.

- Compression supported on data types INTEGER, BYTEINT, SMALLINT, DATE, DOUBLE, DECIMAL(1, 2, 4, 8), CHAR(N) (N<256), FLOAT/REAL(8).

- Compression is NOT supported on VARCHAR, VARBYTE, VARGRAPHIC, TIME, TIMESTAMP, and INTERVAL.

If you want to improve overall Teradata system **performance** we suggest **four areas.**

- **Multi-Value compression** – Saves space and adds speed
- **Partition Primary Index** – Adds speed
- **Multi-statement requests** – Lowers overhead
- **Hire a CoffingDW Consultant** – Saves money and adds tremendous knowledge

Implementing Compression

You can implement compression when you create the table with the CREATE statement or in some cases the ALTER table statement. Here is the Syntax:

```
CREATE TABLE Employee
(
Employee_No      Integer
,Dept            Integer
,First_Name      Varchar(20)
,Last_Name       Char(20) COMPRESS
                 ('Smith', 'Wilson',
                  'Davis', 'Jones')
) Unique Primary Index(Employee_No)
;
```

The ALTER statement can't compress existing columns. It can add new columns and compress them.

```
ALTER TABLE Employee
  ADD Department_Name   Char(20)
       COMPRESS
          ('Sales', 'Marketing',
           'Campaigns', 'HR')
;
```

How Compression Works

Compression works in conjunction with both the Table Header and each data row that has compressed columns. When you create a table, a table header is created on each AMP. It will hold a grid of the compressed columns and the compressed value options. Then, when a row holds a compressed value it will flip a bit in the row overhead to indicate the value to represent.

```
CREATE TABLE Employee
(
Employee_No      Integer
,Dept            Integer
,First_Name      Varchar(20)
,Last_Name       Char(20) COMPRESS
                 ('Smith', 'Wilson',
                  'Davis', 'Jones')
) Unique Primary Index(Employee_No)
;
```

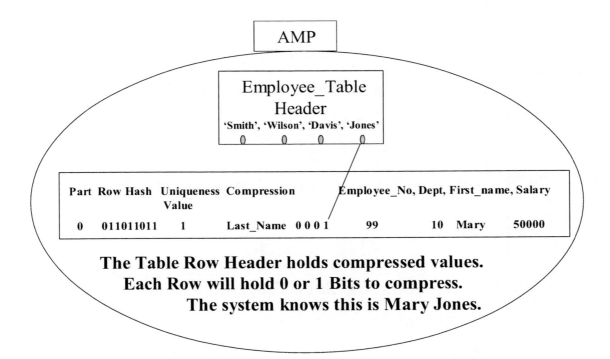

The Table Row Header holds compressed values.
Each Row will hold 0 or 1 Bits to compress.
The system knows this is Mary Jones.

Teradata and ANSI Mode

Teradata was originally written to be compatible with DB/2. As Teradata evolved it was able to include connections to network attached systems. Another evolution of Teradata is the inclusion of ANSI (American National Standards Institute) standards in its functionality and the format of its SQL commands. Teradata works in two modes to take advantage of the functionality of either Teradata or ANSI modes. Here is a summary of the differences of both modes:

18) What differences are between ANSI and Teradata must be taken into consideration? (Choose Three)

Teradata Mode:
- Data compares are **NOT** case specific
- **Allows truncation** of displayed data
- Sets the CREATE Table default to **SET Table**
- **A Transaction is implicit by nature**

ANSI Mode:
- Data compares are **case specific**
- **Forbids truncation** of display data
- CREATE Table default to **Multiset**
- **All Transactions** are **explicit** and require a **COMMIT Work** to End the Transaction

Teradata Mode
Comparisons are **NOT Case Specific**
Allows truncation of display data
CREATE TABLE defaults to **SET**
Each Transaction is **implicit** automatically

ANSI Mode
Comparisons **are Case Specific**
NO truncation of display data
CREATE TABLE defaults to MULTISET
Transactions are explicit and need COMMIT

Teradata Mode Transactions (Called BTET)

Teradata mode considers every **SQL statement as a stand-alone transaction**. This means that if the outcome of the statements is successful, the work is committed to the database. When multiple tables are being updated, multiple SQL commands must be used. Multiple statements can be placed into a single transaction in **3 ways**:

- Place all the **SQL inside a Macro** (Macros are considered one transaction)
- Submit the SQL using BTEQ and place the **semi-colons at the beginning of the next line**
- Use a **BTET** statement to Begin Transaction (**BT**) and End Transaction (**ET**)

When **multiple statements** are placed into a **single transaction** in **Teradata Mode an error** with any statement causes **all of the SQL statements to ROLLBACK** and then all locks are released.

Teradata mode allows 3 types of transactions and they are Implicit, Explicit, and Two-phase commit (2PC).

Below is an example of an **implicit transaction**. An **implicit transaction** is a transaction that **does not begin and end with BT/ET**. **DDL statements** are not valid in an **implicit multi-statement transaction**.

In BTEQ the semi-colon at the beginning of the line makes this one transaction	UPDATE Employee_Table SET Salary = Salary * 1.1 ; UPDATE Department_Table SET Dept_Name = 'Sales' WHERE Dept_No = 10;	In Teradata Mode If any statement fails all statements In the transaction are rolled back!

Below is an example of an **Explicit Transaction**. An **Explicit Transaction** is a transaction that **does begin and end with BT/ET**. When **multiple statements** are included in an **explicit transaction**, you can only specify a **DDL statement** if it is the **last statement**.

Teradata Mode is Called BTET because you can utilize BT to Begin Transaction & ET to End Transaction	BT; UPDATE Employee_Table SET Salary = Salary * 1.1; UPDATE Department_Table SET Dept_Name = 'Sales' WHERE Dept_No = 10; ET;	In Teradata Mode If any statement fails all statements In the transaction are rolled back!

ANSI Mode Transactions

In ANSI Mode the first SQL statement initiates a transaction. The transaction is terminated with a COMMIT, ROLLBACK or ABORT statement, or if a failure occurs. ANSI Mode allows you to submit as many SQL statements as you want and when you want to COMMIT them to the database you use the COMMIT WORK statement. You must have a COMMIT explicitly stated as the last statement of a transaction in order for the transaction to terminate with success.

In **ANSI Mode** if one of the **SQL statements fail** then **only the failed statement is rolled back**. There is **one exception**. If the statement that fails is **a DDL statement** then **all SQL statements in the transaction are rolled back**.

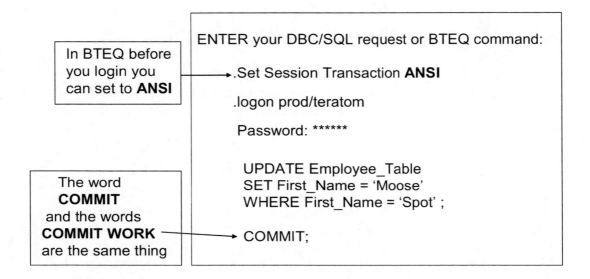

Teradata Mode	ANSI Mode
DELETE FROM Pretend_Table ALL;	DELETE FROM Pretend_Table ALL; COMMIT ;

How you delete Pretend_Table in Teradata Mode and in ANSI mode.

The word **ALL** in the delete is **optional**.

SQRT Function

Below are calculations that show how Teradata utilizes the SQUARE ROOT function.

```
SEL sqrt (16) as sixteen
    ,sqrt (15) as fifteen
    ,sqrt (14) as fourteen
    ,sqrt (15) as twentyfive
```

One Row Returned

Sixteen	Fifteen	Fourteen	Twentyfive
4.00	3.87	3.74	5.00

```
SEL sqrt (-16) as neg_sixteen
```

ERROR - Bad Argument for SQRT Function

INSERT/SELECT on two exact tables.

An INSERT/SELECT is used to insert data from one Teradata table to another Teradata table. This works only if both tables are on the same Teradata system. The command is extremely simple if both tables are defined the same (same columns, same data types in the same order).

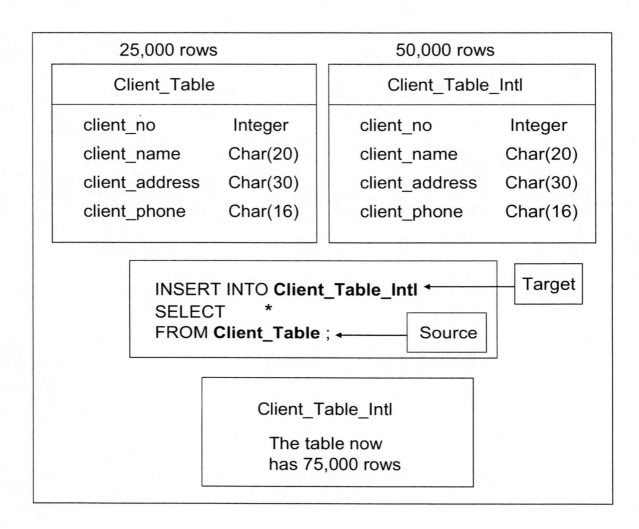

INSERT/SELECT on Tables that Don't Match

An INSERT/SELECT is used to insert data from one Teradata table to another Teradata table. This works only if both tables are on the same Teradata system. The example below will explain that you can't merely say SELECT * because the columns don't match up. You need to **SELECT the columns you want** in the **proper order** of the **target table**.

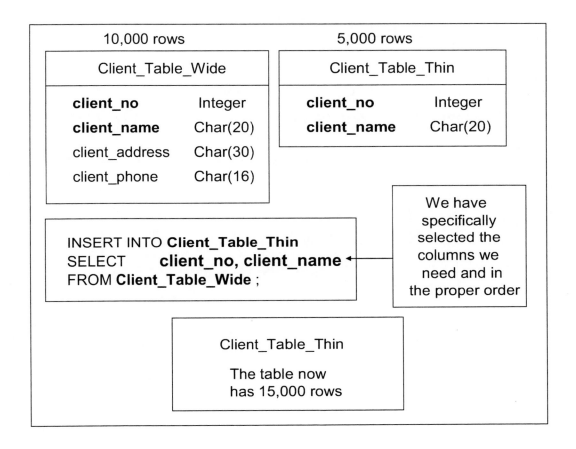

Triggers

Even Winnie the Pooh knows Triggers are wonderful things! A Trigger is built to perform an action when an **INSERT**, **UPDATE**, **DELETE** or **INSERT/SELECT** is performed on a table. You **can't** have a **SELECT fire a Trigger**. Once a Trigger is built it fires automatically without any user intervention. Triggers and any subsequent Triggers constitute a single transaction so if the trigger fails the transaction fails. Triggers are a new form of object in the Teradata database and have a type of "G".

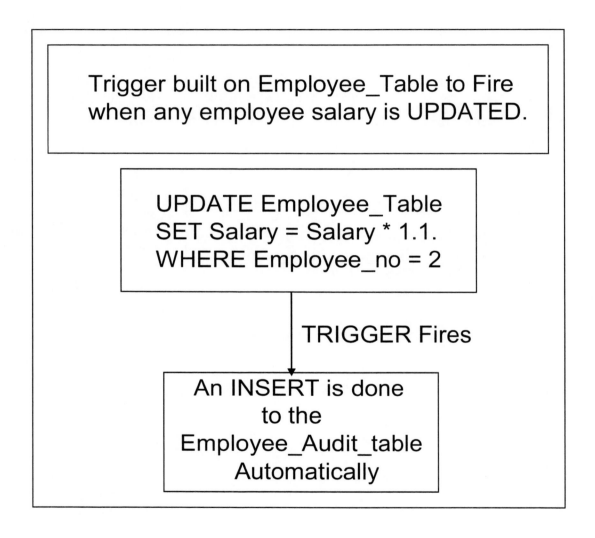

Trigger built on Employee_Table to Fire when any employee salary is UPDATED.

UPDATE Employee_Table
SET Salary = Salary * 1.1.
WHERE Employee_no = 2

TRIGGER Fires

An INSERT is done
to the
Employee_Audit_table
Automatically

Row Triggers or Statement Triggers

A Trigger fires when an action takes place on a Triggered Table. You can demand that the Trigger fires for every row that is updated (Row Triggers) or you can demand that the Trigger only fires for each UPDATE Statement (Statement Triggers). For example sake lets say we put a trigger on a table with 100 rows. If we then updated every row and used a Row Trigger we would have 100 fired Triggers. If we had used a Statement Trigger we would have only fired the Trigger once.

Row Trigger Syntax

CREATE TRIGGER   <Trigger-name>
<u>TRIGGER ACTION</u> {BEFORE | AFTER}
[ORDER <sequence-number>]
<u>TRIGGERING ACTION</u> > {INSERT | UPDATE | DELETE | INSERT/SELECT}
[OF (<column-name>, …)]   ON   <subject-table>
REFERENCING   **OLD AS** <before-imaged-row>
NEW AS <after-image-row>
FOR EACH ROW
[WHEN (*optional condition*)]
(<u>TRIGGERED ACTION</u> { **INSERT | INSERT/SELECT**} ;)   ;

Statement Trigger Syntax

CREATE TRIGGER   <Trigger-name>
<u>TRIGGER ACTION</u> {BEFORE | AFTER}
[ORDER <sequence-number>]
<u>TRIGGERING ACTION</u> > {INSERT | UPDATE | DELETE | INSERT/SELECT}
[OF (<column-name>, …)]   ON   <subject-table>
REFERENCING   **OLD_TABLE** AS   <before-image>
NEW_TABLE AS <after-image>
FOR EACH STATEMENT
[WHEN (*optional condition*)]
(<u>TRIGGERED ACTION</u> { **INSERT | INSERT/SELECT | UPDATE | DELETE | ABORT/ROLLBACK | EXEC** } ;)   ;

Trigger Examples

Our Trigger below is named Emp_Salary_Trigger and it has a purpose. Everytime a row in the Employee_Table has the Salary updated the Trigger will fire. It will capture the employee_no, what the salary looked like before the update, what the salary looked like after the update and the date of the change.

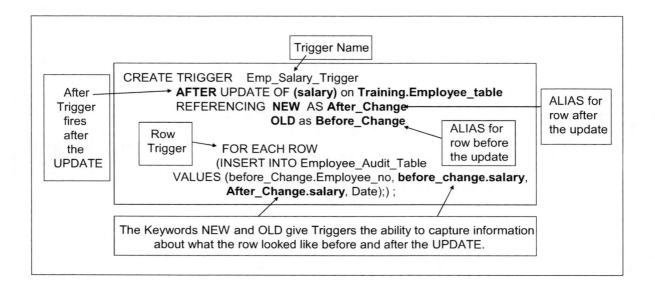

Our next example below is another AFTER Trigger. It fires FOR EACH STATEMENT. We are attempting to capture the CURRENT_TIMESTAMP for our load jobs.

```
CREATE TRIGGER   Cust_Load_Trigger
        AFTER INSERT on Training.Customer_table
            FOR EACH STATEMENT
            (INSERT INTO Load_History_Table
        VALUES ('Customer Table Loaded ' || Current_Timestamp);) ;
```

ORDERING Multiple Triggers in a Sequence

When **multiple triggers** are on the **same table (and are similar in nature)** they will **fire at random** when an **event strikes**. If you decide you want them to **fire in a particular order** you can utilize the **ORDER statement**. Because one Trigger has an ORDER 200 and the other Trigger has an ORDER 300 the ORDER 200 Trigger will fire first. If you don't have an ORDER statement then you can't control which will fire first.

```
CREATE TRIGGER    Dept_Trigger
        AFTER INSERT on Training.Department_table ORDER 200
        FOR EACH STATEMENT
        (INSERT INTO Dept_History_Table
    VALUES ('New Dept Added ' || Current_Timestamp);) ;
```

```
CREATE TRIGGER    Dept_Trigger2
        AFTER INSERT on Training.Department_Table ORDER 300
        FOR EACH STATEMENT
        (INSERT INTO Load_History_Table
    VALUES ('Dept Table INSERTED ' || Current_Timestamp);) ;
```

When there are multiple triggers on the same table and the triggers are similar in nature you can give them an ORDER or sequence in Which to fire. If the ORDER statement is not used then you can't control in which order the triggers will fire. An ORDER statement guarantees firing in the proper order.

Trigger Enable or Disable with ALTER Trigger

Many of the load utilities such as Fastload or Mutliload don't allow Triggers. You can ALTER Trigger to enable or disable a trigger. Before the load takes place you can disable an individual trigger or all triggers on a particular table. After the ALTER TRIGGER command if you place a Trigger Name it will disable the Trigger. If you place a Table Name then all Triggers for that table are disabled. Once the load completes you can easily prepare the Trigger or Table for action with the ENABLED statement.

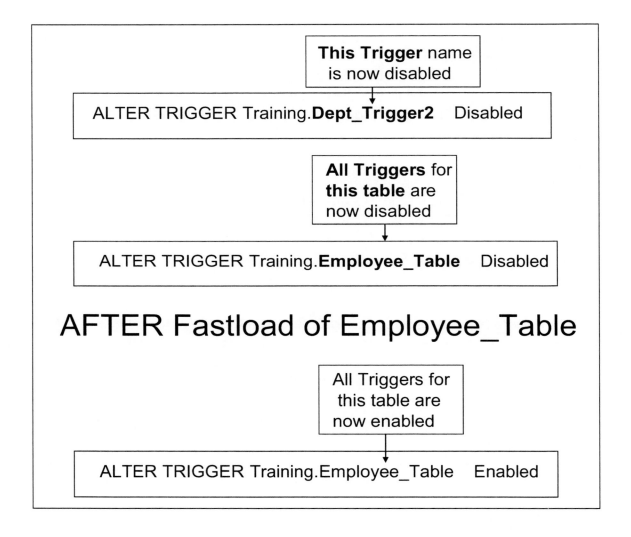

Referential Integrity (RI) Constraint

Referential Integrity (RI) insists that a row cannot be inserted unless the value in the column has a corresponding value existing in another table. This also means a row cannot be deleted if a corresponding value in another table still exists. For example, imagine getting fired and your employer deletes you from the employee table, but forgets to delete you from the payroll table. A RI check can be used to enforce data integrity and prevent this scenario. Referential Integrity does not allow anyone to be deleted from the employee table unless they were already deleted from the payroll table.
are

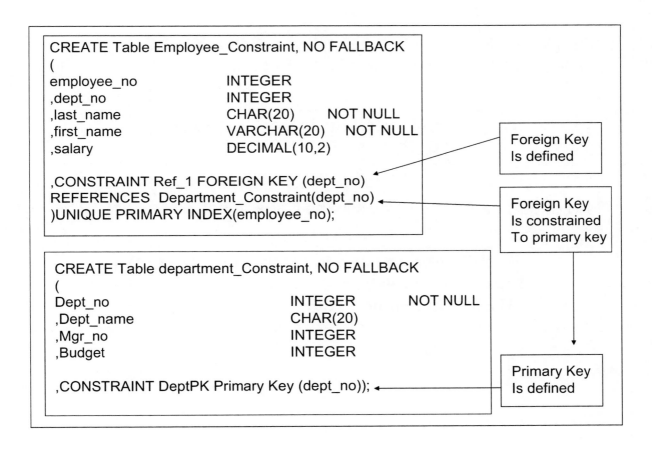

Referential Integrity Insert Error

Here we have decided to insert a new employee into the Employee_Constraint Table. We have our RI set so that every time a new employee is added to the Employee_Constraint Table their department number must match that of the Department_Constraint Table's department number. If you try to add an employee with a department number that does not exist in the Department_Constraint Table then you will receive an error. The new department number must be entered in the Department_Constraint Table first before entering the new employee.

When inserting a row into the Employee_Constraint Table the dept_no must already exist in the Department_Constraint Table.

INSERT INTO Employee_Constraint
(1, **10**, 'Phillips', 'Ryan', 60000);

No department 10 yet exists in the Department_Constraint Table

**ERROR: Aborted due to a non-valid index on Tera_Tom.Employee_Constraint
INSERT Command Failed**

Referential Integrity Insert Number One

Now that we have inserted the appropriate department number into the Department_Constraint Table we are able to put new employees into the Employee_Constraint Table successfully with valid department numbers.

When inserting a row into the Department_Constraint Table first the INSERT Command is completed successfully. Now we are ready to insert our new employee into the Employee_Constraint Table.

```
INSERT INTO Department_Constraint
(10, 'Sales', 1, 200000);
```

```
1 rows processed.
INSERT Command Complete
```

Referential Integrity Insert Number Two

Here we are finally able to insert our new employee into the Employee_Constraint Table because we now have a valid department 10 in the Department_Constraint Table. The constraints that we set up in the create table statement made sure that this employee was able to be entered into this table.

When inserting a row into the Employee_Constraint Table
the dept_no must already exist in the Department_Constraint Table.

INSERT INTO Employee_Constraint
(1, **10**, 'Phillips', 'Ryan', 60000);

Department 10 has been added to the Department_Constraint Table

**INSERT Command Complete
1 row processed.**

Referential Integrity using NULL Values

There is one way to insert our employee into the Employee_Constraint Table before his department number is entered into the Department_Constraint Table. Lets say for example that we have RI set up on an Employee_Table and a Payroll_Table. We want to add the employee's new salary to the Payroll_Table to run some tests and see how much that changes the average salary, or the sum of the salaries in the Payroll_Table before we make the final move and add the employee to the Employee_Table.

If this was the case we would take all of the information and enter it into the Payroll_Table, leaving the Employee_Number (the Primary Key) NULL. This allows us to enter the information into the Payroll_Table so we can use it to see how it will affect the departments payroll without having any problems inserting the new row. Once the decision is made to add the employee to the Employee_Table then we can go ahead and change the Employee_Number from a NULL to the true value.

When inserting a row into the Employee_Constraint Table with a department value that is NULL we are allowed to insert rows Without defining the constraint. Our insert was successful!

INSERT INTO Employee_Constraint
(2, NULL, 'Smith', 'Jerry', 45000);

By making the Dept_No NULL we will not check the Department_Constraint Table for RI.

1 rows processed.
INSERT Completed Successfully

Referential Integrity Deleting a Row

We need to be careful how we handle altering our data in these tables, otherwise we may get an error. In this scenario we cannot insert a new employee into the Employee_Constraint Table without them having a valid department number in the Department_Constraint Table. Here if we decide to take an employee who recently was fired out of the table, we will first need to remove them from the Employee_Constraint Table before we remove them from the Department_Constraint Table.

Another scenario would be if a department was losing funding and we needed to drop that department. We would need to move all of the employees from the Employee_Constraint Table in that department to a new department before we can drop the department from the Department_Constraint Table.

When deleting a row from the Department_Constraint Table the tables RI will prevent us from deleting something from its partner table in order to ensure Referential Integrity.

Delete from Department_Constraint
where dept_no = **10**;

We cannot delete department 10 from the Department_Constraint Table because it still has employees in the Employee_Constraint Table Who are in department 10.

**ERROR: Referential constraint violation: cannot delete/update the Parent Key value.
0 records returned.
DELETE Command Failed**

Referential Integrity Delete Complete

We have taken the appropriate step toward moving our employees by moving them from the Employee_Constraint Table before we do any big altering to the Department_Constraint Table.

When deleting a row from the Employee_Constraint Table we Complete our command successfully.

Delete from employee_constraint
where dept_no = 5;

0 records returned.
DELETE Command Complete

Chapter 24 – Explain

"They always say time changes things, but you actually have to change them yourself."

Andy Warhol

Explain of a Full Table Scan

Teradata retrieves rows in three ways. The fastest is when the Primary Index is utilized in the WHERE clause of the query. The second fastest way is when a Secondary Index is utilized in the WHERE clause of the query. The final way (and the slowest) is a Full Table Scan.

A Full Table Scan means each AMP will read all of the rows they hold for a particular table. Each row is read only once and essentially the entire table is read. You can see if your query is doing a Full Table Scan by using the EXPLAIN facility and looking for the words "all-AMP RETRIEVE by way of an all-row scan".

EXPLAIN
SELECT * From Employee_Table;

1) First we lock a distinct Tera-Tom."psueudo table" for read on a RowHash to prevent global deadlock for Tera_Tom.Employee_Table.
2) Next, we lock Tera-Tom.Employee_Table for read.
3) We do an **all-AMPs RETRIEVE** step from

   Tera-Tom.Employee_Table by way of an **all-rows scan** with no residual conditions into Spool 1 (group_amps), which is built locally on the AMPs. The size of Spool 1 is estimated with high confidence to be 12 rows. The estimated time for this step is 0.03 seconds.
4) Finally, we send out an END TRANSACTION step to all AMPs involved in processing the request.

An **all-AMPs RETRIEVE** step by way on an **all-rows scan** is a
FULL TABLE SCAN

EXPLAIN - UNIQUE PRIMARY INDEX (UPI)

Teradata retrieves rows in three ways. The fastest is when the Primary Index is utilized in the WHERE clause of the query. The second fastest way is when a Secondary Index is utilized in the WHERE clause of the query. The final way (and the slowest) is a Full Table Scan. The example below utilizes the UNIQUE PRIMARY INDEX (UPI).

When you utilize an UPI no spool will be used. Teradata can send the row directly back to the user.

EXPLAIN
SELECT * From Employee_Table
WHERE employee_no = 12;

Primary Index is Employee_no

1) First we do a **single-AMP RETRIEVE** step from Tera_Tom.Employee_Table by way of the **UNIQUE PRIMARY INDEX** "Tera_Tom.Employee_Table.employee_no = 1" with no residual conditions. The estimated time for this step is 0.01 seconds.

-> The row is **sent directly back** to the user as a result of statement 1. The total estimated time is **0.01 seconds**.

A **single-AMPs RETRIEVE** step by way of the Unique Primary Index
Is the Fastest Query Possible!

363

EXPLAIN - NON-UNIQUE PRIMARY INDEX (NUPI)

Teradata retrieves rows in three ways. The fastest is when the Primary Index is utilized in the WHERE clause of the query. The second fastest way is when a Secondary Index is utilized in the WHERE clause of the query. The final way (and the slowest) is a Full Table Scan. The example below utilizes the PRIMARY INDEX which really means it utilizes a NON-UNIQUE PRIMARY INDEX (NUPI). When you utilize a NUPI spool will be used.

Notice that a NON-UNIQUE PRIMARY INDEX is still a 1-AMP Operation.

```
EXPLAIN
SELECT * From Employee_Table2
WHERE Last_Name = 'Coffing' ;
```

Primary Index is Last_Name

1) First we do a **single-AMP RETRIEVE** step from Tera_Tom.Employee_Table2 by way of the **PRIMARY INDEX** "Tera_Tom.Employee_Table.last_name = 'Coffing'" with no residual conditions into Spool 1 (one-amp), which is built locally on that AMP. The size of spool is estimated with low confidence to be 2 rows. The estimated time for this step is 0.01 seconds.

-> The contents of Spool 1 are sent back to the user as the result of statement 1. The total estimated time is **0.03 seconds**.

An **UPI** or a **NUPI** in the WHERE clause is always a **One-AMP Operation**.

EXPLAIN – UNIQUE SECONDARY INDEX (USI)

All queries that utilize a Unique Secondary Index (USI) in the WHERE Clause will result in a two-AMP operation. Teradata retrieves rows in three ways. The fastest is when the Primary Index is utilized in the WHERE clause of the query. The second fastest way is when a Secondary Index is utilized in the WHERE clause of the query. The final way (and the slowest) is a Full Table Scan.

EXPLAIN
SELECT * From Employee_Table
WHERE First_Name = 'Arfy' ◄
AND   Last_Name = 'Coffing'; ◄

UNIQUE SECONDARY INDEX (USI) on
First_Name, Last_Name

---

1) First, we do a **two-AMP RETRIEVE** step from

    Tera_Tom.Employee_Table by way of **unique index # 12**
    "Tera_Tom.emloyee_table.first_name = 'Arfy',
    Tera_Tom.employee_table.last_name = 'Coffing'"
    with no residual conditions.
    The estimated time for this step is 0.02 seconds.
-> The row is sent directly back to the user as the result of statement 1.
    The total estimated time is 0.02 seconds.

A **UNIQUE SECONDARY INDEX** IS ALWAYS A
Two-AMP Operation

EXPLAIN – NON-UNIQUE SECONDARY INDEX

All queries that utilize a Non-Unique Secondary Index (NUSI) in the WHERE Clause will result in an all-AMP operation, but not a Full Table Scan (FTS). It is an all-AMP operation because each AMP has to check its secondary index subtable to see if it has rows that will qualify. If an AMP has rows then it will continue to participate in the query execution. If an AMP does not have any rows then it knows it no longer has to participate. Even though a NUSI in the WHERE clause is an all-AMP operation it can still save a great deal of time because it is NOT a Full Table Scan (FTS).

Teradata retrieves rows in three ways. The fastest is when the Primary Index is utilized in the WHERE clause of the query. The second fastest way is when a Secondary Index is utilized in the WHERE clause of the query. The final way (and the slowest) is a Full Table Scan.

EXPLAIN
SELECT *
From Retail.item
WHERE L_Partkey = 553 ;

Non-UNIQUE SECONDARY INDEX (NUSI) on L_Partkey

1) First, we lock a distinct Retail."Psuedo table" for read on a RowHash to prevent global deadlock for Retail.item.
2) Next, we lock Retail.item for read.
3) We do an **all-AMP RETRIEVE** step from Retail.item by way of **index # 4 "**Retail.item.**L_Partkey** = 553" with no residual conditions into Spool 1 (**group_amps**), which is **built locally** on the AMPs. The size of Spool 1 is estimated with high confidence to be 31 rows. The estimated time for this step is 0.16 seconds.
4) Finally, we send out an END TRANSACTION step to all AMPs involved in processing the request.

A **Non-UNIQUE SECONDARY INDEX** (NUSI) IS an all-AMP operation

But not a Full Table Scan (FTS).

EXPLAIN – What is a Psuedo Lock?

Whenever all-AMPs are utilized in a query a Psuedo Lock must be placed on the table. This sounds like fancy terminology, but all it means is that a "Gatekeeper" is responsible for locking the table for one user at a time. Let me explain this EXPLAIN Terminology.

We know that each AMP holds a portion of a table. We also know that when a Full Table Scan is performed that each AMP will read their portion of the table. If Teradata isn't careful a DEADLOCK can happen. A deadlock is when two different users require multiple locks and one user gets one lock and the other user gets the other lock. Both users require both locks and wait for the other lock to become available. They will unfortunately wait forever unless Teradata breaks one of the locks. This is a deadlock.

A Psuedo Lock is how Teradata prevents a deadlock. When a user does an All-AMP operation Teradata will assign a single AMP to command the other AMPs to lock the table. Teradata actually hashes the table_name and uses the hash map to choose an AMP. This single "Gatekeeper" AMP will always be responsible for locking that particular table on all AMPs. This allows for users running an all-AMP query on the table to have to report to the "Gatekeeper" AMP. The "Gatekeeper" AMP never plays favorites and performs the locking on a First Come First Serve basis. The first user to run the query will get the lock. The others will have to wait.

> **EXPLAIN**
> **SELECT * From Employee_Table;**

1) First we lock a distinct Tera-Tom."psueudo table" for read on a RowHash to prevent global deadlock for Tera_Tom.Employee_Table.
2) Next, we lock Tera-Tom.Employee_Table for read.
3) We do an **all-AMPs RETRIEVE** step from Tera-Tom.Employee_Table by way of an **all-rows scan** with no residual conditions into Spool 1 (group_amps), which is built locally on the AMPs. The size of Spool 1 is estimated with high confidence to be 12 rows. The estimated time for this step is 0.03 seconds.
4) Finally, we send out an END TRANSACTION step to all AMPs involved in processing the request.

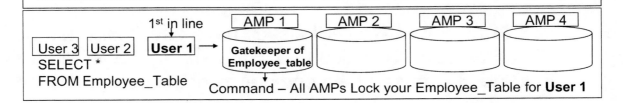

EXPLAIN – Confidence Levels

In the EXPLAIN facility confidence levels have to do with COLLECT STATISTICS. If STATISTICS were collected on a column or index and that particular column or index is used to retrieve rows then Teradata has High Confidence that it can determine the number of rows it will return. If COLLECT STATISTICS was not run and Teradata has no clue to the number of rows it will return it will utilize the phrase NO Confidence. If No Statistics were collected, but Teradata can use Sample Statistics, Dynamic AMP Sampling or Random AMP Sampling then it has a good guesstimate of the number of rows returning and will deliver a Low Confidence phrase.

**EXPLAIN
SELECT * From Employee_Table;**

1) First we lock a distinct Tera-Tom."psueudo table" for read on a RowHash to prevent global deadlock for Tera_Tom.Employee_Table.
2) Next, we lock Tera-Tom.Employee_Table for read.
3) We do an **all-AMPs RETRIEVE** step from Tera-Tom.Employee_Table by way of an **all-rows scan** with no residual conditions into Spool 1 (group_amps), which is built locally on the AMPs. The size of Spool 1 is estimated with **high confidence** to be **12 rows**. The estimated time for this step is 0.03 seconds.
4) Finally, we send out an END TRANSACTION step to all AMPs involved in processing the request.

- **High Confidence** – Statistics have been collected on the columns or indexes being utilized.

- **Low Confidence** – Only Sample Statistics, Dynamic Statistics, or Random Samples have been performed on the columns or indexes being utilized.

- **No Confidence** – No Statistics have been collected or Teradata just can't figure out how many rows will be returned because of the complexity of the query.

EXPLAIN – Execute the following steps in Parallel

In the EXPLAIN facility when the phrase "We execute the following steps in Parallel" is seen then Teradata is performing two different steps simultaneously. An AMP has 80 worker tasks so it can do 80 different things at one time. It can therefore perform different steps of the plan simultaneously if the two steps don't depend on one step finishing first and the other step utilizing the previous' results.

```
EXPLAIN
SELECT dept_no, Employee_No
FROM      Employee_Table
INTERSECT
SELECT  dept_no, Mgr_no
FROM      Department_Table;
```

1) First we lock a distinct Tera-Tom."psueudo table" for read on a RowHash to prevent global deadlock for Tera_Tom.Department_Table.
2) Next, First we lock a distinct Tera-Tom."psueudo table" for read on a RowHash to prevent global deadlock for Tera_Tom.Employee_Table.
3) We lock Tera_Tom.Department_Table for read, and we lock Tera-Tom.Employee_Table for read.

4) # We do the following steps in Parallel

   1) We do an all-AMPs RETRIEVE step from Tera-Tom.Employee_Table by way of an all-rows scan with no residual conditions into Spool 1 (all_amps), which is redistributed by hash code to all AMPs. Then we do a sort to order Spool 1 by row hash and the sort key in spool field 1 eliminating duplicate rows. The size of Spool 1 is estimated with high confidence to be 12 rows. The estimated time for this step is 0.03 seconds.

   2) We do an all-AMPs RETRIEVE step from Tera-Tom.Department_Table by way of an all-rows scan with no residual conditions into Spool 2 (all_amps), which is redistributed by hash code to all AMPs. Then we do a sort to order Spool 2 by row hash and the sort key in spool field 1 eliminating duplicate rows. The size of Spool 1 is estimated with high confidence to be 10 rows. The estimated time for this step is 0.03 seconds.

5) We do an all-AMPs JOIN step from Spool 1 (last-use) by way of a RowHash match scan, which is joined to spool2 (Last Use). Spool 1 and Spool 2 are joined using a merge join with a join condition of ("field_1 = field_1"). The result goes into Spool 3(group_amps), which is built locally on the AMPs. The size of Spool 3 is estimated to be 5 rows. The estimated time for this step is 0.02 seconds.
6) Finally, we send out an END TRANSACTION step to all AMPs involved in processing the request.
-> The contents of Spool 3 are sent back to the user as the result of statement 1. The total estimated time is 0.06 seconds.

EXPLAIN – Redistributed by Hash Code

When two tables are joined the joining rows have to be on the same AMP for the actual join to take place. Since rows are placed on AMPs based on their Primary Index Value quite often Teradata will have to redistribute a table into spool by re-hashing the table by the value in the WHERE or ON Clause. **Redistributed** means there is **data movement**.

EXPLAIN
SELECT First_Name, Last_name, Dept_Name, Mgr_No
From Employee_Table
**   ,Department_Table**
WHERE Employee_table.Dept_no =   Department_table.Dept_no ;

NOT the **Primary Index**
Of **Employee_Table so**
Redistribute by **Dept_no.**

Primary Index
Of **Department_Table**
so keep in place.

1) First, we lock a distinct Tera-Tom."Psuedo table" for read on a RowHash to prevent global deadlock for Tera-Tom.Department_Table.
2) Next, we lock a distinct Tera-Tom."Psuedo table" for read on a RowHash to prevent global deadlock for Tera-Tom.Employee_Table.
3) We lock Tera-Tom.Department_Table for read, and we lock Tera_Tom.Employee_Table for read.
4) We do an **all-AMP RETRIEVE** step from

   Tera-Tom.Employee_Table
   by way of an all-rows scan with a condition of ("NOT(Tera_Tom.Employee_Table.dept_no IS NULL)") into Spool 2

   (all-AMPs), which is **Redistributed by hash code**
   to all AMPs. The we do a SORT or order Spool 2 by Row Hash.
   The size of Spool 2 is estimated with no confidence to be 11 rows.
   The estimated time for this step is 0.03 seconds.
5) We do an all-AMPs JOIN step from tera-Tom.Department_table by way of a RowHash match scan, which is joined to Spool 2 (Last use). Tera_Tom. Department_Table and Spool 2 are joined using a merge join, with a join condition (""Dept_no = Tera_Tom.Department_table.Dept_no"). The result goes into Spool 1 (group_amps), which is built locally on the AMPs. The size of Spool 1 is estimated with no confidence to be 20 rows. The estimated time for this step is 0.04 seconds.
6) Finally, we send out an END TRANSACTION step to all AMPs involved in processing the request. The contents of Spool 1 are sent back to the user as the result of statement 1. The total estimated time is 0.07 seconds.

EXPLAIN – Duplicated on All AMPs

When two tables are joined the joining rows have to be on the same AMP for the actual join to take place. Since rows are placed on AMPs based on their Primary Index Value quite often Teradata will have to redistribute a table into spool by re-hashing the table by the value in the WHERE or ON Clause. However, if one of the tables is **small, Teradata will often duplicate the smaller table in its entirety on ALL AMPs.**

EXPLAIN
SELECT Cust_Name, Order_Total
FROM   Customer_Table, Order_Table
WHERE customer_table.cust_Num = Order_table.Cust_Num ;

| The Primary Index Of **Customer_Table, but** the **table is SMALL.** | **Not** the **Primary Index** Of **Order_Table, but** the **table** is **very large.** |

---

1) First, we lock a distinct Tera-Tom."Psuedo table" for read on a RowHash to prevent global deadlock for Tera-Tom.Order_Table.
2) Next, we lock a distinct Tera-Tom."Psuedo table" for read on a RowHash to prevent global deadlock for Tera-Tom.Customer_Table.
3) We lock Tera-Tom.Order_Table for read, and we lock Tera_Tom.Customer_Table for read.
4) We do an **all-AMP RETRIEVE** step from

   # Tera-Tom.Customer_Table

   by way of an all-rows scan with a condition of ("NOT(Tera_Tom.Customer_Table.Cust_Num IS NULL)") into Spool 2

   (all-AMPs), which is **Duplicated on ALL AMPS.**
   The size of Spool 2 is estimated with high confidence to be 8 rows. The estimated time for this step is 0.03 seconds.
5) We do an all-AMPs JOIN step from Spool 2 (Last use) by way of an all-rows scan, which is joined to Tera_Tom.Order_Table. Spool 2 and Tera_Tom.Order_Table are joined using a **Product join**, with a join condition (""Cust_Num = Tera_Tom.Order_table.Cust_Num"). The result goes into Spool 1 (group_amps), which is built locally on the AMPs. The size of Spool 1 is estimated with low confidence to be **1,632 rows**. The estimated time for this step is 0.05 seconds.
6) Finally, we send out an END TRANSACTION step to all AMPs involved in processing the request. The contents of Spool 1 are sent back to the user as the result of statement 1. The total estimated time is 0.08 seconds.

EXPLAIN – JOIN INDEX

A Join Index pre-joins two tables with columns that are requested when the Join Index is created. The Join Index is never accessed directly by the user in their query, but the Parsing Engine knows about the Join Index and it will decide whether to use it or not. A Join Index is also maintained as the tables are updated. The penalty is additional PERM space, but the benefits are much quicker joins when the tables are joined in user queries. Remember, a Join Index actually pre-joins the two tables and creates another physical table. Only the PE can decide whether to utilize the Join Index in its plan.

EXPLAIN
SELECT First_Name, Last_name
,Dept_Name, Mgr_No
From Employee_Table as E,
Department_Table as D
WHERE E.Dept_no = D.Dept_no ;

A **Join Index** called **Emp_Dept_Join_Index** has previously been created on the two tables.

---

1) First, we lock a distinct Tera-Tom."Psuedo table" for read on a RowHash to prevent global deadlock for Tera-Tom.Emp_Dept_Join_Index.
2) Next, we lock Tera-Tom.Emp_Dept_Join_Index for read.
3) We do an **all-AMP RETRIEVE** step from

Tera-Tom.Emp_Dept_Join_Index

by way of an all-rows scan with no residual conditions into Spool 1 (**group_amps**), which is **built locally** on the AMPs. The size of Spool 1 is estimated with low confidence to be 2 rows. The estimated time for this step is 0.03 seconds.
4) Finally, we send out an END TRANSACTION step to all AMPs involved in processing the request.

Users query and join the actual tables, but the PE can utilize
The **JOIN INDEX in its plan.**

EXPLAIN – BMSMS Bit Mapping

When multiple weakly selective Non-Unique Secondary Indexes (NUSIs) are ANDed together the Parsing Engine (PE) will come up with a plan to use bitmapping. This is how it works. Instead of doing a Full Table Scan on the base table each AMP will look at each NUSI subtable involved with the WHERE Clause and AND Clause. Each AMP will store the base Row IDs of rows where they find a match. They can then build spool based on finding matching Row IDs from the NUSI Subtables. If you see BMSMS (Bit Map Set Manipulation Step) in your explain then you are utilizing a plan of genius.

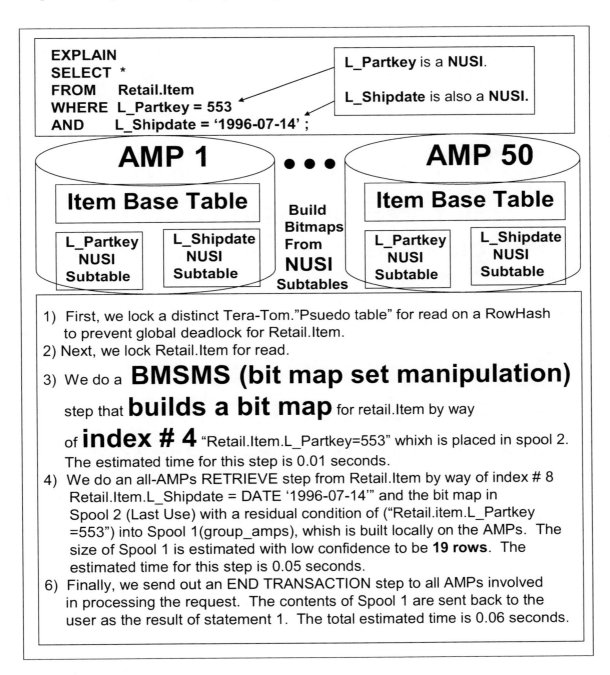

```
EXPLAIN                                      L_Partkey is a NUSI.
SELECT  *
FROM    Retail.Item                          L_Shipdate is also a NUSI.
WHERE   L_Partkey = 553
AND     L_Shipdate = '1996-07-14' ;
```

AMP 1 ••• **AMP 50**

Item Base Table   Build Bitmaps From **NUSI** Subtables   **Item Base Table**

L_Partkey NUSI Subtable   L_Shipdate NUSI Subtable   L_Partkey NUSI Subtable   L_Shipdate NUSI Subtable

1) First, we lock a distinct Tera-Tom."Psuedo table" for read on a RowHash to prevent global deadlock for Retail.Item.

2) Next, we lock Retail.Item for read.

3) We do a **BMSMS (bit map set manipulation)** step that **builds a bit map** for retail.Item by way of **index # 4** "Retail.Item.L_Partkey=553" whixh is placed in spool 2. The estimated time for this step is 0.01 seconds.

4) We do an all-AMPs RETRIEVE step from Retail.Item by way of index # 8 Retail.Item.L_Shipdate = DATE '1996-07-14'" and the bit map in Spool 2 (Last Use) with a residual condition of ("Retail.item.L_Partkey =553") into Spool 1(group_amps), whish is built locally on the AMPs. The size of Spool 1 is estimated with low confidence to be **19 rows**. The estimated time for this step is 0.05 seconds.

6) Finally, we send out an END TRANSACTION step to all AMPs involved in processing the request. The contents of Spool 1 are sent back to the user as the result of statement 1. The total estimated time is 0.06 seconds.

EXPLAIN – PPI Tables and Partitions

PPI Tables are Partitioned Primary Index tables that are designed to prevent a Full Table Scan (FTS). The Employee_Table_PPI table is partitioned by the column Dept_No. Each AMP sorts their portion of the table by Dept_No first and then by Row ID second. This allows for many queries to be satisfied by having each AMP read one or more partitions without having to do a Full Table Scan (FTS). Look for the words "All-AMP RETRIEVE step from a SINGLE PARTITION" and you can bet your query is taking advantage of a partitioned table.

```
EXPLAIN
SELECT * From Employee_Table_PPI
WHERE Dept_No = 20 ;
```

This table is a PPI Table partitioned by Dept_No

1) First we lock a distinct Tera-Tom."psuedo table" for read on a RowHash to prevent global deadlock for Tera_Tom.Employee_Table_PPI.
2) Next, we lock Tera-Tom.Employee_Table_PPI for read.
3) We do an **all-AMPs RETRIEVE** step from **A Single Partition** of Tera-Tom.Employee_Table_PPI with a condition of ("Tera_Tom.employee_able_PPI.Dept_No = 20") with a residual condition of ("Tera_Tom.employee_able_PPI.Dept_No = 20") into spool 1 (group_amps), which is built locally on the AMPs. The size of Spool 1 is estimated with no confidence to be 2 rows. The estimated time for this step is 0.03 seconds.
4) Finally, we send out an END TRANSACTION step to all AMPs involved in processing the request.
-> The contents of Spool 1 are sent back to the user as the result of statement 1. The total estimated time is 0.03 seconds.

Each AMP reads a Single Partition

Group_AMPs, SORT, Eliminating Duplicate Rows, and No Residual Conditions

Here is an explanation of Group_AMPs, Sort, Eliminating Duplicate Rows, and No Residual Conditions.

Group_AMPs means that a subset of AMPs will be used instead of all the AMPs. Teradata will also use the term one_amp to indicate a single AMP.

Eliminating Duplicate Rows indicates that a DISTINCT operation is being done to make certain that there are no duplicate rows in the answer set.

A **SORT** will SORT the data in spool or on each AMP. A Sort/Merge will sort the data on each AMP and then merge the data across the BYNET.

No Residual Conditions means that no other Conditions exist. A Residual Condition would mean a WHERE or AND clause is causing Teradata to further exam row values to see if they qualify.

EXPLAIN
SELECT Distinct Dept_No
From Employee_Table ;

1) First we lock a distinct Tera-Tom."psueudo table" for read on a RowHash to prevent global deadlock for Tera_Tom.Employee_Table.
2) Next, we lock Tera-Tom.Employee_Table for read.
3) We do an all-AMPs RETRIEVE step from Tera-Tom.Employee_Table by way of an all-rows scan with **no residual conditions** into spool 1 **(group_amps),** which is Redistributed by hash code to all AMPs. Then we do a **SORT** to order Spool 1 by the sort key in spool field1 **eliminating duplicate rows**.

   The size of Spool 1 is estimated with high confidence to be 12 rows.
   The estimated time for this step is 0.03 seconds.
4) Finally, we send out an END TRANSACTION step to all AMPs involved in processing the request.
-> The contents of Spool 1 are sent back to the user as the result of statement 1. The total estimated time is 0.03 seconds.

EXPLAIN – Last Use, End Transaction, and Computed Globally

Here is an explanation of Last Use, End Transaction, and Computed Globally.

Last Use means that after the current step the spool will be released. Most people believe that spool is released when the query is done, but Teradata actually releases certain spool files once they are no longer needed.

End Transaction means that the transaction is ending. When the transaction ends there is either a commit or rollback and all transaction locks are released.

Computed globally means that the computations are done at a system level and that they are not computed locally on the AMP.

```
EXPLAIN
SELECT Dept_No
From Employee_Table
GROUP BY Dept_No ;
```

1) First we lock a distinct Tera-Tom."psueudo table" for read on a RowHash to prevent global deadlock for Tera_Tom.Employee_Table.
2) Next, we lock Tera-Tom.Employee_Table for read.
3) We do an all-amps SUM step to aggregate from Tera-Tom.Employee_Table by way of an all-rows scan with no residual conditions, and the grouping identifier in field 1026. Aggregate Intermediate Results are

   computed globally, then placed in spool 3. The size of Spool 3 is estimated with low confidence to be 4 rows. The estimated time for this step is 0.03 seconds.

4) We do an all-AMPs RETRIEVE step from **Spool 3 (last use)**

   by way of an all-rows scan into Spool 1 (group_amps), which is built locally on the AMPs. The size of Spool 1 is estimated with no confidence to be 4 rows. The estimated time for this step is 0.04 seconds.

5) Finally, we send out an **END TRANSACTION** step to all AMPs involved in processing the request.

-> The contents of Spool 1 are sent back to the user as the result of statement 1.

376

Chapter 25 – Stored Procedures

"You don't get harmony when everybody sings the same note."

- Doug Floyd

Stored Procedures

Stored Procedures are different then other objects in many ways and there is a great deal of confusion on exactly what they do. Your worries are over! Here is the scoop.

Stored Procedures are much closer to a scripting or programming language then a view or a macro. The difficult part about Stored Procedures is that they are not meant to bring back rows like a view or a macro. Stored Procedures usually perform maintenance on the system. If you wanted to know all of the customers who placed orders for a particular date you could write a view or a macro and see the result set on your PC in a couple seconds. Stored Procedures are not meant to bring back multiple rows unless you set up a cursor.

Stored Procedures
Contain SQL and Stored Procedure Language (SPL) combined
Must use a cursor to retrieve more than 1 row
May receive parameters and return output values as parameters
Stored in Database or USER Perm Space

We SELECT from a view.	We Execute A Macro	We Call a Stored Procedure
Select * from Emp_View;	**Exec** Mymac;	**Call New_Proc();**

CREATE Procedure

A Stored Procedure is stored as an executable piece of code, but treated like all Teradata objects. The CREATE Procedure command compiles the Stored Procedure at CREATE time. Once compiled it is ready for the CALL and stored in the user database. The object kind is "P".

One of the differences between macros and stored procedures is that although macros can receive input parameters, stored procedures can receive input (through parameters) and provide output (through parameters). In the CREATE PROCEDURE you will have the parameter list only if you have input or output parameters. You will always have a procedure body.

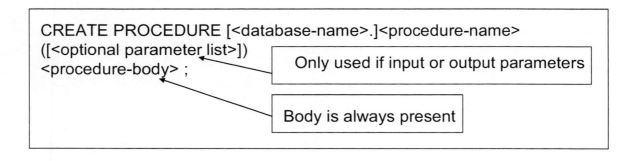

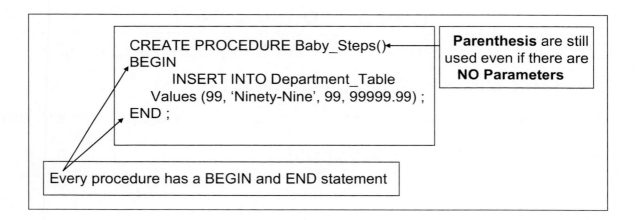

Nesting BEGIN and END Statements

Every Stored Procedure needs a BEGIN and END statement. **The first BEGIN and END** statements only need to say **BEGIN** and **END;**. **Any other BEGIN and END** statements must also be accompanied by a **Label-name:BEGIN** or **END Label-name**.

The next example is for example sake to show multiple BEGIN and END statements and their accompanying labels. We are hard-coding the values we want to INSERT or DELETE. That works great one time, but our next example will show how to pass parameters.

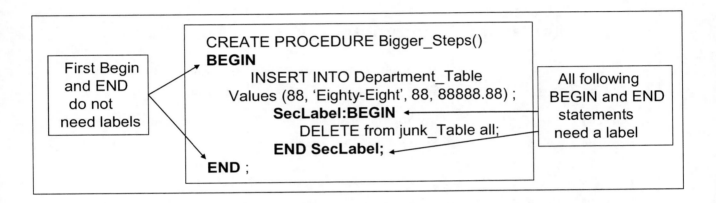

After you have created a procedure you are ready to CALL the Stored Procedure. Don't forget to include the Parentheses.

CALL PROCEDURE Bigger_Steps();

Passing a Stored Procedure Parameters

There are three elements when using parameters with a Stored Procedure. There are three types of elements in Parameter Usage. We have an IN an OUT and an INOUT. They do just what they say. The **IN** passes an **input parameter**, the **OUT** an **output parameter**, and an **INOUT** serve both as **INPUT and OUTPUT** parameters. Our next example will use the **IN** Parameter Usage.

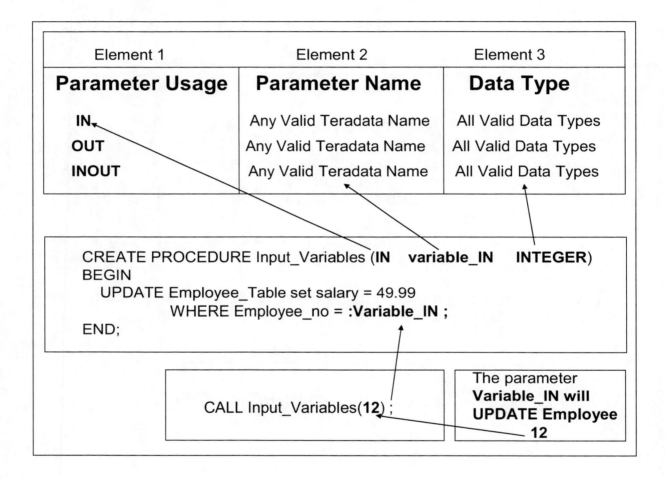

Element 1	Element 2	Element 3
Parameter Usage	**Parameter Name**	**Data Type**
IN	Any Valid Teradata Name	All Valid Data Types
OUT	Any Valid Teradata Name	All Valid Data Types
INOUT	Any Valid Teradata Name	All Valid Data Types

```
CREATE PROCEDURE Input_Variables (IN    variable_IN    INTEGER)
BEGIN
    UPDATE Employee_Table set salary = 49.99
            WHERE Employee_no = :Variable_IN ;
END;
```

CALL Input_Variables(**12**) ;

The parameter **Variable_IN will UPDATE Employee 12**

An Example of all Three Parameters

Our next example will show you how to use the IN and OUT parameters.

```
CREATE PROCEDURE Walking_Proud
  ( IN        Variable1        Integer
  ,IN         Variable2        Integer
  ,OUT        Response_Out  Char(10)
  )
BEGIN
  IF Variable1 < Variable2
        THEN SET Response_Out = 'Variable1 Loses' ; END IF;
  IF Variable1 > Variable2
        THEN SET Response_Out = 'Variable 1 Wins';  END IF;
  IF Variable1 = Variable2
        THEN SET Response_Out = 'Variable Tie';     END IF;
END;
```

Call Walking_Proud(2, 2, **Response_Out**)

Response_Out
_____

Output message → **Variable Tie**

You are required
to include the **OUT**
Variable name when
You make the CALL

DECLARE and SET

Stored Procedures utilize variables and the DECLARE establishes a local variable and a SET will change or set the value for a variable. The DECLARE statement will declare a variable name list and there can be multiple names in the list as long as they are the same data type. If you had five variables with different data types you would need five declare statements. If you had 10 variables with the same data type you would need only one declare statement.

Stored Procedures have stringent requirements on names. You can't have two Stored Procedures with the same name even if they are in a different database. You can't have two variables within a procedure with the same name.

When you utilize DECLARE you can specify a default value that is done automatically each and every time the procedure is run. If there were multiple variables run with the same data type the DEFAULT will apply to all. If not, the variable will contain a NULL value.

Set assigns values to the variable. Even if the variable had DEFAULT or NULL values the SET command allows changes to be made. Our example below will actually pass an IN and OUT parameter to the procedure and then use DECLARE and SET to establish and initialize another variable. Then the two variables can be compared.

```
CREATE PROCEDURE Leaping_Variables
(IN         Variable1 Integer  ◄──────┐  1st Variable is
,OUT        Response_out Char(20)      │  an IN Parameter
)
BEGIN

    DECLARE  Variable2   integer;  ◄───┐  2nd Variable is
    SET Variable2 = 4;  ◄──────────────┘  DECLARED and
                                           SET

  If Variable1 < Variable2
    THEN SET Response_out = 'Variable1 Loses'; END IF;
  If Variable1 > Variable2
    THEN SET Response_out = 'Variable 1 Wins'; END IF;
  If Variable1 = Variable2
    THEN SET Response_out = 'Variable tie'; END IF;
END;
```

ELSEIF for Speed

The ELSEIF is considered one IF statement and it has better speed then our previous example. Our previous example had 3 different IF statements followed by 3 END IF statements. Our query below does not have 3 IF statements, but one ELSEIF.

```
CREATE PROCEDURE My_ElseIF
(IN        Variable1 Integer           1st Variable is
,OUT       Response_out Char(20)       an IN Parameter
)
BEGIN

   DECLARE  Variable2   integer;       2nd Variable is
   SET Variable2 = 4;                   DECLARED and
                                        SET
IF Variable1 < Variable2
    THEN SET Response_out = 'Variable1 Loses';    F
     ELSEIF Variable1 > Variable2                 A
       THEN SET Response_out = 'Variable 1 Wins'; S
        ELSE                                       T
            SET Response_out = 'Variable tie';
END IF;
END;          There is only one END IF statement
```

The Scoop is the LOOP and it LEAVES like a Tree

LOOPS define an unconditional loop. The SQL/SPL loops repeatedly until it comes upon a LEAVE command. Then it exits at the END LOOP. For every LOOP there is an END LOOP. A LOOP does not require a label on the LOOP and END LOOP unless there is a LOOP within a LOOP. That is the Scoop.

```
CREATE PROCEDURE LOOPY
(IN variable1 INTEGER)

BEGIN
  DECLARE Variable2 Integer;
  SET variable2 = 0;

  The_Loop:LOOP
        SET Variable2 = Variable2 + 1;
        IF Variable1 = Variable2 THEN LEAVE THE_LOOP;
        END IF;
          INSERT INTO Proof_Table
            VALUES(:Variable1, :Variable2, Current_Timestamp);
        END LOOP The_Loop;
END;
```

The WHILE and END WHILE

LOOPS use a LEAVE statement to exit the loop, but the WHILE statement has conditional logic built right in. WHILE tests itself with each LOOP and will continue as long as the condition is true. For each WHILE there is an END WHILE. The label name is optional unless there is a loop within a loop.

```
CREATE PROCEDURE Input_Rows
(IN  Var1  INTEGER)

BEGIN
   DECLARE The_Count INTEGER DEFAULT 0;

   BIG_LOOP:WHILE The_Count < Var1
        DO
     SET The_Count = The_Count + 1;
         INSERT INTO Proof_Table
             VALUES(:The_Count, NULL, Current_Timestamp);
   END WHILE  BIG_Loop;
END;
```

INDEX